LEISURE GUIDE

IRELAND

▲ Dunmanus Bay, separating Mizen Head and Sheep's Head, Co Cork

Published by The Automobile Association,
Fanum House, Basingstoke, Hampshire RG21 2EA

Editorial contributors: Jean Boydell (tours);
Professor Terence Brown (Literary Ireland);
Wilfrid Capper (walks in Ulster); Peter Harbison
(A Brief History, A Land of Historic Ruins); David
Herman (walks in eastern Ireland); Ian Hill
(A Taste of the Irish, A–Z Gazetteer, tours); Helen
Livingston (The Shape of the Land); Joss Lynam
(tours); Dáithí Ó hÓgáin (Irish Myth and Legend);
Séan Ó Súilleabháin (walks in western Ireland);
Susan Poole (tours); Brian Smith (The Irish
Horse); Paul Sterry (The Natural History of
Ireland); Jack Whaley (The Country House and
Garden); Tony Whilde (tours).

Editor: Susi Bailey

Edited, designed, produced and distributed by
AA Publishing, Fanum House, Basingstoke,
Hampshire RG21 2EA.
© The Automobile Association 1993
Maps © The Automobile Association 1993

A catalogue record for this book is available from
the British Library

ISBN 0 7495 0639 3
USA edition ISBN 1–55650–556–6
VOCAB No 18364

This book was produced using Quark XPress™,
Microsoft Word™ and Aldus Freehand™ on Apple
Macintosh™ computers. The principal typefaces
used in this book are Clearface and Helvetica.

Colour origination by Daylight Colour Art Pte.
Ltd, Singapore
Printed and bound by William Clowes Limited,
Beccles and London

The contents of this publication are believed
correct at the time of printing. Nevertheless, the
publishers cannot accept responsibility for errors
or omissions, or for changes in details given. The
views expressed in this book are not necessarily
those of the publisher. Every effort has been made
to ensure accuracy in this guide, However, details
do change and the publishers would welcome any
information to help keep the book up to date.

Heights of mountains are given in two forms in
this guide: where a height is mentioned in the text
by a map (such as in the tours), the height is given
in metres, in order to be consistent with the
mapping. Where there is no map (such as in the
gazetteer), the height is given in feet. In general,
measurements are imperial rather than metric.

Introduction: Carrick-a-Rede rope bridge, Co Antrim

Contents

▲ Glenveagh Castle on Lough Beagh, Co Donegal

*Intr**oduction***

Few can resist Ireland's appeal, and few would take issue with the old clichés about the island: the people do seem to have retained an instinctive warmth and hospitality lost by so many nations; the raw beauty of the countryside does have more than its fair share of historic ruins, dating from long before the advent of Christianity; it undoubtedly is a largely rural island where it is possible to escape the more oppressive aspects of late 20th century lifestyle; the musical and literary traditions do have greater currency than elsewhere; the Guinness does taste better ... But Ireland is much more than the sum of its clichés, and the best way to appreciate it is to explore this most beautiful of islands, every corner of which – be it a desolate peat bog, a Georgian city square or a rocky promontory – has something to offer. This book, written largely by people who live and work in Ireland, will enable you to discover more of this most intriguing of islands.

A Brief History

Peter Harbison

The history of Ireland can be seen as that of a conservative, island population reacting to, and trying to come to terms with, new people and ideas from outside, predominantly Britain. These people and ideas were met with the whole spectrum of reaction, from absorption to rejection. The whole process could not have started, however, without the aboriginal settlement of hunters and fishermen. This settlement is likely to have taken place around 8000BC, some time after the last of the Ice Age glaciers retreated, though perhaps not before the umbilical land-bridge between Britain and Ireland was ruptured.

The Great Gaels of Ireland
After millennia of apparent stagnation, the settlers were given a new injection of life around 4000BC by the arrival of farmers who taught them animal husbandry and crop-rearing. These newcomers also built great megalithic tombs in which to bury their dead and lay monumental claims to the lands around them. This Stone Age amalgam of hunter and farmer provided Ireland with the basic gene pool for most of its subsequent

▲ Dún Beag promontory fort on the Dingle peninsula, perhaps of the Iron Age

populations. For the remainder of the prehistoric period, one of the major innovative factors in the country was the development of a Celtic language. How far this language emerged through a peaceful but pervasive interchange of ideas, or through an eruptive arrival of Celtic-speaking warriors, conquering all before them with their superior iron technology, is a question which has yet to find a satisfactory answer.

These 'great Gaels of Ireland', to use GK Chesterton's phrase, remained comparatively

A re-creation of a bogland village is to be found at Glenbeigh, on the Ring of Kerry ▼

undisturbed in their sea-girt bastion while the Roman Empire skittled their Celtic cousins in Gaul and much of Britain. Yet the Roman presence in the larger island to the east did cast its beneficial shadow by sending Christianity, which came to Ireland like a spark from the dying embers of Roman Britain.

The Arrival of Christianity

The national apostle, St Patrick, is largely given the credit for having replaced the pagan Celtic pantheon with the single Christian God. However, it is likely that he had been preceded by other missionaries in the south-east, where the new religion, as well as a knowledge of writing, was probably introduced from England's West Country. Irish society stuck to its pattern of a scattered rural population, and the nearest it came at the time to the towns which had developed in Roman Britain were the monastic foundations. These sprang up in the Irish countryside from 5th and 6th centuries onwards and gradually developed an almost urban character, providing artistic and literary patronage which resulted in great manuscripts and high-quality metalwork. It was from these monasteries, too, that the Irish monks exiled themselves voluntarily in order to preach the Gospel in Britain and on the Continent, where the barbarian invasions of the 5th century had suffocated a burgeoning Christianity.

The Vikings

Towns in the secular sense were first introduced into Ireland by the Vikings, who, as in Britain, descended like a wolf on the fold at the end of the 8th century to play havoc with the monasteries and their treasures. Their influence, however, was largely confined to the coast, where their main contribution lay in founding towns such as Dublin and Waterford, and in the knowledge of trade and shipping which they imparted to the resident population. This latter influence brought Ireland into maritime contact with markets up and down the Atlantic seaboard. The Vikings lost much of their power and impetus after the turn of the millennium, however, by which time they had already begun to integrate with the native Irish and had introduced the first coinage to the country.

The Normans

The Viking towns were, in turn, to form the nucleus for the power base

▲ Ireland's largest Anglo-Norman castle, at Trim in Co Meath, was built in 1172

of their successors, the Normans, who answered the call of an ousted king, Dermot McMurrough, in 1169 to help him to regain his throne, but who promptly used the opportunity to conquer new lands for themselves. Superior arms and armour enabled them to overrun two-thirds of the country within half a century, and to establish an English-oriented presence in Ireland which continues in part to the present day. They built great castles and cathedrals, and settled mainly in the east and south of the country, developing a system of government and land tenure based on the feudal model of their English and Welsh homelands, and which was very different from the Irish legal code prevailing in the rest of the country.

The Irish fought back, however, and, with the population of the Norman towns decimated by the Black Death (1347–50), much of the Norman territory came to be ruled by those descendants of the original Norman lords who by now had become, as the phrase went, 'more Irish than the Irish themselves'. Their power proved a thorn in the side of the Tudor monarchs in London, and Henry VIII dissolved their monasteries to enrich the royal coffers.

The Plantations

In a series of pernicious wars, Elizabeth I overcame Hiberno-Norman and Gaelic opposition in many parts of Ireland and initiated a system of plantation by English immigrants in the south and midlands, which was extended to the north after her death. Resistance in the north finally crumbled when the flower of Gaelic nobility sailed away to the Continent in the face of defeat at Stewart hands under James I. Settlers from Scotland and England

(particularly from the overpopulated city of London) were granted lands which had been expropriated from the native Irish of Ulster, and thus were sown the seeds of discontent which still seethes in the northern province today.

The 17th century saw the stranglehold of English power tightening around the neck of Ireland and, as in the previous century, this also had its religious implications in the wake of the Reformation – the Irish clinging to their Catholic tenets, while the English tried to establish a Protestant hegemony. Twice during the century struggles which held England in thrall spilled over into Ireland. The first involved Cromwell who, though respected as the Lord Protector in Britain, became a hated aggressor in Ireland, where the campaign to establish his Ironside rule and religion lives on in Irish memory as one of barbaric cruelty and destruction. The second was the Stewart struggle for the throne of England against the related but imported William of Orange. The Stewart fight ebbed and died on the battlefields of Ireland at Derry, Aughrim and the Boyne, and with the consequent departure to France of James II and his faithful Irish followers after the Treaty of Limerick in 1691, Ireland headed into a century of glaring contrasts.

The Protestant Ascendancy

The Gaelic-speaking Catholic majority became downtrodden, being denied land, education and the practice of their religion by a victorious Protestant minority. The almost equally disadvantaged Nonconformists, particularly in the north where some of them had only recently arrived from Scotland, started to emigrate to North

▲ 'The Liberator' represented Clare, Kerry, Dublin, Kilkenny and Cork, as well as being Lord Mayor of Dublin

America, thereby setting a pattern for broader sections of the population to emigrate in the following centuries for economic and other reasons. But it was from the ranks of the Protestant Ascendancy that the desire for Irish independence emanated in the last quarter of the 18th century.

The Struggle for Independence Begins

Partial success came in 1782 when Ireland was allowed its own Parliament, with Henry Grattan spearheading a movement towards greater liberty and enlightenment which also restored a degree of religious tolerance. There followed a brief span of 18 years when Dublin became truly the second city of the Empire, achieving an elegance in art and architecture. This was epitomised in the capital's public buildings which were designed by James Gandon and engraved by James Malton, and in the impressive and well-appointed country mansions of the upper classes, standing in their beautifully wooded and landscaped demesnes.

However, the 'insidious' ideas of the American War of Independence and, more particularly, the French Revolution, led patriots like Wolfe Tone to dream of total independence from England, only to have their ideas rudely shattered in an unsuccessful insurrection in 1798. The spectre of an unfettered Ireland which this raised in London circles brought about a bribed Irish Parliament which voted itself out of existence by passing the Act of Union in 1800. Thereafter, the centre of power and wealth – and the society beaux and belles who went with it – moved to London once more, leaving the quality of Irish life very much the poorer. The first three decades of the 19th century saw the rise of Daniel O'Connell, an Irish lawyer who fought one successful campaign to have Catholics admitted as members of the Westminster Parliament, and another to achieve religious emancipation for the Catholic peasants. But his subsequent attempts to regain greater Irish freedom were gradually overtaken by younger radicals whose efforts proved equally unsuccessful in the rising of 1848.

Famine and Nationalism

The three years before this saw the disastrous failure of the potato crop in Ireland, a blight which caused the island's population to be reduced by half in less than a decade. Ireland's small cottier society began to disintegrate, and the second half of the century was characterised by the rise of an increasingly urbanised Catholic middle class. Most Irish towns still bear the hallmarks of their development in the mid-Victorian era, and the increasing self-confidence of the majority religion can be seen in its desire to have its town and village church spire dwarfing that of the established Protestant church! Hand in hand with this went an increasing demand for greater ownership of land by the Catholics who felt aggrieved at having been dispossessed centuries earlier. The Liberal Gladstone took what steps he could in the right direction, and a concomitant movement towards Home Rule might well have finally succeeded had the leader of the powerful Irish Parliamentary party at Westminster, Charles Stewart Parnell, not blunted the campaign's momentum by falling from power as the result of a disastrous divorce case. On such things does the fate of a nation hang!

By one of those curious paradoxes, the mid-Victorian rise in Celtic nationalistic spirit and a revelling in the rediscovery of the country's glorious Gaelic past – symbolised by the sudden craze to model tombstones on the ringed high crosses of a thousand years earlier – was accompanied by a decline in the use of the Irish language. Whereas at the beginning of the 19th century the majority of the

Dublin, 25 April 1916. The Easter Rising was firmly quelled, but the Irish Free State was only six years away ▼

▲ The monastic ruins at Clonmacnoise, centre of religious learning for centuries

26 counties – much to Churchill's disgust – remained uncommitted in World War II, although its neutral stance in the conflict led to its increased stature in the League of Nations after the War, and the acceptability of its troops as part of the United Nations peace-keeping forces in more recent decades.

De Valera introduced a new, and still largely unchanged, constitution in 1937, when Ireland dropped its dominion status. Even when John A Costello declared a republic in 1949, it was still basically an agricultural country heavily dependent on its livestock for foreign revenue. Ireland had remained largely unaffected by England's Industrial Revolution in the 19th century and it was not until the 1960s that the country, in an effort to overcome economic impoverishment and the re-emergence of emigration to an increasingly affluent Britain in the previous decade, developed its own industrial base under the leadership of Seán Lemass. This prepared the way for an economic boom in the 1970s which encouraged the Republic to join the EC in 1973.

The Troubles Today

By this time, however, a shadow had already come over the island. A peaceful civil rights campaign in search of greater equality for the Nationalist/Catholic population in Northern Ireland in 1969 was soon overtaken by terrorist activity which subsequently polarised the two communities in Ulster and created an extremist strife which shows few signs of being resolved. The Hillsborough Anglo-Irish Agreement, signed in 1985 by Margaret Thatcher and the Irish Taoiseach (Prime Minister) Garret FitzGerald, allowed the Republic a toe-hold in the Ulster door. This continues to prove unacceptable to Ulster Unionists, however, who see no justification for this move – and so, despite the best efforts of diplomats and parliamentarians on both sides of the Irish Sea, the 'Irish problem' continues.

Northern Ireland remains an integral part of the United Kingdom and, although by no means without its troubles during the past quarter-century, it continues to provide its citizens with a high standard of living, aided by considerable investment in its industrial base, and the development of its recreational facilities which are now being appreciated by an ever-increasing number of tourists.

population was Irish-speaking, the education system's insistence on the use of English in schools saw to it that English was the well-established dominant language by the beginning of the 20th century, with Irish thriving largely in pockets along the western seaboard. Today, the native language is fighting an uphill battle for survival, although it has been greatly enlivened by popular Irish-language broadcasting in Gaeltacht (Gaelic-speaking) areas which has to compete with the largely English-speaking television stations.

The ever-simmering desire for Home Rule in Ireland was put on ice by the outbreak of the World War I, but not before the Protestant majority in the six northern counties of Ulster had made it clear through Edward Carson that they wanted nothing less than the retention of complete union with the English crown. While many Irishmen enlisted in the British Army to fight and die in the battle against 'the Hun', others more nationalistically minded used the opportunity of English absence to stage a small uprising in Dublin during the Easter weekend in 1916. It was speedily quelled, but the summary execution of many of its leaders proved counter-productive

and those who were previously sympathetic to English rule began to look favourably upon the idea of some form of Irish independence.

The Emergence of the Free State

An Irish Parliament was instituted in 1919 and, after many a bloody skirmish, England offered treaty conditions in 1921 under which the 26 Irish counties with Nationalist/Catholic majorities were to become a free state on the understanding that the six northern counties of Ulster which had a Unionist/Protestant majority should remain firmly a part of the United Kingdom. But while the English approved, not all the Irish averred, as many wanted independence for the entire island. There followed a blood-letting civil war for two years which finally culminated in the acceptance of the treaty terms, although many of the land-owning class retired to England, seeing little fortune for themselves in a free state largely dominated by Catholics. In Ulster, Stormont was built to house the continuing English admin-istration, while the fledgeling Free State developed its own civil service, police force and army to run the new country in isolation. In the wake of an economic war against England in the 1930s the

The Natural History of Ireland

Paul Sterry

Ireland is an ideal destination for anyone with an interest in natural history. The rural landscape, with its wealth of unspoilt habitats, is rich in plants and animals and offers wildlife interest throughout the year.

A Range of Habitats

Wilderness Ireland conjures up images of a land of bogs and marshes, but in reality there are many other contrasting habitats to be found. Huge lakes and unspoilt rivers dominate any map of Ireland and, where shelter permits, the intricate coastline conceals some excellent estuaries. On the west coast, battered by the full force of the Atlantic, there are stunning cliffs and rocky islands, many of them home to some of the finest seabird colonies in Europe. Mountains and moorlands add another inland dimension to Irish wildlife and, in part, make up for the lack of woodland. Although not normally considered an important wildlife habitat, agricultural land also plays a significant role in Irish natural history. Until recently, non-intensive farming meant that flower-rich meadows could thrive and provide breeding sites for, amongst other species, the corncrake, a bird that is highly endangered elsewhere in Europe.

Influences on Irish Wildlife

In terms of numbers of resident species, the flora and fauna of Ireland is impoverished when compared to Britain and mainland Europe. However, this apparent paucity is balanced by the extraordinary range of interesting species that do occur, as well as by the abundance of many of them. Three physical factors have had a special influence on Irish wildlife – the island's geology, its geographical position and its climate.

Ireland bears many of the scars of glaciation, both physically and in its influence on the natural history. At the retreat of the last Ice Age recolonisation from Britain, and hence from Europe, occurred via land-bridges, which slowly disappeared as the ice melted and sea-levels rose. Some plants and animals simply did not make it –

there are no snakes in Ireland along with many other notable absentee animals.

Unlike its relatively recent geological history, Ireland's underlying ancient geology certainly has contributed to the diversity of its wildlife. In particular, the presence of bedrock limestone has allowed a most unusual mixture of plants to become allies. Among the limestone pavements of the Burren, for example, arctic-alpine flowers grow beside Mediterranean species at altitudes close to sea-level.

Ireland's geographical position has also influenced the flora. Several Irish plants originally came from the Iberian peninsula – the so-called Lusitanian influence – while another element of the flora comes from across the Atlantic. Lastly, Ireland's mild, wet climate has also influenced its wildlife. Rain-bearing Atlantic fronts are a feature of the weather and allow plants to flourish, especially in the bogs and marshes – Ireland is called the 'Emerald Isle' for good reason. Mild winters also mean that Ireland is a refuge for countless birds, the numbers of regular visitors being augmented during bouts of severe weather on mainland Europe.

Bogs and Marshes

Bogs and marshes are a characteristic feature of the landscape and are a delight to most naturalists. Indeed, 'bog-trotting' is an eagerly anticipated pursuit for botanists in Ireland keen to search out wetland specialities.

▼ The large marsh grasshopper

Sphagnum moss is a characteristic bog plant and forms dense carpets of deep green, often studded with rosettes of sundew leaves. Lousewort, cottongrasses, bog asphodel and cross-leaved heath are all found in wet areas, while bell heather and crowberry prefer drier sites. Dragonflies and damselflies are characteristic wetland insects, and sphagnum bogs are perfect habitats for Ireland's largest grasshopper, the large marsh grasshopper. Take care when exploring the bogs, however, especially where the moss is bright green and the ground quakes, as a thin crust of vegetation often blankets deep pools.

During the spring and summer, birdwatchers will find breeding birds such as snipe, redshank and meadow pipits. Stonechats prefer drier land and occasionally fall victim to that dashing bird of prey, the merlin. In winter, flocks of white-fronted geese can be seen in many areas, including Lough Naman Bog near Belleek in Co Fermanagh, and predators such as hen harriers and short-eared owls hunt for small mammals.

Peatlands Park, near Dungannon in Co Armagh, is an extremely good area for the bog enthusiast because a boardwalk affords dry access to some of the best areas. Mongan's Bog near Clonmacnoise and Clara Bog near Clara, both in Co Offaly, also have much to offer, as do the marshes and bogs on the shores of loughs Corrib, Conn, Derg and Carra. Bogs grade into moorland and mountain at the Connemara

National Park near Letterfrack; this site has the added attraction for botanists of St Dabeoc's heath, a rare and attractive plant. Dorset heath and Mackay's heath grow on Errisbeg blanket bog near Roundstone.

Freshwater Lakes and Rivers

Bodies of freshwater and river systems are plentiful in Ireland and most are full of wildlife interest. Breeding and wintering birds are found in abundance and a host of unusual aquatic plants thrive.

Swans are the most visible of the wintering wildfowl. All three European species can be found in Ireland in the winter, the most significant being the whooper swans which, like the slightly smaller Bewick's swans, breed in the Arctic. Most of Iceland's breeding whoopers – several thousand in number – come to

▲ The great-crested grebe

Ireland and good places to look for them, as well as Bewick's swans, are at Lough Foyle near Eglinton (an RSPB reserve), Lough Funshinagh near Athlone and Lough Gara near Frenchpark. Large lakes such as Lough Carra near Ballinrobe, Lough Derravaragh near Mullingar and Lough Conn near Pontoon should be searched for wintering wildfowl such as pochards, tufted ducks, goldeneyes, wigeons, teals and mallards.

Glendalough, in the Wicklow Mountains, makes a good base from which to search for moorland birds such as the red grouse, meadow pipit and ring ouzel ▼

▲ A lone rowan tree grows from a grike in the Burren, home of a remarkable flora

Among the more interesting aquatic flowers to be found in Irish lakes is pipewort, a plant with its main centre of distribution in North America. Look for its grass-like flower spikes around the shores of lakes in western Ireland, particularly in Co Mayo.

As with other elements of the Irish fauna, there are fewer fish species than in Britain. Pike, perch and rudd are native and widespread, but roach are local and have been introduced. A notable feature of many rivers, especially on the west coast, are salmon and sea trout in certain seasons.

Turloughs are seasonally flooding, shallow lakes that often dry up in the summer months. Rahasane Turlough near Craughwell is not only good for wildfowl and waders in the winter, but is interesting in its own right as it is one of the best remaining examples of this type of habitat.

Lough Neagh is the largest freshwater lake in the British Isles and is important for waterfowl. Great crested grebes and mute swans breed here and, in winter, tens of thousands of wildfowl arrive, including whooper swans, pintails, teals, shovelers, tufted ducks and pochards. The east side is generally more productive and is also good for waterside plants including Irish lady's tresses and several rare and unusual grasses.

▲ A dense flowered orchid, the Burren

Mountains and Moorlands
Peaks and moors are exhilarating places for walkers seeking the isolation and challenge of these remote and inhospitable regions. For the naturalist, the rewards are perhaps less obvious than in lowland areas, but many of the upland plants and animals are found nowhere else. Irish mountains are not high and there is often a gradual change from bog habitat to moorland, characterised by heathers and purple moor grass, and finally to the hills and mountains that ring the perimeter of Ireland. Although the Wicklow Mountains comprise the largest upland area in Ireland, those in the south-west harbour the most wildlife interest.

Typical birds of upland regions include red grouse, meadow pipits and ring ouzels. The latter are spring migrants to Ireland. Look out for males perched on rocky outcrops – they resemble blackbirds with a white crescent on their breast. For the botanist, the uplands of the south-west are the most rewarding. The drive from Killarney to Kenmare has a quite stunning backdrop, and by exploring bogs, patches of woodland and rocky gullies, you should be able to come across strawberry trees, Irish spurge, large-flowered and pale butterworts, and St Patrick's cabbage, a type of saxifrage. On rainy days, look for the Kerry slug, an attractive species with spotted markings.

Woodland
Ireland is the least wooded country in Europe. Less than three per cent of the land area is covered by natural woodland whereas, in the past, there was nearly 90 per cent coverage. However, large tracts of conifer plantation are appearing, mainly in upland areas, although these monocultures do little to encourage woodland wildlife. This loss in woodland may, in part, explain the scarcity of many resident and migrant woodland birds – for example, redstarts and great spotted woodpeckers are completely absent from Ireland.

Natural woodlands, and especially those in damp and shady areas, are good for lichens, mosses and ferns. Glengarriff Woodland in Co Kerry is a particularly rewarding site comprising mainly oaks with rowan and birch; holly and strawberry trees can also be found here. Any of the woods around Killarney are worth exploring, as are woodlands in the Connemara National Park near Letterfrack and Marble Arch Forest near Enniskillen. The latter site comprises mainly ash woodland in a dramatic gorge setting.

The Burren
Because of its unique nature, the Burren deserves a special mention on its own. It is a large area of rolling limestone hills and eroded pavements in Co Clare. An extraordinary mixture of flowers, more characteristic of the Alps, the Arctic and the Mediterranean, grow side by side, making this a Mecca for any serious botanist. Anywhere between Lisdoonvarna and Ballyvaughan is likely to be good, and Poulsallagh and Black Head are particularly noteworthy areas of limestone pavement.

Specialities of the Burren, including spring gentian, hoary rock-rose, bloody cranesbill, mountain avens and early purple orchid, provide a stunning display of colour in May and June. Many other species can be found growing in the grykes (eroded cracks in the pavements) and include the dense-flowered orchid, limestone bugle and ferns.

The Coast

For many naturalists, Ireland's coast is its glory. So indented is the coastline that nowhere in the island is more than 50 miles from the sea, and the shoreline itself is far from uniform.

▲ A pair of Bewick's swans, winter visitors to be found on the east coast

At first glance, Ireland's estuaries and mudflats may appear featureless and bleak, but in reality they teem with life. Molluscs, crustaceans and other marine creatures are abundant and provide the food on which many coastal birds depend. Estuaries are, perhaps, most rewarding for the birdwatcher during the winter months. The mild temperatures encourage huge numbers of ducks, geese and waders to visit; in spring, many of them fly north to breeding grounds elsewhere in Europe.

Strangford Lough, not far from Belfast, is an outstanding birdwatching site. The mudflats are home to vast numbers of birds which are best viewed from the A20 which runs along its eastern shore. Brent geese, whooper swans, teals, red-breasted mergansers, greenshanks, redshanks and grey plovers are among the species to look out for. There is an observation hide at Castle Espie near Comber.

Equally famous among birdwatching circles are the Wexford Slobs. Much of the area to the north of Wexford Harbour is now a wildfowl reserve and it is the best site on the island for Greenland white-fronted geese, brent geese, Bewick's swans (all winter visitors) and many others.

Not far away from Wexford are two other excellent coastal areas. Tacumshin Lake, near Tomhaggard, drains at low tide to reveal mudflats covered in plants such as glasswort and seablite, and harbours a rich invertebrate fauna. Coastal birds such as gulls, waders and wildfowl are easily spotted, and serious birdwatchers rate it highly as a site for vagrant birds from America in the autumn. Lady's Island Lake, near Rosslare Harbour, is an enclosed, brackish lake with an interesting flora including the rare cottonweed.

Sheltering in the south-west corner of Ireland, Tralee Bay has mudflats and large areas of salt-marsh. Brent geese and wigeon are winter highlights – try visiting the western side of the bay near Lough Gill, itself a good birdwatching spot. Near Tralee Bay is the brackish Akeragh Lough at Ballyheige. The dunes have an interesting flora and the lake is another good place for American vagrant birds in the autumn.

The Shannon Estuary is a vast system of mudflats, salt-marshes and grazing marsh. Waders include huge flocks of dunlins and black-tailed godwits, with the best areas being around Aughinish Island on the south side and Poulnasherry on the north.

Ireland is indeed fortunate is possessing some of the most dramatic coastal scenery in Europe. Many of the inaccessible cliffs and islands, particularly on the west coast, are home to immense colonies of seabirds. Birds such as puffins, guillemots, razorbills, shags and kittiwakes have important colonies here and the sight (and smell) of these lures birdwatchers during the months of May and June. Although by their very nature most of these colonies cannot be approached closely, excellent views can usually be had with the aid of binoculars.

Good sites to visit include the Saltee Islands off Kilmore Quay in Co Wexford, Old Head of Kinsale near Kinsale in Co Cork, Skellig Michael off Ballinskelligs in Co Kerry, Puffin Island off Portmagee in Co Kerry, Horn Head south of Buncrana in Co Donegal, the Cliffs of Moher in Co Clare and Rathlin Island off Ballycastle in Co Antrim. Many of these coastal areas are also home to the chough, an aerobatic member of the crow family with red legs and a long, down-curved bill.

Seawatching is a favourite pursuit of the serious birdwatcher. During periods of strong onshore winds, large numbers of seabirds are pushed closer to the shore than is usual and good views can be obtained. Spring and autumn, when most North Atlantic seabirds are migrating, are the best seasons and most of the sites mentioned above can be good in suitable weather. Look for gannets, shearwaters, storm petrels and skuas. As a bonus, the west coast also offers the chance of seeing basking sharks, huge ocean sunfish and an occasional whale or dolphin.

Great Blasket Island from Slea Head on the Dingle peninsula – good for seabirds ▼

The Shape of the Land

Helen Livingston

Ireland stands on the western edge of the Old World and faces the New World across the Atlantic storms, Europe's last stop before America. The character of its landscape reflects this, and even today there is a sensation that this is an outpost, a frontier land, bathed in the clear light reflected from the great ocean.

The 'Emerald Isle' is green and growing, for lush grass flourishes in the moist climate, fed by rain brought in by westerly winds off the Atlantic, and the Irish landscape has a mysterious, intangible quality that springs from the ever-changing light and shade that is born of its climate. From day to day and even from hour to hour, the light shifts, so that what was the misty outline of a hill becomes a shining reality and then, with another change of mood, a black menacing presence.

But what is a 'typical' Irish landscape? It is impossible to define, for juxtaposed within a short space are mountains and hills, moorlands and pasture. And always there is the landscape of water: lakes and rivers, the curious peat bogs with their brown pools, and the wonderfully diverse scenery of nearly 1,900 miles of coast.

Geology

The variety of scenery is matched by a variety in the rocks underfoot. The oldest rocks in Ireland are found near Rosslare in Co Wexford. They are 2,400 million years old, and are ancient even when compared to the oldest rocks in the world which are about 3,500 million years old. Other ancient rocks break through to the surface in Co Donegal and in parts of Co Mayo and Co Galway. Ireland's youngest rocks, at a modest 15,000 years, are the sands, gravels and clays of the great Ice Age. Ireland has had an exciting geological history: it has been covered by the sea; it has been elevated in mountains on the scale of today's Himalayas; the north-west and south-east parts of the island have been separated by an ocean the size of the modern Atlantic; and much of the country has been buried by glaciers.

In the north, including the counties of Mayo, Sligo, Donegal, Tyrone, Derry and Antrim, the

grain of the land runs north-east to south-west. This is the same alignment as in Scotland and

The Giant's Causeway; there is a similar structure in the Hebridean isle of Staffa ▼

Scandinavia, and reflects the trend of an ancient chain of mountains which ran across these lands some 440 million years ago. These mountains were formed by the violent collision of two crustal plates which joined together the two halves of Ireland. At the same time, molten granite from within the earth was injected into the existing rocks. This granite now forms the Wicklow Mountains and the region to the west of Galway.

In the south-western counties of Kerry and Cork the grain of the country runs approximately east to west, sending long fingers of land out into the Atlantic which are separated by the tapering inlets of Dingle Bay, the Kenmare River and Bantry Bay. Further east, the same arrangement is found in the Galtee and Knockmealdown mountains. These ridges and valleys are the remains of ancient folds in the rock, folds which were creased into the strata 300 million years ago, the result of the formation of another mountain range, this time well to the south of Ireland.

Between about 65 million and 30 million years ago, lava upwelled on to the surface and spread over the land to form the Giant's Causeway and Antrim Plateau. At about the same time, the granite of the Mourne Mountains was injected into the rocks of the area and volcanoes erupted. Long extinct, these now form isolated hills such as Killteely Hill in Co Limerick.

Common Irish Rock Types
Limestone is the most widespread rock in Ireland, the familiar grey stone of walls and cottages. It covers the whole of the midland region, yet over most of this area it is unseen at the surface, buried beneath glacial clays and sands. Occasionally, the limestone juts through to make steep hills, as at Ben of Fore and others in nearby Co Westmeath. But where the limestone forms moorlands raised above the surrounding countryside, the landscape is dramatic. The Burren in Co Clare has the largest expanse of bare limestone pavement in western Europe, and smaller stretches of limestone upland are found in Co Sligo, Co Fermanagh and Co Cavan.

Formed about 350 million years ago, limestone was laid down in the sea, later to be elevated as land above sea-level. It contains many marine fossils: look for sea shells, corals and broken stems of sea lilies.

Limestone is a strange rock, hard and resilient yet susceptible to being dissolved in rain-water, and rain-water is far from rare in Ireland! Enormous quantities of limestone have disappeared, literally washed away, which explains why Irish limestone generally forms lowlands. In some areas only isolated blocks of this rock are left, such as the dramatic mountain of Knocknarea, just to the west of Sligo.

'Lost rivers', a feature of limestone terrain, are common. South of the Marble Arch Caves in Co Fermanagh, the Owensbream River flows on to limestone rock where it sinks into the ground under a 130ft high cliff. It re-emerges at the Marble Arch Caves. In other places such 'sinks' are mere boggy hollows – as at Geevagh in Co Sligo and on the Burren in Co Clare. Ireland has a vast hidden landscape of limestone caverns, only a small fraction of which have been explored. Some caves are open to the public, allowing visitors to explore in safety and to see the great stalactites and stalagmites, many stained brown and orange due to impurities in the rock. Such caves include Marble Arch Caves in Co Fermanagh, Mitchelstown Caves in Co Tipperary and Aillwee Caves on the Burren in Co Clare.

Limestone pavements, so magnificent in the Burren, developed through the solution of the rock by rain-water once the protective covering of soil was ripped off by the glaciers of the great Ice Age. These bare rock surfaces are divided into blocks which are separated by deep fissures known as grykes, the latter harbouring rare and beautiful flora.

Sandstone is found mostly in the south and south-west and in the Belfast region. It is a rock of warmer hue than the cool grey limestone, and was formed by sand and gravel being laid down some 400 million years ago, making it slightly older than the limestone. Sandstone does not dissolve in rain-water, and is a strong rock. In the south-west it forms the east–west hill and mountain ranges, between which the limestone forms the lowlands.

Quartzite, which forms the gleaming white peaks of such mountains as Errigal (Co Donegal), the Great Sugar Loaf (Co Wicklow), Croagh Patrick (Co Mayo) and the Twelve Bens of Connemara (Co Galway), is virtually indestructible under the moist Irish climate. Compact and resistant, it is ancient sandstone which has been altered by great heat and pressure so that it

▲ The distant Maumturk Mountains

Elements of Scenery

In Ireland it is rare to be out of sight of hills. They hover on the horizon as a blue haze, sharpening into clearer profile as rain approaches. They break up the central plains and the moorlands, and reach their apogee along the west coast where they face the Atlantic breakers. Here some of the hills fall sheer into the surf – as with the massive 2,000ft high cliffs of Slieve League in Co Donegal.

Irish mountains frequently rise almost from sea level, and this endows them with a more lofty quality than they otherwise might possess. And how varied they are! They range from the quartzite peaks of Donegal (including Muckish and elegant Errigal), sufficiently

is composed almost entirely of the grey-white mineral silica.

The dark, fine-grained rock known as basalt was formed by a succession of lava flows oozing on to the land and blanketing the surface, thereby producing the familiar hexagonal columns of the Giant's Causeway and Antrim Plateau.

Distinctive and speckled granite, made underground where molten rock was injected into the crust, contains large black, white and pink crystals. It is hard and usually forms high ground – examples are the Wicklow Mountains and Mountains of Mourne.

The Great Ice Age

The imprint of the Ice Age is stamped clearly on Ireland's landscape. Glaciers spread out from the main mountain masses, so that only the highest peaks protruded above the ice and snow. Glaciers transformed river valleys into U-shaped troughs – Glenmalure in Co Wicklow is a fine example, as is the Gaddagh Valley beneath Carrantuohill in Co Kerry. At the coast, glaciated valleys made fjords or long, deep, winding arms of the sea. Killary Harbour, between Co Mayo and Co Galway is a superb example.

Corries, or great mountainside hollows, were gouged out of the mountain-tops by ice. Coumshingaun, in the Comeragh Mountains of Co Waterford, is probably the most spectacular Irish corrie, with a backing cliff 1,300ft high. Other noteworthy corries are Coomasaharn in Co Kerry, the hollow containing Lough Bray in the Wicklow Mountains, and the hollows cut into the north face of

▲ Yeats made this distinctive mountain, Benbulben (520m), in Co Sligo, famous in verse; it is spectacular in profile, too

Slieve Corragh in the Mourne Mountains.

The rock removed from the corries and valleys was left behind in the lowlands when the ice melted, thus conspicuous small hills of glacially deposited sand, gravel and clay can be found amid the pastures of central and southern Ireland.

isolated from one another to give breathing space and impart an air of fantasy to the whole, to the Mountains of Mourne, granite domes which cluster together in rounded solemnity; and from the Wicklow Mountains, which are an older granite range, crouching together to the south of Dublin, to the sandstone Macgillicuddy's Reeks of Kerry, which stand as a great ridge thrusting towards the Atlantic, and the Twelve Bens of

Connemara, quartzite peaks watching relentlessly over western Galway.

The rock-strewn moorlands are wild uplands of sweeping solitude, their character varying with the rock from which they are made. There is bleak sandstone moorland above Windy Gap in Killarney, brooded over by the summits of Macgillicuddy's Reeks, and the bare waste of the limestone Burren in Co Clare, which seems to embrace the sky. North-west Mayo, the most remote and lonely moorland of them all, is carved across ancient twisted rocks where black turf-cuttings punctuate a seemingly uninhabited land.

The moorlands drop down slowly to the plains, so that isolated pockets of pasture, surrounded by rough stone walls, shoulder away the moors and cultivated land takes over. This chequer-board of green fields, divided by stone walls or by deep hedges and crossed by great rivers, is the quintessential rich landscape of the 'Emerald Isle'. It is a landscape largely inherited from the Ice Age, the soils of the midlands having been formed on glacial clays.

Small hills among the pasturelands are Ice Age features: winding ridges, often followed by roads keeping to a dry course, are the fossilised casts of rivers which flowed beneath huge sheets of glacial ice. Such ridges are particularly common in the Tuam region of Co Galway. Other small rounded or oval hills, which cluster together making for a broken lowland terrain, are found in a great swathe of land from Co Down through Armagh, Monaghan, Cavan, Leitrim and Sligo to Mayo.

In Ireland water is never far away and it contributes much to the excitement and beauty of the scenery, from moorland stream, dark bog-pool or inland lake, to the vast indented coast. There are always reflections of landscape and sky, or movement and flashes of light.

Irish rivers on their way to the sea frequently languish in lakes. The mighty River Shannon is a prime example, flowing through a whole series of lakes including Lough Ree and Lough Derg, before passing into its lengthy estuary and out to the Atlantic. Such rivers, winding over the glacial deposits which cover the lowland limestone of the midlands, have no steep gradient down which to flow. They spread out, seemingly unconfined by any valley, and whenever the topography permits they form the lakes. Often, as is the case around Lough Oughter in Co Cavan, rivers and lakes merge together in a marshy, reedy maze of channels and swamps. Such regions are scarcely far removed from the peat bogs.

Peat bogs, which provide Ireland's one huge natural resource – turf for burning, and agricultural and garden peat – are brooding, lonely places. Today, this landscape is fast disappearing as commercial cutting gobbles up the peat at a phenomenal rate. The largest peat bogs in Ireland are in the midlands, where they developed on the uneven land left behind by the glaciers. These raised peat bogs started life as lakes in enclosed hollows surrounded by lush vegetation. The lakes slowly filled up with plant debris. Fen woodland gave place to bog moss and the whole habitat became wetter and more acidic. The blanket bogs of upland areas, such as the flat summit of Ben Bulben in Co Sligo, also developed because of an accumulation of plant debris in the moist, mild climate.

There is a gentle sadness and an inexpressible longing in the landscape of the peat bogs. Away from huge commercial extraction you can still savour this quality, where neatly stacked turf fresh from the cutting and the black cut surfaces themselves are the only signs of humanity under wide skies.

The landscape of water reaches its most magnificent and its most varied along Ireland's 1,900 miles of coast.

The east coast faces Britain and mainland Europe across the Irish Sea, so that the full wrath of waves that have travelled thousands of miles across the ocean does not reach it. Thus, mudflats, sandy beaches and low cliffs are found in many places, as in those areas between south Wexford and Dundalk Bay.

The western coast of Ireland is the final rampart of Europe, and along this seaboard is an amazing variety of coastal scenery. There are deep sea fjords, such as Lough Foyle with the spectacular mountains at its mouth, and lovely Killary Harbour, winding far inland, and there are the glaring white sands of the Connemara beaches, formed of silica sand eroded from the quartzite rocks of the area. There are also the ramparts of Slieve League in Co Donegal, the towering isolated cliff of Croaghaun on Achill Island, and the great wall of the Cliffs of Moher in Co Clare, which, at less than half the height of Slieve League, achieve an impressive magnificence because they are so vertical. Then there is the wide, long estuary of the Shannon, with its rocky coves and its inner mudflats, and finally, where the grain of the land is at right angles to the coast, there are the hill promontories and long tapering inlets of the south-west, reaching the climax of their beauty along the coast of Kerry.

Looking down Killary Harbour in Connemara, considered by some to be Ireland's finest fjord, near the village of Leenane – the setting for the film, *The Field* ▼

The Country House and Garden
Jack Whaley

Although heritage houses with landscaped gardens are quite rare in Ireland, there are, fortunately, some splendid exceptions where very fine houses are matched by equally stunning gardens – Mount Stewart in Co Down and Malahide Castle in Co Dublin being just two.

The 'Big House' in History
In times past the 'big house' was nearly always accompanied by its walled garden. These gardens were usually sited at some distance from the house so that a large expanse of wall did not impose itself upon the view from the house. Pinched circumstances, however, left the owners of many of the large houses with little choice but to cut back somewhere, and that often meant the abandonment of walled gardens. Gone today are many of these old families who were unsuited to present-day commercialism, and who were forced to sell off their estates or struggle unsuccessfully to avert the inevitable decay of their homes and lands. Ruined castles which were once the seats of great families are therefore commonplace throughout the island.

After the advent of the Irish Republic, a state of hostility raged between the large landowners and

▲ Mount Stewart House and Gardens

the new government. As with most newly emergent nations, there eventually came about a compromise with some tolerance conceded on both sides so that now, instead of trying to tear down the fabric of a colonial regime, those in government have come to realise the potential of what was previously regarded as a foreign culture. As a result, many of the large private properties – including their fine gardens – have now passed into state ownership. Those under the direction of the Office of Public Works and other public bodies in the Republic have been developed with sensitive discernment, and now provide a tourist attraction of wide appeal.

The Stately Homes of the North
The National Trust operates in Northern Ireland and has its headquarters at Rowallane in Co Down. Visitors to this old demesne, its gardens having been developed by the family owners before it became a Trust property, enter a driveway planted with towering rhododendron bushes. The gardens, including an arboretum, spread around the house and also feature a walled garden of quite exceptional quality. Many plant varieties have been developed and raised here, and carry the name of the garden. The house, however, is not generally open to the public as it contains the administrative offices of the Trust.

Another National Trust property, and one which must rank among the jewels in its crown, is Mount Stewart on the shores of Strangford Lough. The early 19th-century house with its vast Ionic portico was built close to the site of an earlier house, around the same time as the first Marquis of Londonderry gained his title. Inside the house (open to the public), the visitors' book contains many notable names, including those of the then future King George VI and the present Queen Mother who visited the house when they were the Duke and Duchess of York. In 1977 Lady Mairi Bury, the last member of the family in residence, presented Mount Stewart to the National Trust,

Azaleas and other acid-loving plants thrive at Rowallane Gardens, Co Down ▼

▲ The gardens at Bantry House have the added attraction of views over Bantry Bay

although she continues to live there today.

The garden at Mount Stewart is unrivalled in Ireland. The architectural settings designed by Lady Londonderry are as eye-catching as the plants. The latter include many rare and tender items whose survival is made possible by the Gulf Stream conditions existing around this coastal area. In the vicinity of the old driveway, a collection of choice species and hybrid rhododendrons provides a succession of colour. Facing the house, a large artificial lake has a waterside walk lined with specimen trees and shrubs around its entire perimeter. At the northern extremity of the lake can be seen olive trees which were grown from seeds obtained from the Mount of Olives. East of the house stands the Temple of the Winds which was erected by the first Marquis. Its architect, James Athenian Stuart, specialised in neoclassical architecture and this work, apart from his other masterpiece at Shugborough in Staffordshire, is the only accurate replica of the famous Athenian Tower of the Wind.

Journeying South
Dublin can be reached by a two-hour drive through the scenic valleys bordering the Mourne Mountains. On the northerly outskirts of the city, and nestling in the picturesque village of Malahide, is the historic castle of the Talbot family. The estate and its famous garden, containing a unique collection of Australasian plants, is now owned by Dublin County Council, since 800 years of continuous occupation of Malahide Castle by the Talbot family ended in 1973 with the death of Lord Milo Talbot. The castle is open to the public and contains examples of various periods of architectural design with furnishings to match. The threads of history are woven into the lives of this family which lost 14 of its members in the Battle of the Boyne.

Venturing a few miles south of Dublin and just inland from the coast lies the Powerscourt demesne, a magnificent garden with breath-taking views of the mountains around. The mansion of the Powerscourt family has largely been destroyed by fire, but a visit to the extensive landscaped gardens with their giant trees, lakes, fountains and waterfalls is an absolute must.

Into the Midlands
The Irish midlands, while of no great intrinsic beauty in themselves, do contain one or two places rich in distinction. One of these is Birr Castle, which possesses gardens which contain a comprehensive collection of trees and shrubs. (The castle itself is not open to the public.)

Across the Slieve Bloom Mountains lies Emo Court. This Palladian mansion, for many years the seat of the Earls of Portarlington, is situated six miles out of Port Laoise towards Dublin beside the village of Emo. It was designed for the first Earl of Portarlington by James Gandon, the celebrated architect of the Custom House and Four Courts in Dublin. Emo was the only country house he designed. Building began in 1790 and was sufficiently advanced to allow habitation in 1793, but by then costs had considerably overrun estimates and the matter of interior decoration had to be deferred. It was not until 1830 that Louis Vulliamy was engaged to execute the grandiose decoration.

The grounds are a fitting match for the magnificence of the house. A very extensive garden containing a wide variety of trees and shrubs has been built up by the present owner, Cholmeley Harrison. The grounds are open daily during season and the house can be viewed by appointment.

Estates of the South-West
Heading south again, some particularly fine scenery is encountered in the well wooded and watered valleys of Co Cork. At Glengarriff near the border with Co Kerry, time should be taken to visit Bantry House, poised to provide a panoramic view of Bantry Bay. The house is famous throughout the world for its furnishings, including tapestries which once belonged to Marie Antoinette.

Out in Bantry Bay and reached by a ferry service, Garinish Island is a gardners' paradise. Here can be seen the most tender of the exotic plants introduced into Ireland, and the antics of playful seals on the rocks around the island provide a spectacle few will forget.

A Land of Historic Ruins

Peter Harbison

▲ The most wonderfully positioned of Irish ruins, Dún Aengus, in the Aran Islands

To say that Ireland is a country in ruins is very far from the truth, but it is fair to say that it is a land rich in historic ruins which provide a visual record of Irish architectural achievement, a cross-section and elevation illustrating the island's historical and cultural ups and downs.

Passage-tombs and Megaliths

These ruins take us as far back as the Stone Age around 3000BC when, half a millennium before the pyraminds were built, the Irish 'took the edge' off them, as it were, by erecting 'round pyramids' – hemispherical passage-tombs where the dead were buried in chambers near the centre of a great man-made mound, just as the pharaohs were to be interred in Egypt some five centuries later. None of these passage-tombs is more famous than Newgrange (Co Meath), one of Europe's first great masterpieces of architecture, where the rays of the sun climbing above the horizon on the shortest day of the year penetrate the cavernous recesses of the tomb-chamber within.

Newgrange is only one amongst hundreds of Ireland's megalithic tombs, although it stands at the more sophisticated end of the range, counterbalanced by the simple three- or four-legged dolmen which captivates us with its graceful charm worthy of a modern abstract sculpture.

All of these 'great stone' tombs are presumed to be pre-Celtic, but the Celtic warriors in their turn made their contribution to the Irish landscape by building stone fortresses for the living, usually circular in shape with high walls, as at Staigue in Co Kerry. However, few can match the barbaric magnificence of Dun Aengus on the Aran Islands in Galway Bay, where the defenders saved themselves a lot of toil by perching a set of semi-circular walls on a precipitous cliff-edge where no attacker could climb the 200ft from the raging waters of the Atlantic Ocean below.

Monastic Remains

Redolent of more peaceful preoccupations are the remains of the Christian monasteries which enrich the serenity of rural Ireland at places like Monasterboice (Co Louth), Clonmacnoise (Co Offaly), Devenish (Co Fermanagh) and Kells (Co Meath), once the home of the famous book now preserved in the library of Trinity College, Dublin. Their most conspicuous monuments are the slender round towers which rise heavenwards to a height sometimes reaching 100ft, and in which Ireland has a virtual monopoly. Bell-towers (or campaniles) in essence, they served to call the devout to worship, as a store for the monastery's treasured reliquaries and, like a beacon, to encourage the flagging spirits of the pilgrim on his or her final steps to pray at the shrine of the founding saint.

Standing frequently almost literally in their shadow on the same sites are the great high crosses of stone. Their characteristic ring supported the cross-arms and doubtless doubled as a cosmic symbol surrounding a representation of the crucifixion which nearly always takes up the crucial central position at the junction of arms and shaft. The crosses themselves are decorated with high-relief figure sculptures illustrating scenes from the Old and New Testaments, exhorting the faithful to reflect on the content of the Bible story, and encouraging popular piety in monk and laity alike.

A third element frequently found in these early monasteries is, not unnaturally, one or more small churches, often unadorned but occasionally providing delightful examples of the carver's imaginative craftsmanship in the Romanesque style of the 12th century. The simple abodes of the ascetic monks who erected these wonderful monuments have rarely been preserved, although examples of beehive huts are occasionally found on islands off the west coast which they once inhabited.

The same 12th century which saw the popularity of Romanesque churches also experienced two significant historical changes which were to add a whole new dimension to Ireland's monumental heritage. The first of these was the arrival of the new Continental monastic orders – the Cistercians, Dominicans and later the Franciscans, among others – who brought order into the layout of the monasteries, in contrast to the piecemeal building which had prevailed in the earlier Irish establishments. Those Irish who wanted to live the life of monastic contemplation no longer flocked to the old Irish monasteries, which were gradually abandoned one by one, and they thronged instead to the new order monasteries.

These later monasteries were characterised by a long and lofty church (with a tower) placed on one side of an open, restangular cloister-garth which provided circulation to the more domestic parts of the monastery. They remained in use for centuries until they were dissolved by King Henry VIII, although some may have retained their roofs until Cromwell provided the final death-blow.

Norman Castles

The second important event of the 12th century was the arrival of the Norman barons, which led to the construction of massive castles such as Carrickfergus in Co Antrim and Trim in Co Meath which are, however, more compact than some of their great Welsh counterparts. The Normans also built a host of lesser fortifications to enforce their claims to the lands which they so speedily conquered from the hapless Irish. Some of these castles were rendered obsolete with the advent of the cannon around the 16th century, but others continued to carry out their vital defensive function as late as the 17th century when they were made harmless and instead became the skeletons which can be seen standing sentinel in town and countryside today.

Tower Houses

Following the general European trend in the later part of Middle Ages, the Irish of the 15th and 16th centuries came to build smaller tower houses as status symbols for their families, and they often surrounded these with bawn-walls to keep their cattle in at night. The passing of the Gaelic aristocracy in the 17th century, however, led to their decline, although castles and bawns of English and Scottish inspiration were built at the same time in the northern counties by the planters who had settled there, and more spacious mansions started to be built in other parts of the country too.

Forts and Stately Homes

Later fortifications are rarer, one of the great exceptions being the splendid star-shaped Charles Fort near Kinsale in Co Cork, built around 1680. The fear of a Napoleonic invasion to attack England through the back door of Ireland led to the construction of the most recent fortifications, the early 19th-century Martello towers most numerous along the east coast, and some stout defences to prevent a crossing of the River Shannon at places such as Banagher in Co Offaly.

Some of the medieval castles were adapted for more gracious living conditions in the 18th century, of which Malahide Castle in Co Dublin is a fine example. That same enlightened century saw the construction of some splendid country houses for the Ascendancy gentry, of which Westport House in Co Mayo and Castletown in Co Kildare are excellent representatives and which are normally open to the public. Others sadly suffered depredations during the civil war in the early 20th century, or fell prey to the impoverishment of their owners. A decline in the numbers of the Protestant population in Ireland also led to the deconsecration of a number of attractive 19th-century churches – but they, like the other monuments from prehistoric to medieval times discussed above, are a reflection of the ever-changing historical circumstances which are common to all nations the world over.

These pages: Staigue Fort, on the Ring of Kerry, is roughly 2,500 years old

A Taste of the Irish Ian Hill

Breakfast and beyond

First-time travellers may be stunned by the Irish farmhouse breakfast. First come plates of wheaten bread, soda bread, hot toast, freshly rolled pats of buttercup-yellow butter and pots of home-made raspberry, strawberry and damson jam. This is followed by hot porridge swimming in buttermilk, topped with cream and dredged with demerara sugar, and then a 'gentleman's' (two eggs) or 'lady's' (one egg) fry, with two rashers of fried (not grilled) bacon, two pieces of fried potato bread, a slice of fried soda bread and sometimes even fried bull's testicles!

Not all breakfasts will be as overpowering as this, but few will be far short of it. Although the Irish do not eat 'lunch', they may eat 'dinner' at that time and follow it in the evening with high tea.

Dinner (or lunch) may consist of an Irish stew (lamb, leeks, carrots, potatoes, lots of salt) or boiled Ballymoney or Limerick ham with cabbage, onions and simple white sauce. This could be followed by apple tart and cream, and washed down – if the traveller can develop a taste for it – with buttermilk, the liquid left when the makings of butter are removed from the milk.

After dinner, and if feeling a little peckish before high tea, the traveller may have quite a search for the traditional afternoon tea with its big pot of strong tea and choice of half a dozen kinds of bread and scones. An old-fashioned stately hotel is the best bet. There may be soda bread, made on a griddle from baking soda, flour, salt and buttermilk; wheaten bread; apple soda and currant bread; and beautiful barm brack, a yeast bread full of currants which should, ideally, be toasted in front of an open fire and smothered in butter. And high tea? Well, this is rather like breakfast all over again, with maybe a chop thrown in for the missing porridge, and another three types of bread and assorted home-made jams.

Restaurants and Festivals

Of course, Ireland is not all like this. There are excellent, sophisticated restaurants in the major cities. Dublin has its 'Left Bank' brasserie area on the River Liffey's right bank at Temple Bar, while Galway's is by the quays and Belfast's is between the Opera House and the university. There is also a handful of dazzling young chefs turning the island's freshest farm, sea and lake produce into the lightest of temptations, as well as Georgian country houses producing poached wild Atlantic salmon with a fruit-based sauce and steamed new potatoes in the spring and summer. In the winter look for woodcock, snipe, wild duck and hare, with redcurrant sauces from the old estate gardens.

Nowadays there are several dazzling fish restaurants serving nothing but the freshest wild salmon and trout, plus brill, hake, turbot, plaice, crab, lobster and scallops. Mussels, oysters and Venus clams do not, unlike salmon and trout, suffer by being farmed, but enthusiasts should head for Galway with its native flat oysters, the stars of the first of the county's two September oyster festivals, at Clarinbridge. The other, the Galway Oyster Festival, takes place two weeks later in Galway city. Kinsale's International Gourmet Festival during the first week of October is Co Cork's suitable rival.

Strangford in Co Down has no food festival yet, but its Galway Hooker Regatta in June is a splendid time to compare the north's oysters, scallops and mussels with those of the west.

Seafood

Oysters should ideally be accompanied with brown wheaten bread, farmhouse butter and a slice of lemon; mussels steamed open over a bubbling mixture of parsley, celery, onions, fresh ground pepper and white wine; and scallops sizzled in butter and bacon fat, and served with the brown bacon scraps which produced the fat. Dublin Bay prawns (*Nephrops norvegicus* or the Norway lobster) should be

Irish baking has much more to offer than just soda bread, delicious though it is ▼

boiled and dipped in melted butter, or split and first sizzled in butter, then dashed with whiskey and flamed as the whiskey heats. To finish, toss in ¼ pint (150ml) of whipping cream, heat up and serve. The real lobster (*Homarus gammarus*), treated similarly but with the flesh removed from the shells for cooking and then replaced in the shell for serving, is fit for its culinary title of the 'Dublin lawyer'.

Traditional Fare

Many younger chefs have lost the shame their predecessors attached to traditional dishes, often dismissed as peasant food. Irish stew, drisheen (black pudding), cruibeens (boiled pigs' trotters), colcannon (mashed potato, leek, butter, cabbage, cream and nutmeg), champ (mashed potato, chives and butter), Dublin coddle (a stew of sausage, bacon, onion, sliced potato and ham-bone stock) and beef in Guinness (as boeuf à la bourguignonne, but with stout), are making daring appearances on fashionable menus. More restaurants specialising in native fare cannot be far behind.

Barm Brack

1 teaspoon fresh yeast
2oz (50g) caster sugar
¼ pint (150ml) lukewarm milk
1 teaspoon mixed spice
8oz (250g) plain flour, sieved
1 egg
pinch of salt
6oz (200g) mixed sultanas,
currants, raisins and candied peel
2 teaspoons sugar

Cream the yeast and sugar, and leave to froth in the milk. Rub the butter into the sieved flour, caster

sugar and spice. Make a hollow in the top and add the yeast mixture and the beaten egg. Beat for 10 minutes with a wooden spoon to form a dough. Work in the fruit and salt by hand and knead. Put in a warmed bowl, allowing it to rise to double its size in about an hour.

Knead again, place in a lightly greased circular baking tin (7in or 15cm) and leave for a further half-hour. Bake in a pre-heated oven at Gas Mark 6 (400°F, 200°C) for 45 minutes. Finally, when baked, glaze with syrup made from 2 teaspoons of sugar dissolved in 3 teaspoons of boiling water.

Boxty

Boxty on the griddle, boxty in the pan,
If you cannot make your boxty, you'll never get your man.

8oz (250g) raw potato
8oz (250g) boiled and mashed potato
8oz (250g) plain flour, sieved
1 teaspoon baking powder
1 teaspoon salt
2oz (60g) butter, melted
¼ pint (150ml) milk

Grate the raw potatoes on to a cloth, then wring out any liquid, keeping it so that it separates into a clear liquid with the starch lying at the bottom. Discard the clear liquid and mix the starch with both the grated raw and the cooked mashed potatoes. Mix in the sieved flour, baking powder, salt, melted butter and enough milk to make a good dough. Knead gently on a floured board. Divide into four and make four flat, round cakes. Mark, but do not cut each cake into quarters. Bake on the griddle.

▲ Fresh salmon and trout such as these are to be savoured throughout Ireland

Hot Irish

A specific palliative against the common cold, and a recommended preventative against it in winter.

boiling water
1 teaspoon demerara sugar
1 large measure Irish whiskey
slice of lemon
6 cloves
pinch of cinnamon and/or nutmeg

Fill a whiskey glass with very hot water, then discard this and fill the glass to two-thirds with fresh boiling water. Dissolve in the sugar, add the whiskey, then add the lemon slice, the cloves, the cinnamon and a little grated nutmeg. Savour the heat, inhale the marvellous aromas and enjoy!

Irish hospitality is hard to beat ▼

Irish Myth and Legend

Dáithí Ó hÓgáin

Ireland is an outstanding reservoir of folklore in the modern world. Until recently communities relied on their own resources for education and entertainment, and as Irish people have always had a taste for style and metaphor in their speech, the traditional stories which they tell one another are usually longer and more elaborate than those of other countries. The Irish language has the oldest vernacular literature in Europe, with beginnings in the 6th century AD, and the interplay of literary and oral traditions has led to a great richness of lore.

The Irish Heroes

The hero-tales of Ireland are celebrated for their antique aura as well as for the strange mixture of tragedy and humour in them. For instance, medieval Irish literature tells of the super-hero Cú Chulainn, who while still a boy slew a fierce hound and grew up to be a great and handsome champion who could overcome whole armies. Yet, despite all his glory, there are burlesque accounts of him, such as the 'battle-frenzy' which caused his face to become savagely ugly and his body to revolve within its skin. This hero is the leading character in the Ulster Cycle, a group of tales which centre on Eamhain Mhacha (Navan Fort), near Armagh.

Further south, at Tara in Co Meath, the sacred site of kingship, ancient rituals have left their imprint on the many stories of the King Cycle. Principal among these is the account of how Cormac Mac Airt came to Tara as an unknown youngster and reigned there as the wisest and best of all rulers. It is said that he was born after his father had been slain in battle by the usurper, Lughaidh Mac Con. When he was seven years of age, he was advised by a druid to go to Tara, and as he approached that stronghold he met a woman who was weeping. She explained to him that Lughaidh had killed her herd of sheep because they had grazed on one of the royal fields. Coming into the presence of the usurper, young Cormac declared that the proper judgement would have been one shearing of the sheep for one grazing of the field. Those who were present were so impressed by this that they deposed the usurper and installed Cormac as king.

It is said that on the Hill of Allen in Co Kildare stood the fortress of the celebrated Fionn Mac Cumhaill. Fionn was originally a Celtic symbol of the seer-poet, but for more than a thousand years stories have been told all over Ireland which represent him as the leader of a colourful band of hunter-warriors, known as the Fianna troop. We are told that, as a little boy, he got his great knowledge by tasting a sacred salmon from the Boyne River, and that he saved Tara from a demonic being who came at November to destroy the citadel with burning breath. Fionn had the

Legend has it that the Hill of Tara was the palace of the High Kings of Ireland ▼

gift of seeing into past, present and future by placing his thumb in his mouth and chewing it.

The folklore of the north-west preserves the memory of the mythical champion Lugh, well known to the European Celts who named Lyon, Leiden and many other places after him. In Ireland he is the grandson of the tyrant Balar, who had a baleful eye which destroyed all on which it gazed. Balar ordered the newly born Lugh to be put to death, but the child was stolen away by the smith Goibhniu and reared in secret. When he came of age, Lugh met his grandfather in battle and shot the eye from his head before Balar could uncover it. Balar was slain and his oppressive army defeated, and Lugh founded the harvest festival (called after him 'Lughnasa') at the hill of Ushnagh in Co Westmeath, then regarded as the focal point of the country.

Mythical Women

Ireland has traditionally been described as a woman, who becomes a beautiful young maiden in times of prosperity but is an ugly hag in times of misery and distress. Several mounds and hills are said to contain palaces of the lustrous otherworld folk called the *sí*, and folklore tells of golden-haired queens who preside over their subjects there. The idea that an otherworld patroness cares for the fortunes of Irish families has led to the widespread Irish belief in the banshee (*bean sí*, literally 'woman of the otherworld'), whose ghostly voice is heard to call out in lamentation when the death of an Irish person is imminent.

Patron Saints

Every part of Ireland has its patron saint, and many places preserve the custom of visiting a holy well dedicated to the saint on his or her feast-day. The best-known pilgrimage site in Ireland is Croagh Patrick, a towering, conical mountain in west Mayo where Patrick, the national saint, is said to have fasted for 40 days. His fast was successful in gaining from God the privilege that he himself should be allowed to judge all the Irish people on the Last Day! Equally popular is the cult of St Brigid, patroness of children and of animals, whose cross, made from straw and rushes, is hung from the walls of many houses.

The Mermaid Folk

Along the north and west coast, all the way from Antrim to Kerry, a legend is told of how a man once

▲ An Arthur Rackham illustration of the childhood of Fionn Mac Cumhaill

found the cloak of a mermaid, and as a result she followed him home and became his wife. They lived happily together and had children, but one day she found her cloak in the house and returned to the sea. Folklore thus claims that some local family or other are descendants of the mermaid. Most individuals cannot boast of such extraordinary ancestry, but the general tendency is for Irish people to claim to be descended from native kings and nobles. Genealogical lore was very popular, and it is still customary to consult a particular elderly person who is an expert at tracing the history of local families.

Legends in Song and Sport

Ireland is famous for its music and song. In the Irish language, plaintive love-songs are in greatest demand, while ballads in English range from humorous to patriotic topics. Poets have traditionally been held in very high regard, as it is said that they get their gift from the *sí*, or fairy people, and that their verses have magical power.

The Irish people are much addicted to sport. Perhaps the two oldest and most popular sports are horse-racing and hurling, the latter believed to be the fastest field game in the world. Indeed, this very point is stressed in a folk legend from Tipperary. We are told that two young men, one a splendid horseman and the other an accomplished hurler, once vied for the affections of a beautiful lady. She promised that she would marry whichever of them could with greater expedition have a love-letter sent to her from one end of the county to the other. Accordingly, the horseman had his companions arranged in relays in order to hand the letter on to each other as their mounts tired, while the hurler sewed the letter into his *sliotar* (hurling ball) and struck it a long distance to a team-mate, who struck it to the next man, and so on. It is claimed that the hurler vanquished his rival, but it all depends on by whom, and for whom, the story is told.

The Irish Horse
Brian Smith

Breeding

The Irish dream of producing the best horses in the world – and they generally do. Names like Golden Miller, Limerick Lace, Arkle, Durlas Eile, Dundrum and Boomerang are legendary. Ireland's natural advantages of 'good bone-producing' soil, equitable climate

Tried and tested as a working animal before the age of mechanisation, the Irish Draught is characterised by its docile temperament, courage, soundness and stamina, but its outstanding feature is its ability to pass on to the Irish hunter and showjumper excellent jumping ability.

▲ A prize-winning Irish Draught horse

and the uncanny affinity of its people with horses are all exploited to breed the best.

Two types of native animal, the Irish Draught and the Connemara pony, nurture future dreams. When crossed with the thoroughbred horse, the former can produce showjumpers like Dundrum, Limerick Lace and Boomerang.

Connemara is a land of mountains, lakes and bog along the Atlantic seaboard. Here the Connemara pony has emerged with qualities prized worldwide – hardiness, agility, intelligence and first-class jumping ability. International visitors come to the capital of Connemara, Clifden, each year in August for the Connemara Pony Show, the shop window of the breed.

Famous Studs

Some of the world's best thoroughbred stallions are found in Ireland. Sadler's Wells is top of the international league of stallions; he stands at Coolmore in Co Tipperary, Europe's largest stud, which charges vast fees for his services. In 1987 Coolmore purchased Ahonoora for £7 million – money well spent as his son, Dr Devious, won the 1992 English Derby.

National Hunt racing (over jumps) is close to the Irish heart. Dawn Run, the most famous daughter of Coolmore stud's Deep Run, won her first race at Tralee in 1982, ridden by her 63-year-old owner, Mrs Charmian Hill, before emulating at Cheltenham the triumphs of the great Arkle 20 years earlier. In the museum at the Irish National Stud, near the Curragh (Co Kildare), visitors can see Arkle's skeleton on display. The stud provides breeders with access to top quality stallions at an affordable fee. Among its purchases in 1979 was the stallion Ahonoora, sold to it for £200,000 to cover a debt at the Playboy Club in London. He proved a good investment!

The most famous Irish-bred horse is Red Rum. In 1965 he was born at Rossenara Stud in Co Kilkenny, and in 1977 became the only horse ever to win the Aintree Grand National three times. Even in retirement, reports on his health make news.

Racing

In the 19th century, racing across country – steeplechasing – frequently resulted from wagers, spectators often taking a hand in the outcome. John Dennis, known as 'Black Jack', was on one occasion pelted with stones by partisan supporters of another rider during a race, and at the last fence – a wall 5ft high – he found an ass and cart pulled across it. However, with a prodigious leap he flew the double obstacle.

At Punchestown racecourse, 20

▲ Ireland has produced many top showjumpers – both equine and human

miles from Dublin, some of the character of those turbulent days is recalled each April at the National Festival of Steeplechasing. Although no other venue offers its splendid clay banks, excellent National Hunt racing is available elsewhere, such as at Fairyhouse, north of Dublin (Irish Grand National, April) and Leopardstown, in a Dublin suburb (Handicap Hurdle, January; Champion Hurdle and Gold Cup, February; Phoenix Stakes, August). For summer visitors, racing festivals are held at Killarney (July), Tralee (August) and Listowel (September), all in Co Kerry. W B Yeats once attended the July meeting at Ballybrit in Galway:

There where the course is,
Delight makes all of the one mind,
The riders upon the galloping
horses,
The crowd that closes in behind.

The only official sea strand racing in Europe takes place in August at Laytown, north of Dublin. Few racecourses can match the beauty of Gowran Park, in Co Kilkenny, a short distance from where Paddy Mullins, Ireland's leading National Hunt trainer, has his stables. Pre-eminent, however, is the Curragh with its catalogue of classic races – 2,000 Guineas and 1,000 Guineas (both in May), Derby (June), Oaks (July) and St Leger (September).

The National Stud at Tully ensures the continuity of quality bloodstock ▼

Hunting and Riding in Ireland

The interest in hunting among the gentry in the 18th and 19th centuries was all-consuming. 'What do you do in Meath in the summer?' someone asked Lady Fingall, whose husband was Master of the Meath Hunt from 1888 to 1891. 'We just wait for the winter,' she replied. Instead of paying the bills, much of the gentry's money went on lavish hospitality. 'Humanity' Dick Martin could reputedly fight a duel before breakfast, ride all day to hounds over 6ft walls and entertain lavishly in the evening.

Many of the hunts are famous – for example, the Kildares, the Meaths, the stag-hunting Ward Unions, the Galway Blazers and the Scarteen in Co Tipperary. Hunting can be pursued daily from October to March, although the best known packs limit the number of visitors. Hunt secretaries advise on hiring horses locally, and some hotels arrange hunting with local packs on request.

Available to the more active are residential equestrian centres which offer varied programmes of tuition and cross-country riding. The more adventurous can take to the trail rides of Connemara, Donegal, Sligo and Kerry.

Showjumping and Eventing

A judge at an early showjumping competition held at the Royal Dublin Society Horse Show told one lady, upon asking what mistakes she had made, that her horse had jumped well but that he disliked her hat! The RDS Horse Show held in early August now attracts

international showjumpers. Millstreet International Horse Show in Co Cork follows in August and again in October, while 500 other showjumping events are held in the summer, ranging from the largest in towns and cities like Galway (July), Cork (June), Balmoral in Belfast (May), Kilkenny (July), Ennis and Limerick (August), to village competitions.

If for showjumpers all roads lead to Dublin, for eventers they lead to Punchestown in May when major international competitions take place. Eventing is a growing sport in Ireland and at venues north – Rademon in April and Loughanmore in October – and south – Moorhill and Skevanish in April, Ballinlough Castle in August, Castletown, Dollanstown Stud, Kilcooley Abbey and Templemartin in September, and Blarney Castle and Glenealy in October – some of Ireland's emerging stars can be seen.

Other Equestrian Sports

Visitors to Ireland can watch polo free of charge in Dublin's Phoenix Park, home of one of the world's oldest clubs, every Tuesday, Thursday, Saturday and Sunday from May to mid-September. In north Co Dublin, American-style trotting races are becoming popular and in West Cork trotting ponies are raced along local roads.

Horse Fairs

At the many horse fairs traditional aspects of Irish life blend with the need to sell horses. Cahirmee in Co Cork (July), Spancil Hill in Co Clare (June) and Ballinasloe in Co Galway (October) read like a roll call of locations where famous horses have been sold – Cahirmee claims it sold Marengo, Napoleon's charger. But the 'fun of the fair' has always been present to make palatable the surrender of the horses.

Literary Ireland

Professor Terence Brown

Very few writers in history have given the world images and phrases which have become universally known. Cervantes's Don Quixote tilting at windmills is one such image, as is Shakespeare's Hamlet with his skull. At least two Irish writers have also managed this feat: Jonathan Swift whose Lemuel Gulliver among the little people has given us the adjective 'Lilliputian' and Samuel Beckett, whose play about two scholar-tramps waiting at evening for a mysterious figure who never arrives made the phrase 'waiting for Godot' synonymous with futile expectation everywhere. Both these writers are names that may not immediately be associated in the public mind with Ireland. Swift, the author of *Gulliver's Travels*, is often reckoned an English writer and Beckett, who wrote much of his work in French (including the first version of *Waiting for Godot*), is claimed for modern French and international letters.

Swift and Beckett are not the only Irish writers who made so impressive a contribution to English or international literature

that their national origins became almost forgotten. For instance, it would be impossible to conceive of English drama without the names

▲ The redoubtable George Bernard Shaw

of Farquhar, Congreve, Sheridan, Wilde and the Dublin-born George Bernard Shaw. The last of these almost single-handedly revived English-language theatre in the first years of the 20th century. And English literature without the Irish-born Oliver Goldsmith, Laurence Sterne and Iris Murdoch would surely have been a lesser thing.

The Roaming Tradition

The Irish literary tradition is one in which exile and emigration have played decisive parts. Countless young men and women have left Irish shores to seek a literary fortune in the English capital. For others Europe, and especially Paris, where James Joyce published his master work, *Ulysses*, and wrote his last work, *Finnegans Wake*, has served as a lodestar for the artistically ambitious. It was there, for example, that Beckett settled in the 1930s. Such men and women did not go abroad simply because London or Paris offered Irish writers more congenial or professionally secure environments for literary production. Rather, one senses that Irish writers were obeying an ancient Irish impulse and satisfying a deeply engrained wanderlust. The Irish have always been travellers. Early legends

Swift's Gulliver wakes to find his problems small in scale, but constraining ▼

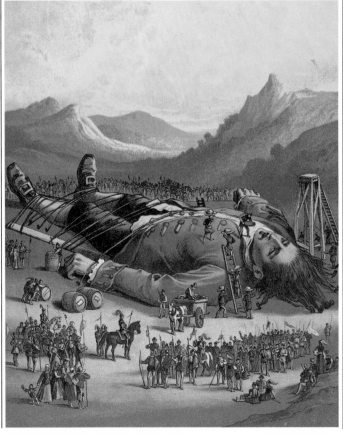

include tales of fabulous journeys to the western isles in the quest for the land of the ever young, which may have taken Irish sailors to the shores of Greenland and Newfoundland. More recent emigrants have travelled to the Americas and to Australia. Not surprisingly, nostalgia and homesickness is one of the great themes of Irish literature – whether it is the 6th-century St Colmcille, remembering from exile on the remote Scottish island of Iona his days in Derry, or W B Yeats declaring as he walked the pavements of 19th-century London, 'I will arise and go now, and go to Innisfree'.

Following Yeats's Footsteps

Innisfree is a small island in a small lough in Co Sligo. It is in the heart of what is now known as 'Yeats Country'. This is an Irish region where the poet spent much of his childhood, and which Yeats evoked unforgettably in his poetry and drama. It is a real enough place, composed of Sligo town and its surroundings, the rocky outcrop of Ben Bulber mountain to the north of the town, Rosses Point, the streams flowing into Glencar Lake, and the little town of Dromahair in nearby Co Leitrim. In Yeats's poetry it is translated into a country of the mind, partly through its association with the myths of the prehistorical Celts, and partly through Yeats's power as a poet to invest it with mystery and magic. It is a landscape of solitude and loneliness, and of bare rocks and ruined trees, where at twilight the human and the fairy worlds might mingle.

Place-names in Literature

The name Innisfree comes from the Irish *inis fraoigh*, meaning 'heather island' and the poem's title depends, in both its English and Irish form, on a place-name with evocative associations. Indeed, the Irish literary tradition is one in which places and place-names have played a decisive part. In pre-Christian Ireland where the bards had an honoured and powerful place in society, a poet was required to undergo a protracted apprenticeship, part of which involved retirement in a darkened cell in which he committed to memory the lore and legendry of the topography of all the country. This lore of places highlighted an island people's fascination for Ireland's distinctive regions and extraordinarily variegated landscape, a fascination which is perennial in Irish literature as a whole. Even today, we think of Seamus Heaney's Co Derry, John Hewitt's Glens of Antrim, Patrick Kavanagh's 'stony grey soil of Monaghan', and, of course, of Joyce's Dublin.

Irish Society in Literature

The landscape of Ireland is not only exceptionally beautiful and varied, its

◀ W B, son of the accomplished artist, John B Yeats

▲ 'I will arise and go now, and go to Innisfree'

colour of life in Wicklow, Mayo and on the Aran Islands. Many writers indeed saw in the life of the Irish countryside an image of the essential Irish identity, which Anglicisation and political oppression could never quite destroy. What none of them could escape observing was that in Irish rural life the story-teller was passionately esteemed and that good talk was highly regarded everywhere. Synge's masterpiece, *The Playboy of the Western World* (1907), celebrates the power of the spoken word and of story-telling when a young man is afforded hero status in a Mayo village simply because he recounts in increasingly colourful terms how he has slain his tyrannical father. Irish literature, from the 8th-century epic tale of the Iron Age hero Cú Chulainn, the *Táin Bó Cuailgne*, to Samuel Beckett's trilogy of compulsive anecdote, *Molloy*, *Malone Dies* and *The Unnameable*

achievements and glory of his king or chieftan, but was also expected to curse his enemies. The power of satire was much feared, and it was believed that well-chosen satiric words could bring blisters to a man's face and an inventive nickname could destroy him. Gaelic literature contains much harsh invective and biting satire, but it was the 18th-century English-language writer Jonathan Swift, who in 1729 published what is perhaps the most devastatingly satiric work by any writer anywhere: *A Modest Proposal for Preventing the Children of Poor People in Ireland from Being a Burden to Their Parents or Country, and for Making them Beneficial to the Public*. In this brief but brilliant treatise Swift, in the persona of an economist and a concerned citizen, proposed that the children of the poor should be raised for the table, and that such fare would especially be appreciated by the landlords of Ireland since they had already consumed most of the parents. Swift's satire in this work is so savage, so near the bone indeed, that many readers have been repelled by his vision, failing to respond to the work's fierce ironies.

place-names a kind of poetry; it is also the site of a turbulent and often violent history. Its great 18th-century houses and deserted villages of the western seaboard symbolise a social order that until recent times was fraught with division and conflict (an ancient quarrel continues in the north). Many Irish writers have turned to the image of the ancestral house as a metaphor of caste and family consciousness, and of the pressures of history at work on dynastic inheritance. Maria Edgeworth at the end of the 18th century in *Castle Rackrent* made the history of a feckless family of landlords a metaphor of the bad old days, which also expressed her deep anxiety about the future of her own family's estate at Edgeworthstown in Co Longford. In this century, Elizabeth Bowen in *The Last September* (1929) and in the account of her own house in north Cork, *Bowen's Court* (1942), offered an elegy for the Anglo-Irish caste, which had been overtaken by revolution.

Other writers wrote not of the aristocratic world of the 'big house', but of the life and experiences of the Irish country-folk. William Carleton, who grew up in the Clogher Valley of Co Tyrone in the 19th century, recorded the existence of the pre-Famine Irish. In the 20th century the dramatist John Millington Synge expressed the vibrant speech and theatrical

▲ Swift; cleric, pamphleteer, satirist, poet and champion of the Dublin poor

(1951–3), is a literature in which narrative plays a major part. Behind much writing lies the voice of the story-teller and the gossip of the pub, as does the structure of the folk tale, the swiftly circulating rumour or joke.

The Power of Satire
In ancient Gaelic Ireland the poet had a duty to honour in words the

From Desperate Times
A Modest Proposal is, however, only a particularly shocking example of something which Irish literature often provides – an extreme situation that draws from a writer an extreme response. A desperate history has provoked a literature of desperation, often ironical, black-comic, learned and witty, conscious of the tragi-comic in most human situations, and a cry of protest in the name of human survival. Samuel Beckett, who was awarded the Nobel Prize for Literature in 1969 (the third Dubliner to be so honoured after Yeats and Shaw), was once asked why Ireland, a small country with a small population, had produced so many remarkable writers. He replied, 'When you are in the last ditch, there is nothing left but to sing'. Swift would have understood. So too would all those poets over the centuries whom Yeats imagined in his poem 'Under Ben Bulben' as singing 'the indomitable Irishry'.

Gazetteer

Ian Hill

▲ St Colman's Cathedral and shopfronts, Cobh, Co Cork

Each entry in the Gazetteer has an Irish
National Grid reference included under the
heading. An explanation of how to use the
Irish National Grid is given on pages 114–15.

ACHILL ISLAND
CO MAYO
MAP REF: F60

The bridge over Achill Sound links Ireland's largest island to the mainland. Guarding the southern entrance to the Sound is pirate Grace O'Malley's elegant 15th-century tower house, Carrickkildavnet Castle, looking south to Clew Bay's island-studded waters. The main road runs west through Keel with its two-mile-long beach, its little sheep-cropped golf course and tiny brown trout lake, to Dooagh with its beach sheltering under Moyteoge Head. The road ends above Keem Bay where basking sharks plough the Atlantic's summer waters and Croaghaun (2,192ft) dominates the horizon before descending to the 2,000ft, four-mile-long cliffs above the sea.

On Slievemore's slopes (2,204ft), on the tiny road north to Doogort, lies the Colony, which was established in 1834 to convert the west's Catholics to the Protestant faith.

The Atlantic Drive – a series of coastal roads – takes in much of the island's best scenery, weaving between tiny green fields, brown and purple bog, wild fuchsia hedges, intricate stone walls, and isolated thatched, white-washed cottages. The Folklife Centre in Dooagh gives an informative picture of what life was like here a hundred years ago.

ADARE
CO LIMERICK
MAP REF: R44

The lichen-splashed stone walls of three 15th-century abbeys and a

▲ Off Achill's safe beaches the only sharks, basking ones, are harmless

13th-century castle complement the very English beauty of Adare's thatched cottages which line the tree-fringed streets of this tranquil village. The Trinitarian priory (AD1230), the only surviving dedication to the Trinitarian canons in Ireland, lies in the main street, and the Augustinian priory (AD1315) can be found on the edge of town. Both are still partly in use as parish churches, the former by the Catholic Church and the latter by the Church of Ireland. Behind the Trinitarian priory is a restored medieval columbarium devised for 200 doves. The quiet Augustinian cloisters still bear the arms of branches of the Fitzgerald clan. Two medieval chapels and the Franciscan friary, with its 72ft tower, stand in the middle of the golf course in the grounds of Adare Manor. This was built for the Earl of Dunraven in the Gothic style in the early 19th century on the site of a 17th-century house. The manor is now a luxury hotel, and the work of architect Augustus Pugin (who also designed the Houses of Parliament in London) can be admired in the great carved chimney piece of the Great Hall.

The Desmond Castle, dating from at least the 17th century, is best viewed from the 14-span, 15th-century stone bridge over the River Maigue, a good salmon and trout river.

AHERLOW
CO TIPPERARY
MAP REF: R82

The secluded and beautiful Glen of Aherlow lies between the dramatic

▲ Scant pasture for Achill's sheep

peaks of the ridge of the Galtee Mountains, the highest inland ridge in Ireland, and the wooded slopes of Slievenamuck on the edge of the Golden Vale. The R663 (off the Tipperary–Cahir road) runs west along the valley of the River Aherlow to Galbally village with its imposing main square, brightly painted houses and fine views of the summit of Galtymore. At 3,018ft Galtymore is the highest point in the Galtee range. The ruins of the Franciscan Moor Abbey with their dominant 70ft tower lie at the head of the glen near the village, and date from the 15th century.

Once an important pass guarding access from Tipperary to Limerick, the vale's isolation also made it a natural refuge for the outlawed and the dispossessed who hid in the caves on the slopes of the Galtees. St Berrihert's Kyle, on the south side of the Glen, contains some interesting early gravestones.

ANNAGHDOWN
CO GALWAY
MAP REF: M32

Annaghdown is reputedly the site of a monastery founded by St Brendan the Navigator and governed by him until his death in AD577, and that of a nunnery founded by his sister Brigid. Lying off the N84, on the south-east shore of magical Lough Corrib, it is dotted with enigmatic remains, many of them pertaining to the 12th-century cathedral and its associated Augustinian nunnery. The remains of the nunnery can be seen north-west of the simple Gothic rectangular cathedral walls, the latter containing a fine Romanesque window taken from the nearby 15th-century priory, whose remains stand just to the west.

ANNALONG
CO DOWN
MAP REF: J32

Annalong's pretty granite harbour, built in a natural fissure in the Mourne Mountains, has a cheery dockside pub, a restored 19th-century water-powered corn-mill and a little barn museum with old farm and domestic instruments and artefacts. There is a marine park, an attractive coastal walk and a slipway beside the mill. The awesome backdrop of the mountains – with their tiny steep fields, each bounded by a tracery of hand-built granite walls – dominates the tiny harbour which is crowded with fishing boats, especially in summer when the local 'skiffs' prepare for the short herring season. Slieve Bignian (2,449ft) attracts energetic walkers.

ANTRIM
CO ANTRIM
MAP REF: J18

Just four miles north of Belfast's International Airport, one of Ireland's finest round towers points skyward in Antrim's suitably named Steeple Park. Built around the 10th century, where Patrick's disciple, Aodh, had first raised his monastery five centuries earlier, the tower reaches a height of 93ft from a base 50ft in circumference, with walls 4ft thick. The doorway, 7ft off the ground, is evidence of the need in those days to have a secure refuge from marauding Vikings.

Sir John Clotworthy, later Lord Masseerene, built a castle here in 1662, and although it was burnt down in 1922, a turreted gateway opposite the town's 1762 court-house leads to the former castle grounds. Now a public park, these still show some of the delights designed by Le Nôtre (who also devised Versailles). The Six-Mile Water river meanders through the park, and many of the original vistas, walks, canals, fish ponds and trimmed lime hedges can still be seen. A Viking mound, a Norman motte and Clotworthy House, formerly a 19th-century coach-house and now an arts centre with open-air theatre, are extra attractions.

At the other end of the High Street from the court-house stands All Saints Church (Anglican), a rarity in Ulster in that part of it dates back to the 16th century. Its graveyard is the burying place for one of Antrim's famous sons, the writer and evangelist Alexander Irvine (1863–1926). In the intriguingly named Pogue's Entry, off Church Street, is his birthplace, featured strongly in his novel *My Lady of the Chimney Corner*.

Shane's Castle estate (on the A6), home of Lord O'Neill, houses a narrow-gauge steam railway and nature reserve.

ANTRIM COAST ROAD
CO ANTRIM
MAP REF: D30

Architect Charles Lanyon (who gave Belfast its best 19th-century buildings) designed the magnificent Antrim Coast Road in the 1830s. However, it was left to Scottish engineer William Bald to devise practical methods which simultaneously blasted away the cliff rock and had it drop precisely in position to form the foundations of the very road itself. The construction provided famine relief work, created easy access to the nine previously isolated Glens of Antrim, and gave the north a most beautiful corniche, referred to prosaically on maps as the A2, with riveting views around every corner.

◀ On the slopes above Annalong's harbour are the narrow tracks down which huge granite slabs were hauled for shipping to Liverpool

ARAN ISLANDS
CO GALWAY
MAP REF: L80

Thirty miles west of Galway, in the often storm-tossed Atlantic, the three Aran Islands maintain and offer a glimpse of life on the very edge of the once known world, despite the summer influx of visitors. A few cows and hens, a pig and a goat here and there comprise the local livestock. Although there are bigger boats now, the essential fishing craft is still the black *currach,* a strong, light construction of tarred canvas stretched over a bent wooden frame.

Legendary Cú Chulainn slew Ferdia, by the ford which gave Ardee, with this 1207 castle courthouse, its name ▼

The Irish playwright JM Synge (1871–1909) was fascinated by the islands, as was American film-maker Robert Flaherty. The latter's classic production *Man of Aran,* filmed in the 1930s, is shown twice daily in the Halla Ronan in Kilronan, on Inishmore ('big island'). The other two islands are Inishmaan ('middle island') and Inisheer ('eastern island'). Inisheer has a small folk museum beside the Ceard Shiopa, one of the outlets for the islands' famous hand-knitted oiled-wool sweaters.

There are flights from Galway's airports, and ferries from Galway itself and Rossaveal to Inishmore, from Doolin to Inishmore and Inisheer, and in summer from Spiddal to all three islands.

Settled by Christians in the 6th century, the islands are dotted with early Christian remains, haunting memorials to a spare asceticism. Teampall Chiaráin and Teampall Mionnáin on Inishmore are the most moving. The most significant remains, however, go back much further to a long-forgotten age. Dún Aengus, a semi-circular stone fort, stands on Inishmore with its back to a 300ft cliff, its date and grim significance remaining unknown. Nearby Dún Oghil, Dún Onaght and Doocaher share the same mysteries.

ARDARA
CO DONEGAL
MAP REF: G79

Ardara is an excellent spot for buying traditional tweeds and hand-knitted sweaters (mostly made to Donegal designs) from a host of shops on the two narrow hilly main streets running down towards the point where the Owentocker River runs into Loughros More Bay. Westwards, the road runs out to Loughros Point,

▲ Ardmore's sandy bay looks east

with its breath-taking views, and along a narrow peninsula separating Loughros More Bay from its little sister Loughros Beg. The Owena River (to the north) is noted for its sea trout, while the Essaranka Waterfall, the Maghera Caves and the Slievetooey Mountains are other attractive diversions.

ARDEE
CO LOUTH
MAP REF: N99

The square stone tower of the court-house in the main street of Ardee, situated on the main Slane–Carrickmacross road, was once the largest fortified home in Ireland. Called alternatively Ardee Castle, it was built by the splendidly named Roger de Pippart during the early 13th century. Both James II and William III slept in the castle on their way to the battle of the Boyne, though not, historians are quick to point out, on the same night. Hatch's Castle in Market Street dates from the same era.

Both the St Mary's churches, Catholic and Anglican, are built on the sites of much earlier churches,

Over time 'island of the east', *inis oirthir* in old Irish, became Inis Oirr. The Ordnance Survey anglicised it to Inisheer, the current pronunciation ▼

FABRIC CRAFTS

The intricate patterns of the true Aran sweater – at once a fashion imperative and a style beloved of plump and hearty red-faced, Guinness-drinking folk singers – have, some say, been used to identify bodies long drowned at sea, sadly a common enough occurrence off those storm-swept islands. If this was so it is fitting enough, for the traditional patterns, because they were handed down by example and by word of mouth from mother to daughter over the generations, became as much a part of a family's inherited genetic fingerprint as any gene. Some symbols are obvious enough – for example, the cables represent fishermen's ropes, while the diamonds are the mesh of their

In J M Synge's play, *Riders to the Sea*, each dropped stitch identifies a drowned son, lost at sea ▼

nets. Others are drawn from Christian and pre-Christian art – from church walls and gravestone slabs, and from the enigmatic carved swirls of an earlier Celtic time.

For a time the designs stood still. In recent years, however, younger designers have taken the basic shapes and stitches, drawn on natural dyes from the landscape about them, and have created new landscapes on wool, echoing the mists and bogs, the bog cotton and the heather, the soft hills and shimmering lakes, and the peaked mountains and the tumbling cliffs.

The 19th century saw the heyday of Irish lace, but the craft never really disappeared and certain styles (such as Carrickmacross) never lost their popularity. The solid areas were once made of muslin or cambric, depending on the ultimate purpose of the object; later, cotton and nylon were adopted. Now Carrickmacross is noted for its appliqué lawn on net,

▲ Aran style from Blarney, Co Cork

while the Good Shepherd Convent in Limerick uses Brussels net. Hand crocheting, also still much in demand, was first brought to Cork from Paris around 1770.

The spinning of sheep's wool for yarn saw the start of the tweed industry, whereby the material was warm enough, rain-resistant enough and hard wearing enough to be of use to working people through the long misty winters of the west. Like linen, lace and wool sweaters, tweed garments are now a fashion designer's delight.

Institutions such as the Kilkenny Design Centre in the Republic of Ireland and the complementary Craft Development Agency in Northern Ireland now offer marketing expertise to many workers in other natural crafts such as ceramics, glass blowing, basketry, wood carving and metalwork.

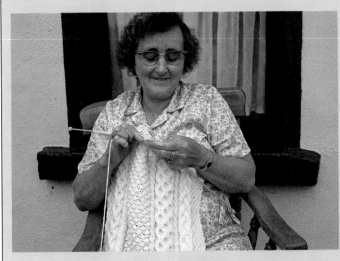

that of the former being where de Pippart built a monastery in 1209. A plaque on the bridge over the River Dee commemorates the mythical warrior Cú Chulainn's victory over his one-time friend Ferdia.

ARDMORE
CO WATERFORD
MAP REF: X17

The resort of Ardmore, on Ardmore Bay and hard by Ram Head, has a fine small beach and an excellent round tower, amongst Ireland's most perfect. Inside are a series of projecting stone grotesques. Carved reliefs set into the remaining walls of the adjoining 12th-century cathedral depict biblical scenes, and the carvings on two upright stones, also within the cathedral walls, are

in the ancient Ogham script.

The area has close associations with St Declan, a 5th-century missionary, and St Declan's Stone (at the south end of the beach) marks his reputed landing place. It is said that crawling beneath the stone guarantees to cure rheumatism in all but sinners – an interesting caveat. St Declan's Well, and his reputed burial place in 9th-century St Declan's Oratory, are places of pilgrimage on the saint's day, 24 July.

ARDNACRUSHA
CO CLARE
MAP REF: R56

Built in the late 1920s, the great dam and hydroelectric power station at Ardnacrusha lie two

miles north of Limerick. The waters of the Shannon have been funnelled into nine miles of canal to provide much of the nation's power, and the station and dam are still an awe-inspiring sight, particularly for the mechanically inclined.

ARKLOW
CO WICKLOW
MAP REF: T27

A small fleet of trawlers in the harbour and the Arklow Maritime Museum in St Mary's Road provide evidence of the town's great maritime past. But it is as a weekend holiday resort that Arklow comes into its own today. The castle on the bluff above the river mouth is that of an Ormonde fortress destroyed by Cromwell.

ARMAGH
CO ARMAGH
MAP REF: H84

Armagh's importance stretches back into the mists of Celtic mythology when the golden-haired Queen Macha – whose likeness, perhaps, is captured in a bare-breasted stone figure in the Protestant cathedral – had her palace built at Eamhain Mhacha (Navan Fort), two miles west of the present city centre. Ulster's fabled Red Branch Knights had their base at Armagh too. A politically astute St Patrick then chose this place for his main church in AD445, and the city subsequently developed into a centre of Christian learning, producing, amongst other artefacts, the great Book of Armagh which is now held in Trinity College Library, Dublin. Brian Boru, killed at the Battle of Clontarf, is buried in the city. His grave is marked by a simple stone on the Church of Ireland Cathedral, which, though originally constructed in 1268 and improved in the 1770s, was incongruously 'restored' in the Gothic style in 1834. Small and simple, its nave is askew to the chancel in reverence to the angle of Christ's head on the cross.

ROAD BOWLS

Bored English soldiers, tossing cannonballs along Irish country roads, are presumed to be the originators of the Irish game of 'bullets', just as their equally bored officers are credited with inventing snooker in Indian messes. In bullets, or road bowls, a 28oz metal ball is hurled in an underarm fashion (after much circular flailing of arms) along a set course of a mile and a half along the back roads of Co Armagh and Co Cork. The winner, as in golf, is the one who accomplishes the distance in the least number of shots, providing the ball stays in play. In Armagh the thrower is preceded by a brave and agile handler who stands on corners, legs akimbo, thus marking the spot where the ball should touch down to take the applied spin and thus round the corner. In Cork the ball navigates corners by sailing over the hedges.

The ecclesiatic capital of all Ireland, Armagh is an elegant Georgian town which owes much of it presence to the work of locally born architect Francis Johnston (1761–1829), who also designed many of Dublin's most beautiful buildings. The green sward of The Mall, once the city's racecourse and now its tranquil park and cricket ground, was built to Johnston's design. Around it are many charming buildings including the neo-classical court-house, the intriguing County Museum and the Museum of the Royal Irish

Francis Johnston's 1790 Observatory ▼

Fusiliers. Beside the Observatory, the Planetarium has computerised star shows and mock-ups of a range of space craft.

The medieval core of the city is best seen from the tower of the Protestant Cathedral from which the plan of the narrow winding streets is quite apparent. Across a valley, the ebullient shape of the twin-spired Catholic Cathedral, with its two stone bishops presiding over an imposing stepped approach, takes pride of place. The blue interior is lavishly decorated with angels and Irish saints.

In the grounds of the Archbishop's demesne stand the Archbishop's Palace (now council offices), a small neo-classical temple built for Archbishop Robinson, the ruins of a Franciscan friary and the newly restored stables, open to the public as a window on bygone days.

Other windows to the past are provided by two delightful National Trust properties within easy reach of Armagh: Ardress House, near Loughgall, a gentleman farmer's residence with excellent plasterwork by the 18th-century Dublin stuccodore Michael Stapleton; and The Argory, overlooking the River Blackwater near Moy, which dates from the 1820s and which retains its acetylene gas plant and a delightful pianola organ.

ASHFORD
CO WICKLOW
MAP REF: T29

In the Devil's Glen, a mile north of the pretty little village of Ashford which stands on the N11, the River Vartry rushes along a shrub-covered rocky chasm and plunges 100ft in a great cascade into the Devil's Punchbowl. Beside the waterfall, constructed walks provide safe and delightful viewing of both water and glen. Also near the village are the noted Mount Usher Gardens, open to the public. The gardens

▲ Mount Usher and 'wild' garden

were originally planned as a 'wild' garden in the late 19th century, and contain a great many rare and interesting shrubs and trees, amongst them a number of subtropical varieties.

ATHENRY
CO GALWAY
MAP REF: M52

The grim, austere bulk of Meiler de Bermingham's castle (dating from 1240) still dominates the southern approaches to Athenry, the 'ford of the kings', once the point where the kingdoms of the O'Kellys, O'Flahertys and O'Heynes met. Bermingham built for defence, not comfort. Parts of the medieval wall and most of the north gate of the old town are still visible, as is the weathered 15th-century market cross right in the middle of town.

Bermingham also founded the nearby Dominican priory, whose church with its elegant stone tracery can still be seen. Little of the later Franciscan friary (15th century) has survived.

ATHLONE
CO WESTMEATH
MAP REF: N04

The rich, fruity voice of the tenor Count John McCormack (1884–1945) once epitomised everything expected of the Irish.

By Athlone weir, the Count was born ▼

BIRTHPLACE OF
COUNT JOHN McCORMACK
WORLDS FAMOUS TENOR

▲ King John's Castle, Athlone

His gramophone, on which you can play his records, rests with other arcane devices in Castle Folk Museum. The house where he was born was in the Bawn off Mardyke Street.

Athlone, guardian of the main Shannon crossing point since the 12th century, also has other claims on the traveller's attention. The Anglo-Norman castle, squat, polygonal and solid, which withstood the advances of William III's army for a week, is the focal point of the town. Once attributed to King John, but built in fact by one John de Grey, it now houses the town museum. The Duke of Wellington also lived in the area for a while.

Just opposite the castle, on the other side of the Shannon, stands the bulky presence of of the Church of St Peter and St Paul (1937) with its typical twin spires, Italianate dome and attractive stained-glass windows by Harry Clarke, the most

notable of modern Irish stained-glass artists.

Oliver Goldsmith's family had associations with Gothic St Mary's Church, and Lissoy, his childhood home, is but nine miles north.

ATHY
CO KILDARE
MAP REF: S69

The rectangular turreted bulk of the solid 16th-century White's Castle (now a private home) sits quite imposingly by the bridge (1796) over the River Barrow in the heart of Athy. The bridge's name, Crom-a-Boo, derives from the battle cry of the Fitzgeralds, Earls of Desmond, one of whom was governor here in the 1420s. At Ardscull, north-east of Athy, is one of the largest Norman mottes in the country, dating from the 12th century. Ballitore, eight miles to the east, is a Quaker settlement where Edmund Burke was schooled.

AVOCA
CO WICKLOW
MAP REF: T27

There is not in this wild world a valley so sweet
As that in whose bosom the bright waters meet

Thus Thomas Moore's poem and song immortalised the Meeting of the Waters in the Vale of Avoca, three miles north of the village of Avoca, where the Rivers Avonmore and Avonbeg meet to form the Avoca. By the corn-mill in the village, Avoca weavers welcome visitors. From the top of the Motte Stone, a mile north, you can see as far as the Welsh coast on a clear day.

▲ The salmon-rich River Moy, Ballina, always popular with anglers

BALLINA
CO MAYO
MAP REF: G21

The ruins beside Ballina's modern cathedral, with its attractive stained glass, are those of a 1427 Augustinian friary, but the town is more justly famed as an angling centre for salmon fishermen tackling the River Moy, at the mouth of whose estuary the town stands. There is also attractive sea angling in Killala Bay where the French, 1,100 of them under General Humbert, landed in support of the 1798 rebellion. To the south, Lough Conn provides good brown trout fishing. Many of the big estates in the area (such as Mount Falcon) advertise traditional salmon angling holidays.

On the road to Lough Conn, half a mile south-west of Ballina, stands the Dolmen of the Four Maols, marking the grave of four foster brothers who were found guilty of the murder of Ceallach, their tutor and Bishop of Kilmore-Moy, in the 6th century. The bishop's brother had them hanged at Ardnaree, across the river.

BALLINASLOE
CO GALWAY
MAP REF: M83

Ballinasloe, at the western end of the Grand Canal, was the site of many skirmishes during the Elizabethan wars. Its more popular fame, however, rests with its October Horse Fair which, with Killorglin's Puck Fair and Ballycastle's Auld Lammas Fair make up the three great fairs of Ireland. Its origins disappear into the mists of time, but it was formally licensed in 1722 and by the end of the 18th century had become one of the three great horse fairs of Europe, buyers from all the great European armies coming to purchase on a grand scale. As many as 6,000 horses changed hands on a single day; according to tradition, one of them was Napoleon's horse, Marengo. Pretty Aughrim, four miles south-west, was the site of one of William III's decisive victories over James II's Jacobite forces on 12 July 1691.

BALLINROBE
CO MAYO
MAP REF: M16

Lough Mask House, four miles from the little angling centre of Ballinrobe on the Robe River, and near the junction of Lough Mask and Lough Carra (joined by an underground river), was the residence of Captain Charles Cunningham Boycott (1832–97). He was a land agent who was 'sent to Coventry' by his tenants due to his appalling and callous behaviour during the Land League Wars, thus giving us the modern-day term 'boycott'. Near by are the ruins of Lough Mask Castle. The town also has an attractive and popular racecourse.

BALLINTOBER
CO MAYO
MAP REF: M17

With the exception of only five weeks during the Famine years, Balintober's Abbey, founded by the Augustinians in 1216 on the site of a church started by St Patrick in AD441, has never ceased to celebrate Mass. Somehow missed out for closure during the Reformation, and although vandalised by the Cromwellians in 1653, the Abbey has continued in action for over 750 years. The much-ruined cloister dates from the 15th century, but the main restoration work of church and chapter house began after Catholic emancipation in the 1840s. The pilgrimage road to Croagh Patrick passes the Abbey. The interior is whitewashed and simple, and the de Burgo Chapel (now a craft shop) was originally built for the tomb of Theobald of the Ships (Tioboid na Long), son of Grace O'Malley, the 'Pirate Queen'. He was murdered near by in 1629.

Downing Fullerton, Ballintoy's owner, founded Downing College, Cambridge ▼

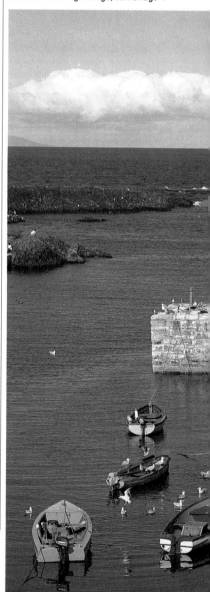

BALLINTOY
CO ANTRIM
MAP REF: D04

Ballintoy's little stone harbour, a good place from which to set off on a boat trip to see the Giant's Causeway, is built beside rows of old lime kilns. The little village itself, dominated by the white church tower which serves as a beacon both to worshippers and to sailors and fishermen, is approached by a little winding road from the A2, the main Ballycastle–Bushmills road. On the road stands a curious house built to his own design by a seascape painter, who added cubic room by cubic room, each with its own window, in order to give himself more and more views of the stunning coastline.

Just along the road towards Ballycastle, the Carrick-a-Rede rope bridge hangs from Easter until September. Originally devsied to enable salmon fishermen to get to their great fixed-engine fishing nets, nerve is all that is needed to cross the 60ft-long bridge which sways 80ft above the waves.

Just before you reach Carrick-a-Rede, Larrybane (NT) lies in a disused lime quarry, with excellent walks, views and a summer tourist information service. Also in the safe hands of the National Trust is the magnificent strand of White Park Bay, just west of Ballintoy. At the far north-west corner of the bay Portbraddan, a cluster of attractive white buildings – one of them reputedly the smallest church in Ireland – nestles just beneath the cliffs. The thatched church, no more than 6ft by 10ft, contains references to several religions, but is dedicated with appropriate whimsy to St Gobhan, the patron saint of builders.

BALLYBUNION
CO KERRY
MAP REF: Q84

In March 1919 Marconi made the first east–west wireless telephonic transatlantic communication from Ballybunion to Cape Breton, Nova Scotia. A stone outside this popular resort town marks the spot. Apart from golf, fishing and hot seaweed baths, the town's main attraction is its splendid beach, divided by a promontory on which stands the remaining wall of a Fitzmaurice castle. The 6ft-thick wall, with its five windows and two large holes, has become the town's symbol.

At the southern end of the beach near Cashen Bay and the mouth of the Feale River (both teeming with wildfowl) can be found several interesting caves. A fenced-off blow-hole, through which the sea may be heard crashing 100ft below, is called the Nine Daughters' Hole as legend has it that a 13th-century O'Connor chief threw his nine daughters into it on hearing that they were to elope with Norsemen. There is a fascinating Heritage Museum at Rattoo, which also has a fine round tower.

BALLYCASTLE
CO ANTRIM
MAP REF: D14

Ballycastle, the port of departure for Rathlin Island, is really made up of two towns, the hilly inland part with its unspoilt shop-fronts, fine Diamond and country fair, and the few streets down by the busy little harbour. Scotland, just 14 miles away, can be seen on a clear day. The Glenshesk and the Ballyvoy rivers join just above the town and there are fine walks (part of the Ulster Way) up Knocklayde Mountain (514ft), which dominates the skyline.

There are excellent tennis courts and good rock fishing down by the long beach and close by, on the A2 towards Cushendun, are the ruins of Bonamargy Priory whose graveyard attests to many bloody battles in past centuries. The most famous of the warriors buried here is Sorley Boy McDonnell, scourge of Elizabeth I.

An angular modern memorial by the harbour marks where Marconi's team made some of the first cross-water radio transmissions to Rathlin Island to give knowledge of shipping movements to Lloyds of London.

The town's fame, however, rests with the late August Oul (or Auld) Lammas Fair, one of Ireland's great fairs. Originally a horse and hiring fair for the people of the glens, from Rathlin and from Scotland, the fair still has its horses and ponies, but it is now a general excuse for music and revelry, the crowds overflowing from the pubs into the thronged Diamond. Almost compulsory purchases are dulse, a dried edible seaweed rich in iodine, and Yellow Man, a bright yellow, sweet, hard candy.

▲ Roads in Ireland are not simply there for cars; they often provide pleasant walking, as here, near Ballyconnell

BALLYCONNELL
CO CAVAN
MAP REF: H21

Beside Ballyconnell's fine 17th-century Protestant parish church and leaning against its wall is the fascinating carved Toomregon Stone, showing, at its apex, two hands pressed against a morose or perhaps unconscious head. Some archaeologists believe that the hands are those of Abbot Briccéne, a famous surgeon of Toomregon Monastery, the ruins of which can be found 2½ miles south. The head is said to be that of a warrior who lost his memory, having been wounded in the head at the Battle of Mag Roth in AD637, and Briccéne is said to have healed him. For others the stone is of the Earth Mother.

Ballyconnell's dreams of prosperity once hung on the fate of the unsuccessful Ballyconnell–Ballinamore canal which linked the Shannon to the Erne along the Woodford River. A massive restoration operation is reopening the waters from Limerick to Belleek, this time for boat cruises rather than barges.

BALLYMONEY
CO ANTRIM
MAP REF: C92

'Planted' by Scots during the 17th century who established its linen industry, its wide main streets and its fine Georgian houses in Charlotte Street, the market town of Ballymoney sits just south of the largest slice of bogland in the north. Three miles north-east at Conagher (just off the B86) stands the ancestral home of William McKinley, 25th President of the United States.

BALLYMORE
CO WESTMEATH
MAP REF: N24

From the 602ft summit of the Hill of Uisneach five miles east of the little village of Ballymore and almost half-way between Mullingar and Athlone, it is possible to see some 20 of Ireland's 32 counties on a clear day. Once regarded as the centre of the country, the hill was the seat of a great May Day fire cult and was occupied by St Patrick (who built a church there) and by Brian Boru (who built fortifications). To the south of the hill, the Catstone was identified by Giraldus Cambrensis, an early geographer, as the very centre or the very navel of Ireland – *umbilicus Hiberniae*.

BALLYSHANNON
CO DONEGAL
MAP REF: G86

As long ago as the 12th century, Cistercian monks were harnessing the power of the mighty River Erne as it rushed through the narrows at Ballyshannon to the sea. In the 1950s, the governments on both sides of the border came together to harness it again in a vast hydroelectric power station at Cathleen's Falls, demolishing the old bridge, narrowing the narrows and building a containing reservoir. Out of town, on the Rossnowlagh Road at the remains of the Cistercian Assaroe Abbey, enthusiasts have renovated two of the monks' original waterwheels, giving the visitor an opportunity to compare and contrast technology across the ages. The town itself still has some attractive Georgian shop- and house-fronts, and the imposing archway entrance to the 18th-century English garrison barracks.

Inish Saimer, a little island in the Erne estuary, is perhaps where Ireland's early colonists, the Scythians, landed around 1500BC. Kilbarron Castle, four miles north, was the castle of Michael O'Clery, chief of the Four Masters who chronicled Ireland's history in the early 17th century.

BALTINGLASS
CO WICKLOW
MAP REF: S88

From the summit of Baltinglass Hill (1,258ft) there are splendid views of the busy town of Baltinglass nestling below, and of the Wicklow Hills to the east. Three passage graves with Bronze Age burial chambers, two of which contain incised stones, and a substantial cairn are other hilltop attractions. The outer ring of stones suggests Iron Age defences.

In what was then called Vallis Salutis (the Valley of Salvation) on the east bank of the River Slaney, lie the 12th-century remains of a Cistercian abbey founded by Dermot MacMurrough, King of Leinster. The tower is an early 19th-century addition.

BANDON
CO CORK
MAP REF: W45

Founding the town of Bandon on the Bandon River in 1608, the then Earl of Cork, having defeated all the local clans, erected walls around it and banned Roman Catholics and nonconformists. Some fragments of the walls survive, as do the Anglican Kilbrogan Church (1610), the oldest post-Reformation Church of Ireland Church in Ireland, and the town stocks.

Kinneigh round tower (go west to Enniskean on the R586, then take the L190) has a most curious

Bandon, on the beautiful Bandon River, still has stocks and a whipping post ▼

appearance, the first 18ft of its 68ft height being hexagonal rather than round. Bealnablath (reached by going further north on the L190, then right on the L40) is where Michael Collins, head of the Irish Free State, was ambushed and assassinated in the Civil War of 1922. Ballinascarthy (to the south-west of Bandon, on the L63) is the ancestral home village of Henry Ford, of motor car fame.

BANGOR
CO DOWN
MAP REF: J58

Although Bangor's most revered treasure, the oldest-known Irish hymn manuscript, the Bangor Antiphonary (from the seventh century) rests in the Ambrosian Library in Milan, Italy, and of the Abbey from whence it came, St Comgall's of the Regular Canons, there is not a trace, the seaside town now has other attractions. Its second era of prosperity came with the opening of the Belfast, Holywood and Bangor Railway. The line's entrepreneurial backers offered free first class season tickets to new householders, and thus a flourishing seaside resort was born, complete with stuccoed Victorian and Edwardian villas.

Although these houses are now probably owned by Belfast's commuting classes, there are still facilities beside the spanking new marina for trips around the bay, ice-cream parlours, band concerts on the promenade, a host of tall guest-houses and that slightly raffish air turn-of-the-century resorts manage to maintain. The surrounding hills are dotted with golf courses, the bays are filled with yacht clubs and tourist information is available from an attractive stone tower by the harbour, built as the customs house in 1637. Bangor Abbey parish church was constructed in 1616 around a 15th-century tower.

BANTRY
CO CORK
MAP REF: V94

The French fleet came to Bantry twice; in 1689 it came to aid the exiled James II and was repulsed, while in 1796, in aid of the rebellion, a storm prevented its landing. The Irish revolutionary hero Wolfe Tone, after whom Bantry's main square is named, was on board a ship during the latter attempt. He was to write later, regretfully, 'We were close enough to toss a biscuit ashore'.

Today the town has a healthy mix of fishing, agricultural markets and tourism to support it, and the French and others who travel west are made more welcome than ever. Many head for Bantry House, a mellow red-brick mansion built in 1750, still a family home but open to the public. Owned originally by the Earls of Bantry, it sits, commanding wonderful views, in superb gardens in the town's wealthy southern suburbs. Chippendale furniture, bookcases belonging to Marie Antoinette, mosaics from Pompeii and Gobelin tapestries are amongst the attractions which also include an Armada Interpretive Centre in the stables.

Horse-riding, golf, and sea and freshwater fishing facilities are excellent in the area, and an adventure centre caters to the more daring. The 19th-century fortifications on Whiddy Island help to disguise the well-landscaped storage tanks for the island's oil tanker terminal. The Tim Healy Pass – named after the first Governor of the Irish Free State, who was born in the town – affords spectacular views of Mizen Head and Sheep's Head, two of the more spindly of the fingers of land stretching out into the Atlantic.

A donkey poses for the camera above scenic 21-mile-long Bantry Bay, dotted with inlets. Warmed by the Gulf Stream, sub-tropical plants flourish ▼

BELFAST
MAP REF: J37

Belfast is a young city even by Irish standards, its prosperity coming first with linen and later with ship-building and those manufacturing industries which grew in association, such as rope-making and heavy engineering. Today, just a few of the grand linen houses survive as office blocks behind the ebullient white Portland stone of the City Hall building. The latter was designed by Sir Brumwell Thomas, whose talents lay as much in borrowing ideas as in invention – a glance at its dome will bring St Paul's Cathedral to mind. Completed in 1906, it replaced the White Linen Hall as the City Hall. Each of the four corners is surmounted by a tower, while the grand entrance hall leads to an octagonal vestibule and a sweeping staircase constructed from no less than three types of marble. A fine mural by John Luke celebrates the city's traditional wealth-generating industries. Outside is a Garden of Remembrance, a stern statue of Queen Victoria and a memorial to those lost on the *Titanic*, a Belfast-built ship. Sir Brumwell, knighted for his efforts, still had to sue the corporation for his fee.

With your back to the City Hall, turn left down Wellington Place and look toward the plain elegance of the Royal Belfast Academic Institution, 'Inst' to its familiars and devised in 1814 (for no fee) by Sir John Soane.

The city's youth is in evidence if you look up the modest street canyons – green hills can be seen at the end of many. In front of the City Hall is the quiet calm of the Linen Hall Library, a public subscription library with its 18th-century origins lying in the enquiring and dissenting minds of the burgeoning city, members of the Belfast Society for Promoting Knowledge. Like many of the best buildings in the city – for example, Queen's University, Clifton House, Crumlin Road Prison, the County Court-House in Crumlin Road, Northern Bank in Waring Street, St Paul's Church in York Street, Trustee Savings Bank in Victoria Street and Sinclair Seamen's Church – the Linen Hall Library was designed by Charles Lanyon, his son or his partner, WH Lynn. Its collection of printed material, both ephemeral and weighty, makes up the most complete record of the city's recent and often turbulent history, right up to the present day.

If you look to your right, two vast

▲ Frank Matcham, the leading theatrical architect of his day, designed his 1845 Grand Opera house with flair, with onion-domed rooftop ventilators as well as gilt elephant's heads decorating the auditorium in oriental extravagance

LINEN

When, after the revocation of the Edict of Nantes (1685), the Huguenots fled to Ireland, they brought with them specific industrial and technical skills which were to supplement and mechanise a linen tradition which had existed in Ireland since the Bronze Age. Specifically, the Huguenots brought the skills of making damask, a mix of weft and warp, which was to revolutionise the Irish linen industry. The damask so made was then embroidered, crocheted, edged and painted. Led by Louis Crommelin, linen overseer to William of Orange, many Huguenots settled in south Antrim and Armagh, mostly around the valley of the River Lagan. Others went to Connaught.

At first this was a rural industry, and flax (from which the linen is processed) was grown as a crop beside weaver's cottages, among the food crops. Not cut, it was harvested by hand, pulled up by its roots, then 'retted' (almost rotted) in summer-warm, stagnant, man-made pools, creating a stench that carried half-way across Ulster. The slimy bunches of half-rotted flax were then laid out to dry. Afterwards, with basic engines often driven by water power from streams, the flax was broken down, spun into thread, woven into cloth and bleached. A beetling mill (NT) at Wellbrook, Co Tyrone demonstrates how the cloth got its sheen.

With mechanisation came the growth of bigger and bigger mills, the concentration of resources and workforce in Lisburn and Belfast, and the prestige of a cloth which was sold to the kings and queens of Europe.

Having lost out in the post-war years to man-made fabrics, linen thread and cloth are once again in demand for high-cost fabrics, and the work of designers such as Paul Costello has put linen on the world's fashion catwalks.

modern cranes – Samson and Goliath in the city's argot – dominate the skyline over the much diminished but still active ship-building yards. Nearer the docks, at the end of High Street, the Albert Clock tower, complete with Prince Albert in Garter robes, leans just enough from the vertical (a result of its sinking foundations) to make it notable. Nearer the City Hall in Chichester Street, a handful of handsome late-Georgian houses survive.

While facing Inst, turn right and then left into College Square North. In the premises of the Belfast Philosophical Society, the Old Museum contains an interesting theatre and exhibition space.

If you turn left from Inst you can be dazzled by the gilt and plush snug, the system of ordering involves pressing a bell, thus waggling a striped flag in a series of devices in the ceiling and attracting the bar-person's attention. The foot rail comprises part of an early central-heating system and the lighting is still courtesy of gas mantles. Legend links the Crown's snugs by tunnel with the Grand Opera House, thus enabling stage-door johnnies to spirit away the ladies of the chorus for oysters and Black Velvet – a cocktail of champagne and Guinness. There are many other atmospheric old pubs in the narrow passages around High Street, once the city's docks: Kelly's Cellars in Bank Street was a haunt of the United Irishmen; while White's Tavern in Wine Cellar Entry is the city's oldest.

Ireland) is a 20th-century building in Donegall Street on the edge of the city's 'Fleet Street'. St Malachy's (Roman Catholic, 1884) in Alfred Street has a wonderful fan-vaulted ceiling. Knockbreda parish church (1737), the city's oldest, lies in the suburbs and was designed by Richard Cassels, who also designed Leinster House (the Irish Parliament) and many of Dublin's other fine houses. The ceiling is starry-blue. The Elmwood Presbyterian Church, opposite Queen's University, has a fine tracery spire and is now an elegant concert hall.

Out in the southern suburbs – in the area surrounding Queen's University, its entrance tower echoing that of Magdalen College, Oxford – are the Arts Theatre, the

▲ Snugs added 1855, faience front in 1889, the 1839 Crown was designed by the Byrnes, local architects, and not, as in legend, by publican Flannagan's son Pat. The upper Corinthian pilastered façade dates from its Railway Hotel days

interior of the Grand Opera House. Designed by Frank 'Matchless' Matcham in 1895, the private boxes are covered in vast elephant heads. Sarah Bernhardt and Orson Welles strode the boards; today it is likely to be the stars of the Royal Shakespeare Company or the Scottish Ballet.

Across the road stands one of the most ornate pubs in these islands, the Crown Liquor Saloon (one of the few pubs to be owned by the National Trust), an extravaganza of tiles, stained-glass windows, marble counters, ornately carved 'snugs', nickel match-striking plates and Victorian mottoes. When seated in a

The city gives the impression that it is one of pubs and churches. St George's (Anglican) in High Street has a splendid portico taken from Ballyscullion House. Sinclair Seamen's Church (1857), Corporation Square, has a pulpit made from a ship's prow and the organ bears port and starboard lights. The First Presbyterian Church (1783), in Rosemary Street, has an elegant elliptical interior – and frequent lunchtime concerts. St Anne's Cathedral (Church of

Lyric Theatre, the Crescent Arts Centre, the Botanical Gardens (with its splendid curvilinear Victorian glass-house and Tropical Ravine), and the accompanying Ulster Museum and Art Gallery. The Museum has informative displays on Irish history and a unique collection of artefacts rescued from the wreck of the Spanish galleon *Girona*, almost the last of Spain's once great Armada, which came to grief near Giant's Causeway in 1588. One of the most poignant of

STANDING STONES

The fields of Ireland's farms are dotted with huge stones, sometimes standing alone, sometimes in seemingly untidy piles, sometimes in circles of five to fifteen in number and, more occasionally, arranged in lines. Sometimes the solitary standing stones (gallans) are plain, while occasionally they are inscribed with the Celtic swirls of the La Tène culture or the short straight incisions of the Ogham script. The stones, standing upright in honour of the old gods, sometimes also have Christian symbols added at a later date.

The parallel lines of stones at Beaghmore, originating from two circles, must have had a phallic significance, and there can be little doubt that the great stone at Turoe had similar associations. Archaeologists have postulated that others had ritual, funerary or primitive calendar functions. Many will have had different significance to different peoples over the aeons, depending on the intertwined forces of the power struggles and religious strengths of the time. Certainly there is no standard size for a standing stone – a few inches or several feet, there are countless examples of all sizes. At Lough Gur the lines of stone mark the road, but then what did the road mark? At Punchestown, Co Kildare, a tall stone marked a grave. Finn MacCool's Fingers in Co Cavan must surely have had some ritual significance, as must those found near the great religious sites such as at Tara in Co Meath, or the nearby ring forts. Perhaps some may even have allowed for a complex game, or have been placed to commemorate a specific event of great importance, a battle won, a death or a birth? Archaeologists may speculate, but then so can the passing visitor.

Called either Giant's Graves or Druid's Altars, Ireland's dolmens, usually consist of three sturdy uprights on which is balanced a massive capstone. They, and other tombs, are sometimes found in hollows, while at other times they are silhouetted against the skyline. They may lie in someone's front garden, in a farmer's field, deep in an unexplored wilderness, or close to a city, such as the Giant's Ring, near Edenderry on the edge of Belfast's suburbs. In all, over 1,250 megalithic tombs survive across the island.

Ogham (the word rhymes with

By Drombeg Stone Circle are huts and hearth, with a trough for boiling food ▼

▲ The three uprights once supported the great 100-ton capstone, Europe's heaviest, at Browneshill megalithic portal tomb, east of Carlow town

▲ The 1840 Palm House, another of Charles Lanyon's triumphant designs

'poem') stones, or more precisely stones bearing the incised ogham writing, present a more specific task of interpretation. Ogham uses a system of up to five straight strokes and notches which comprise a 20-character alphabet, derived, it has been proved, from Latin. The script, which is read from the bottom upwards, was used from the 4th to the 7th centuries. The inscriptions are now easily deciphered if the incisions are not damaged by time, design or accident, and usually record some style of family tree.

A map of Ireland's stone circles will show them grouped in loose clusters, being found more especially in West Cork, Limerick, Tyrone, Fermanagh and Londonderry than in other counties. None in Ireland is as famous as Stonehenge, just as none of the alignments is as well known as those at Carnac in Brittany. However, in groups they can have a compelling presence, Beaghmore and Lough Gur particularly so. As elsewhere, archaeologists and astronomers have noted specific references to positions of the sun in different seasons, hardly surprising in civilisations dependent on the seasons for the availability of both food and light. In general, the circles are thought to date from the Bronze Age, around 2000BC.

these artefacts is a slender gold ring given to a young soldier by his beloved on his departure from Spain. It bears the inscription: 'No tengo mas que dar te' ('I have nothing more to give you'). The Museum's Art Gallery has works by Irish artists including Paul Henry, Sir John Lavery, William Conor and Jack Yeats, plus works by Camille Pissarro, Walter Sickert, Stanley Spencer and Henry Moore.

Further out, on a hill above the Lagan, past pretty Shaw's Bridge and Barnett's Park, stands the great enclosure called the Giant's Ring, which contains a most impressive dolmen at its very centre. The banked enclosure, almost 200yd across, is formed by a 12ft-high, 20ft-thick earthwork dating from 2000BC or earlier. As recently as two centuries ago the good citzens of Belfast used the grassy bank as a natural grandstand, watching horses racing just inside its rim: six circuits made a most convenient two miles.

Across the city, the Transport Museum in Whitham Street contains a collection of trams, early cars and penny farthing bicycles, as well as Old Maeve, the largest steam locomotive ever built in Ireland.

(However, there are plans to move the collection to the Ulster Folk and Transport Museum at Cultra.) Further east, Stormont was once the seat for Northern Ireland's Parliament, and dominates many fine views.

A massive redevelopment plan, which will open up the city's dockside areas and turn the River Lagan's banks into a series of riverside parks, new housing projects, water sports centres and areas of entertainment, will take several years to complete. When it succeeds, it will have turned much of the city around to face a river it has turned its back on for centuries.

The Minnowburn, near Shaw's Bridge ▼

▲ When Sir L Parsons had Birr Castle (1620) he called the town Parsonstown

BEAGHMORE
CO TYRONE
MAP REF: H68

Unlike many other stone circles, those at Beaghmore, high on the windy slopes of the Sperrin Mountains and north-west of Cookstown, are not rings of tall massive slabs. Instead, they are large circles arranged in three pairs, consisting of quite tiny stones. They have projecting straight alignments and one has its whole circle filled with smaller stones. The paired circles and projecting alignments obviously suggest sexual rituals. Despite the smallness of the stones, they are none the less more impressive than other larger constructions, due perhaps to their moody isolation. Discovered by turf cutters, they date from the Bronze Age, although a stone axe-head found near by implies a Neolithic presence as well.

BELLEEK
CO FERMANAGH
MAP REF: G95

At the western limit for cabin cruisers of the navigable Erne, the tiny village of Belleek, centred around its fine, imposing stone pottery factory just by the bridge, is almost the most westerly village inside Northern Ireland. Oddly, the border slices through the edge of the town. Known as a good base for pike fishing in Lough Erne and for the spring salmon, charr and three unique trout species in Lough Melvin, Belleek's main attraction lies in the production of its unique Parian chinaware which is collected by enthusiasts throughout the world. Its lustrous cream colour and the delicacy of the pottery

▲ Castle Caldwell felspar clay began the Belleek pottery's trade in 1857

basketwork – skilfully woven from thin strands of pliable china clay, and then decorated with flowers and shamrocks – are amongst its chief qualities. A tour of the working factory with its accompanying museum, shop and coffee shop is recommended.

BIRR
CO OFFALY
MAP REF: N00

Umbilicus Hiberniae (Navel of Ireland) was the name applied to Birr by writers in ancient times. Indeed, the Seefin Stone, now displayed in the attractive Georgian setting of St John's Mall in the town, once stood on the road south to Roscrea marking, it was said, the very centre of Ireland. Add to this the well-planned tree-lined streets, Emmet's Square, another Georgian Mall, Oxmantown, golf, trout fishing in the Camcor and the Little Brosna rivers and Birr Castle itself, and the town's attractions are many. Dooley's Hotel in Emmet's

Birr Castle's 100 acre demesne has the world's highest (34ft) box hedge ▶

Square was set on fire by carousing members of the hunt in 1809, thus earning them their name, the Galway Blazers.

The castle, the one visible today having been built in the early 17th century, was originally a fort which passed through the hands of Normans, Cromwellians, Jacobites and Williamites. It dominates the town today, and inside its walled demesne are many splendid and exotic trees.

The remains of the third Earl of Rosse's remarkable telescope, the world's largest when it was built in the mid-19th century, can be seen in the grounds of the castle which are open to the public all year round. Arthur Bell Nicholl, who was rector of Birr, married Charlotte Brontë (whose father came from near Banbridge, Co Down) in 1854.

BLESSINGTON
CO WICKLOW
MAP REF: N91

Granted a charter of incorporation by Charles II in 1669, Blessington, with its one broad main street, stands on the tip of Poulaphouca, Dublin's reservoir. Now a weekend retreat for affluent Dubliners, it was once a staging post for the coaches between Carlow and the capital. Downshire House, a splendid Georgian hotel on the main street, was once the residence of the Marquis of Downshire.

Russborough House, a wonderful mansion designed in part by Richard Cassels, contains the Beit Collection, possibly the finest art collection in Ireland which includes works by Velázquez, Goya and Murillo. Open to the public from Easter to October, it stands just south of the town.

BRAY
CO WICKLOW
MAP REF: O21

Bray has one of those traditional seaside resort settings, with a long beach curling towards the shelter of Bray Head at its southern end. Its

prosperity, like many others of its kind near capital cities (Dublin is just 12 miles north), came with the railway age. The esplanade runs for 791ft, and there are fine views from the top of Bray Head and from the cliff walk at its base. No. 1 Martello Terrace, at the northern end of the esplanade, was James Joyce's family home from 1888 to 1891 and is indeed featured in his novel, *A Portrait of the Artist as a Young Man*. It is not open to the public.

BRUGH NA BOINNE
See Dowth and Newgrange

BUNCRANA
CO DONEGAL
MAP REF: C33

Buncrana, the Inishowen peninsula's largest town, nestles in the shelter of hills and looks down over wide Lough Swilly. An excellent wide beach runs three miles south to Fahan. There are fine walks along the banks of the rushing, tumbling River Crana. By Castle Bridge across the Crana lie the remains of an O'Doherty castle, burnt by English soldiers when, in 1608, Hugh Boy O'Doherty had mistakenly expected help from an invading Armada from Spain. Nearby Buncrana Castle was built in 1717 and housed an unhappy Wolfe Tone (1763-98), captured whilst preparing to invade with the French fleet in 1798.

The most spectacular views in the area are from Dunree Head, by the lighthouse where the anti-Napoleonic Martello tower gun emplacements were greatly extended during the First World War to defend the convoys which sheltered here while preparing for the Atlantic run. Fort Dunree Military Museum, spectacularly placed, traces the development of coastal defences since the early 19th century.

There is a Bronze Age burial cairn at Crocahaisal two miles north, and a dolmen at Gransha to the south. The town has a Vintage Car and Carriage Museum which is open daily during the summer months.

BUNDORAN
CO DONEGAL
MAP REF: G85

Tullan Strand, at Bundoran on the south shore of Donegal Bay, has been promoted as one of Europe's cleanest beaches. The long strand and the fantastically shaped rocks near by, given equally fantastical names such as the Fairy Bridge, the Wishing Well and the Puffing Hole, are amongst the reasons why the resort's population swells from 1,700 in winter to 20,000 in summer. The finely situated golf course on Aughrus Head and breakers ideally suited to surfing are others. In the cliffs to the west are the Lion's Paw Caves with more bizarre rock shapes. By Finner Church, between Tullan Strand and the Fairy Bridge, is an imitation standing stone which was erected to Flaherty, reputedly the local King of the Fairies.

BUNRATTY CASTLE
CO CLARE
MAP REF: R46

Bunratty's present castle, now synonymous with medieval banquets and a folk village, was built by Sioda MacConmara in the mid-15th century. The castle was given to the nation in 1954 by Lord Gort who had had it meticulously restored and wonderfully furnished. The 25-acre folk park adjoins the castle, creating a living museum of traditional Irish village life with a village street, 25 houses, a pub, a blacksmith, a draper's shop and a printer's workshop.

Six miles north, the Craggaunowen Project in the grounds of Craggaunowen Castle, creates an earlier Ireland. A crannog (an artificial island) has been created in the middle of a small lake in what is thought to have been the traditional way 2,500 years ago. Other exhibits demonstrate how ancient strains of crops were cultivated and how, in a cooking hole, up to 250 gallons of water can be boiled in just 30 minutes by throwing in stones heated in a fire. The 'Brendan' boat, in which explorers crossed the Atlantic in 1976–7 to show how St Brendan most probably completed the journey long before Columbus, is also there.

There have been castles at Bunratty, once an island, since the Vikings fortified it. The present castle was built in the mid-15th century by Sioda MacConmara ▼

THE BURREN
CO CLARE
MAP REF: M20

The shallow seas where Ireland now stands were rich in shell-life 300 million years ago. The shells became limestone, and in turn the limestone became the base on which Ireland grew. It is only in the Burren, however (the Irish word, *boireann*, means rock), that this base limestone has been left exposed – 500 square miles were scraped clean of topsoil by the glaciers of an ice age 15,000 years ago. The rains and the Atlantic spray and mists then dissolved away holes and fissures, leaving a landscape consisting of a clean pavement of off-white limestone. There are few lakes – merely a shallow acre or two of water in grassy hollows here and there, fed from underground streams and drained by others. They are called turloughs, and beneath the great pavements of limestone the underground streams continue carving out caves almost measureless to man.

Small amounts of soil accumulated in fissures and, thus sheltered, a myriad of plants (many more accustomed to being seen in alpine valleys) now grow. The Burren is a botanist's delight: rock roses and foxgloves are everywhere; mountain avens (*Dryas octopetala*) thrives even by the roadside; bloody cranesbill (*Geranium sanguineum*) and maidenhair fern flourish in the warmth stored in the rocks; and juniper survives in the grykes (fissures) between the clints(slabs) of the limestone pavement.

Four miles north-east of Lisdoonvarna, on the slopes of 1,134ft Slieve Elva (the Burren's highest peak) is the chasm which leads into the Pollinagollum cave system, one of Ireland's largest. Organised guided tours of the Aillwee Cave system – providing a 3,400ft underground walk – near Ballyvaughan, are well signposted. Ruined Corcomroe Abbey, dating from the 13th century, is situated just outside Ballyvaughan and is most attractive.

The best way to see the area is to follow part or all of the Burren Way, from Lisdoonvarna to Ballyvaughan. The area is rich in tombs (there are over 70 of them), the most picturesque being the Poulnabrone Dolmen. Near the Gleninsheen wedge-tomb, a mile north, a farm boy found a splendid gold collar dating from 700BC which is now held in the National Museum in Dublin. Circular earthworks, today used to fence in cattle, can also be found everywhere.

There are excellent views across the Burren from the O'Brien family seat at Leamanagh, near Kilfenora, now an attractive ruin.

BUSHMILLS
CO ANTRIM
MAP REF: C94

The distillery at Bushmills, possessor of the oldest extant licence to distil whiskey anywhere in the world, dates at least from 1608. From that day, the crystal-clear waters of St Columb's Rill have been combined with malt and barley to produce a unique series of triple-distilled, mainly malt, whiskeys. Visitors may start and finish their tour of the distillery in an interpretive centre based in the old malt-drying kilns, and may wish to sample a wee dram, or 'half 'un afore ye go'. The River Bush, which flows through the village past stone mills and under lovely old bridges, is noted for its salmon fishing. The

▲ Bushmills Distillery makes three fine whiskeys; note the 'e' in the Irish

river once generated power for the world's first hydroelectric tramway which ran from Bushmills to the Giant's Causeway between 1883 and 1949. A replica passenger vehicle can be examined in the Giant's Causeway Visitor Centre.

CAHERDANIEL
CO KERRY
MAP REF: V55

Donal's stone fort, which loosely translates into Irish as Caherdaniel, still stands outside this delightful little village which is well placed on the N70, or Ring of Kerry, as it is known, as it circles the Iveragh peninsula. The village overlooks Derrynane Bay where stand the ruins of Derrynane Abbey in the wooded grounds of Derrynane House, now a national monument. For many years this was the home of Daniel O'Connell, more popularly known as 'The Liberator'. The House contains O'Connell's duelling pistol and a blunderbuss owned by patriot leader Robert Emmet, hero of the 1803 rebellion.

Near by there are wedge-tombs and Stone Age graves, relics of the Beaker people who mined copper hereabouts 4,000 years ago.

CAHIR
CO TIPPERARY
MAP REF: S02

Cahir (also spelled Caher) Castle, on a rock in the middle of the River Suir, is all that a storybook castle should be; the square keep, the crenellated walls and the barbican gateway are fit for the silver screen.

But all was not always so. The original, built in the 15th and 16th centuries by the Butlers, an Anglo-Norman family, had to withstand a siege by the Earl of Essex in 1599 which left a few cannonballs embedded in the walls. The Office of Public Works has excellently restored the castle, and inside are fascinating displays of weaponry.

CAPPOQUIN
CO WATERFORD
MAP REF: X19

The Cistercian monks of Mount Melleray, two miles north of Cappoquin, have been here since 1832, clearing the land and

▲ They who claimed Butler's Castle, Cahir impregnable? Shamed thrice!

farming, virtually self-sufficient in their Trappist silence. A guest-house run by the monks makes no formal charge, although offerings are welcome.

Cappoquin House, destroyed in 1923 but restored with great attention to detail in a replica of its 1779 original, is approached through an imposing gateway and along a lengthy drive. South of the market town, on the banks of the Finisk (a tributary of the Blackwater), stands Dromana House, a mansion built by the Villiers Stuart family on the site of a previous castle.

CARLINGFORD
CO LOUTH
MAP REF: J11

Louth's loveliest village, with its white-washed cottages – some decorated eccentrically by a local primitive painter – and feast of castles, shelters on the Cooley peninsula side of Carlingford Lough. The local oysters deservedly have a festival held in their honour. Besides imposing King John's Castle (1210), which towers over the little harbour, and Taafe's Castle (16th century), there is a curious little 15th-century fortified house called The Mint. The Cooley Mountains, rising to 1,935ft in Slieve Foye, the highest peak of Carlingford Mountain, are a walker's paradise – try the 19-mile Táin Trail.

Narrow Water Castle, Carlingford Lough, built in 1560 for £361 4s 2d ▶

CARLINGFORD LOUGH
CO DOWN/CO LOUTH
MAP REF: J11

This striking sea lough runs between two beauties; the Cooley Mountains to the south and the Mourne Mountains to the north. Both provide excellent walks and drives as do both the lough's shores – through Carlingford and Omeath in the Republic of Ireland, and through Warrenpoint and Rostrevor in Northern Ireland. Cranfield, a little beach resort of caravans and small hotels at the lough's mouth, is where the Vikings once landed. Offshore is the once defensive Blockhouse Island, now a bird reserve (mostly for terns). Formidable Green Castle, standing amidst farm buildings and grassy fields north of Cranfield,

commanded the mouth of the Lough from the mid-13th century.

Warrenpoint has a fine promenade, a yacht club, a windsurfing school, an attractive square (usually with a fun fair) and a reputation for good ice-cream. The original 16th-century Old Narrow Water Castle, a pretty little waterside tower house to the town's east by the golf club, has changed hands many times. The more recent, crenellated Narrow Water Castle(1840) on the hill above houses an interesting art gallery in its cellars. The Cloughmore Stone (above Rostrevor in Kilbroney Park) is, according to legend, a rock thrown by Finn MacCool.

CARLOW
CO CARLOW
MAP REF: S77

Carlow, well situated on the River Barrow, has a curious and well documented incident in its past. A Dr Middleton, having leased the 1207 castle in order to turn it into a mental asylum in 1814, decided on an open-plan ward system which would have been most progressive in its day. He used gunpowder to achieve this purpose, but destroyed the building, even riddling the outer walls (which had withstood Cromwell's cannons) with holes.

The classical polygonal court-house, designed by Sir Richard Morrison in 1830, is of great charm as are many of the houses in Dublin Street. Carlow Museum (behind the town hall) contains local artefacts including the gallows. The capstone of Browne's Dolmen, weighing 100 tons and which can easily be found two miles to the east, is said to be Ireland's heaviest.

CARRANTUOHILL
CO KERRY
MAP REF: V88

The broad top of Carrantuohill (3,414ft), the highest peak in the curiously named Macgillicuddy's Reeks and in all Ireland, affords splendid views across the mountains, lakes and inlets of the Iveragh peninsula, itself circumscribed by the Ring of Kerry drive. The recommended approach is from the north, starting at Gortbue School by the entrance to Hag's Glen, travelling up the glen to the Devil's Ladder, and passing between Lough Gouragh and Lough Callee.

CARRICKFERGUS
CO ANTRIM
MAP REF: J48

Carrickfergus is still dominated by the bulk of the great de Courcy Carrickfergus Castle which overlooks the harbour and marina. John de Courcy's work began in 1180 on a rocky promontory, and the castle saw engagements against the French and John Paul Jones, founder of the American Navy. One of the best preserved Anglo-Norman castles in the island, it now houses a Military Museum; medieval fairs are held during summer months. A plaque on the wall marks the landing place of William of Orange in 1690.

St Nicholas's 12th-century parish church has delightful stained-glass windows with St Nicholas (Santa Claus) complete with sled and reindeer. At Boneybefore, close by, is a cottage museum to US President Andrew Jackson whose family lived in the village before emigrating in 1765.

CARRICKMACROSS
CO MONAGHAN
MAP REF: H80

Noted for its lace, a display of which may be seen in the town museum in the old market house (now council offices) at the top of the broad Main Street, Carrickmacross has many fine Georgian houses and traditional shop-fronts. At one end of Main Street stands the rather cold 1844 court-house which was designed by William Caldbeck, and at the other end is the 200-year-old St Finbar's Church with its octagonal spire. The stunning stained-glass windows in St Joseph's Church, built in the Gothic Revival style between 1861 and 1897, were produced in the 1920s by Harry Clarke. The ten stations of the Cross include a portrait of Stalin as the Antichrist. Patrick Kavanagh, poet and novelist, was born at Inishkeen, six miles north-east.

CARRICK-ON-SHANNON
CO LEITRIM
MAP REF: M99

The smallest county capital in Ireland, Leitrim's Carrick-on-Shannon (always shortened locally to Carrick) is an important base for the leisure hire-cruising industry. These boating enterprises replaced the town's original dependence on the waterborne transportation industry of previous ages.

There are some pleasant pubs, shops with traditional fronts, and a scattering of Georgian houses and doorways. There is good fishing

When American privateer John Paul Jones took HMS *Drake* off Carrickfergus Castle in 1778, Belfast, sympathetic to the American Revolution, cheered ▼

noted rock-climbing centre, with horseshoe cliffs – rising to 1,288ft in a superb glacial cirque – in the shadow of 2,597ft Fauscoum. Crotty's Lake (to the north) is named after an 18th-century highwayman and folk-hero, William Crotty, who was hanged at Wexford.

◀ Carrick-on-Suir and Ormonde Castle

locally, mostly for non-game species (although there is some trout angling), plus golf and hunting in the area. A few miles out of the village is a placid waterland of bird life, deserted houses and abandoned castles. Jamestown has more attractive Georgian houses, and Dumsna has a plaque recording where Anthony Trollope lived whilst writing *The McDermotts of Ballycloran*. Lough Key Forest Park and Boyle's 12th-century Cistercian abbey ruins (N4, west) are also most attractive.

CARRICK-ON-SUIR
CO TIPPERARY
MAP REF: S42

Ormonde Castle, the finest Elizabethan manor house in Ireland, is Carrick-on-Suir's chief attraction. Gabled and mullioned, it was built by 'Black Tom' Butler, tenth Earl of Ormonde, as a 16th-century addition to a 15th-century castle. Open to the public in the summer months, the house has a magnificent Long Gallery and fine plasterwork. Anne Boleyn's mother, Margaret, was a daughter of the seventh Earl.

To the north, off the R697 in the tiny village of Ahenny, are two of Ireland's finest high crosses. On the surviving 14th-century town walls at Fethard, north-west on the R706, is one of the country's frankest *sheila-na-gig* figures (an explicit female fertility idol), plus a little Folk and Transport Museum.

In the Comeragh Mountains at Lough Coumshingaun, there is a

▲ Tranquil waters, Carrick-on-Shannon

CARRIGALINE
CO CORK
MAP REF: W76

Drake's Pool in the Owenboy estuary, below this charming village which overlooks Cork Harbour, was where Sir Francis

Drake hid his ships from the larger Spanish fleet in 1587, thus living to fight another day and defeating the Armada the following year.

In the little perpendicular church there is a curious lead effigy to a Lady Newenham. Balla Castle, to the north, is reckoned to be the oldest inhabited castle in Ireland. Monkstown Castle, also to the north, was built by a thrifty Elizabethan lady who insisted that the builders buy all their provisions from her – her total costs when work was completed thus came to but one groat. Crosshaven, across the bay, is a pleasant yachting and sea angling centre.

CARRIGART
CO DONEGAL
MAP REF: C13

Rosapenna golf links, founded by the fourth Earl of Leitrim in 1893, vies with the seven-mile Atlantic Drive, a circuit of the Rossguill Peninsula, for first place amongst Carrigart's attractions. There is also a fine beach in the inlet to Mulroy Bay. At Downies (or Downings) there is a pleasant little well-used harbour and an excellent tweed shop and factory, McNutt's. The location of Meevagh church, north, is said to have been picked by St Columba when his tired donkey laid down and died here.

THE AMERICAN CONNECTION

The great wave of emigration from Ireland to America took place during the famine years in the middle of the 19th century, but there had been another one before that which was just as significant. In the 18th century, families of Scots-Irish planters in the northern counties, denied access to markets and high office by the English, upped and left. From their descendants came at least a dozen US presidents. The ancestral homes of these presidents are listed below (an asterisk denotes a home which is open to the public): Andrew Jackson (7th President), Boneybefore, Carrickfergus, Co Antrim* and Ballyclare, Co Antrim; James Knox Polk (11th), Coleraine; James Buchanan (15th), Deroran, Co Tyrone*; Ulysses Simpson Grant (18th), Dergina, Co Tyrone* ; Chester Alan Arthur (21st), Cullybackey, Co Antrim*; Grover Cleveland (22nd and 24th); Co Antrim;

Benjamin Harrison (23rd); William McKinley (25th), Conagher, Ballymoney, Co Antrim; Theodore Roosevelt (26th), Larne, Co Antrim; Woodrow Wilson (28th), Dergalt, Strabane, Co Tyrone*.

President Ronald Reagan's great grandfather, Michael Regan, was born in Ballyporeen, Co Tipperary; the Kennedys, who left Ireland in the 1820s, had their ancestral home in Dunganstown, Co Wexford. Richard Nixon's family has roots in Dublin and Tipperary. Another less celebrated Irishman also entered the White House. He was Major-General Robert Ross, from Rostrevor in Co Down where his life is commemorated with an obelisk. Fighting for the British, he defeated the Americans at the Battle of Bladensburg, then entered the Capitol to eat the victory dinner intended for President Madison. The Ulster American Folk Park outside Omagh, Co Tyrone has details of these and many other Irish-American links – literary, political, religious and financial.

▲ St Patrick's Cross, Cashel

CASHEL
CO TIPPERARY
MAP REF: S04

On the Rock of Cashel, looming 200ft over Cashel's north side, is perhaps Ireland's most important historical site. The 200 acres of the rock, floodlit at night, are dominated by a round tower and dramatic church ruins. The 85ft round tower dates from the 10th century, while Cormac's Chapel, an excellent example of pre-Norman Romanesque style, with dragons on its doorway and serpents on its sarcophagus, dates from 1127. Also on the Rock are the serene cathedral of St Patrick with its 93ft nave and 85ft tower, and the 15th-century Vicars Choral Hall, the only one of its kind in Ireland. A figure on one face of the original cross is reputed to be that of St Patrick. Brian Boru, St Patrick and Henry II visited the Rock for their various reasons, and the site was where the kings of Munster were crowned.

The traveller should not, however, neglect Cashel town. Cashel Palace, an 18th-century mansion and deanery, is now a hotel retaining excellent panelling and a fine staircase. The Protestant cathedral dates from 1749–84, while Quirke's Castle, opposite the town hall, dates from the 15th century. Somewhat spartan, the cathedral boasts a fine organ and glorious stained glass. The Catholic St John's Church is much grander. The GPA-Bolton Library off Main Street dates from 1744. Cashel Folk Village re-creates 19th-century town life, and the Bothan Scóir, a rebuilt cottage, does the same for the 17th-century.

Athassel Priory, a medieval abbey lying four miles south-west of Cashel off the N74 near Golden, dates from the 12th century. Golden itself has a circular tower house built on an island in the Suir.

CASTLEBAR
CO MAYO
MAP REF: M19

The Earls of Lucan, whose ancestor John Bingham founded Castlebar (Mayo's county town) in the 17th century, used the shaded, leafy Mall as a private cricket ground. Around the Mall are the 1830 court-house with its curious cast-iron pillars, and the attractive black-and-white painted Methodist Hall with its lancet windows. John Wesley laid the Hall's foundation stone in 1785. The Imperial Hotel is where Michael Davitt and Charles Stewart Parnell founded the Land League in 1879 to protect tenant farmers from eviction. Gas still lights the lamp over the front door of their Victorian establishment.

There is a very well preserved round tower, complete with stone cap, at Turlough (four miles north-west).

St Patrick baptised pagan kings and made a bishopric here on Cashel's Rock ▼

ROUND TOWERS

Built as bell-towers, watch-towers to enable warning to be given of advancing Viking raiders, and to act as defensible store-houses for valuables, Ireland's round towers (about 70 of which survive in recognisable form) date mainly from the 9th century. A bell would have given warning of the Viking ships, and the chosen few and the church valuables – for they are usually associated with churches – would come in from the fields and from their places of worship and prayer. They would then climb up the ladder to the doorway (normally quite a few feet off the ground), pull up the ladder, bolt the door and sit out the siege in probably quite uncomfortable conditions.

Elegant yet solid structures, their heights vary from 50ft to 120ft. For stability, and perhaps even for elegance, they taper heavenwards. Usually they were stone capped, although few of the stone caps have survived the centuries.

Inside each one, a spiral staircase hugs the walls, and the narrow windows – few in number – indicate the line of the stair. The windows usually look out on the four compass points. The best surviving towers include those at Antrim (Co Antrim), Ardmore (Co Waterford), Scattery (Co Clare), Cashel (Co Tipperary), Clondalkin (in the Dublin suburbs), Cloyne (Co Cork); Devenish Island (Co Fermanagh), Kildare (Co Kildare), Monasterboice (Co Louth) and Roscrea (Co Tipperary).

12th-century tower, Devenish Island ▼

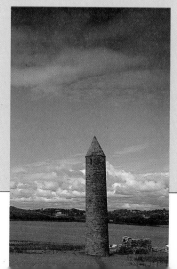

CASTLEISLAND
CO KERRY
MAP REF: R00

Castleisland, now known principally for its locally quarried red marble, was the home and base for the powerful Earls of Desmond. The remains of their once impregnable castle, which then stood on an island surrounded by a moat which was built by dividing the waters of the River Maine, is just a stump at the Killarney end of the town.

Crag Cave at Ballyplymouth (two miles east) contains, apart from stalagmites and stalactites, a number of features which the tour guides weave into tales of Irish mythology. There are rushing underground streams, and the caves continue for over two miles. Desmond's Grave, near Knight's Mountain (north of the town) in the Glanaruddery range, marks the grave of the 15th and last Earl. 'Desmond's Howl' is the name given to the wind as it whistles by.

CASTLEREA
CO ROSCOMMON
MAP REF: M68

Birthplace of Felim O'Conor, last High King of Ireland in the 12th century and of Douglas Hyde, first President of Ireland in the 19th century, the small market town of Castlerea was also the home town of Sir William Wilde, Oscar Wilde's father.

Clonalis House, west of the town on the banks of the River Suck, was the O'Conor ancestral seat. The 'new' Clonalis House (1878) replaces an earlier one which was built in 1700. The House (open to

▲ Clonalis House Castlerea

the public in summer) contains fascinating archive material from a family which produced 11 of Ireland's High Kings.

At Frenchpark, eight miles north of Castlerea, are what remains of 14th-century Cloonshanville Abbey and of an 18th-century Palladian mansion, once the seat of Lord de Freyne. Douglas Hyde's grave is also in the demesne.

CASTLEROCK
CO LONDONDERRY
MAP REF: C73

Near Castlerock, a pleasant and quiet resort on Londonderry's north-east coast, at a crossroads on the Coleraine–Downhill road, stands Hezlett House (NT), a thatched cottage dating from 1690. Downhill (also NT) was the demesne of Frederick Augustus Hervey, Bishop of Derry, Earl of Bristol. His house is in ruins but the classical rotunda of Mussenden Temple, which he had built for a close relation, Mrs Mussenden, stands right on the cliff edge.

Immensely rich, the eccentric Earl Bishop asked plump clergymen to jump hedges or race along the strand to determine who should be appointed to a living. There was also speculation concerning his relationship with Mrs Mussenden.

CASTLETOWNBERE
CO CORK
MAP REF: V64

More formally known as Castletown Bearhaven and less formally as Bear Haven this, the Beara Peninsula's chief town, was the natural sheltered haven in the sound between Slieve Miskish to the north and Bear Island to the south, for the British Atlantic Fleet up to 1937. Now Bear Haven is a holiday centre for rock climbers, deep-sea anglers and botanists. Dunboy Castle, to the south-west, was the last castle to hold out against the English after the Battle of Kinsale in 1601. Nearer the town are the ruins of Puxley Castle, home to the copper barons, the Puxleys, on whom Daphne du Maurier based her novel *Hungry Hill*. The views from Hungry Hill (2,251ft) itself, complete with 700ft waterfall, are stupendous.

CASTLEWELLAN
CO DOWN
MAP REF: J33

Castlewellan's broad, attractive tree-lined streets and squares were laid out by the Annesley family in the mid-18th century. They also built the Scottish baronial style castle a century later, conceived the impressive arboretum and constructed a fine stable block, the latter two now situated in the 1,100-acre Castlewellan Forest Park in the foothills of the Mourne Mountains. There is also a trout lake near the castle which is surrounded by mature beech and oak, a hunting ground in the early autumn for lovers of wild edible fungi.

Castletown Bearhaven (close to Walk 15) provides a haven for sailors ▼

▲ St Columcille's House, Ceanannus Mór, with three tiny rooms under the vaulted roof, can be entered. The key is kept at Long Church View, 100 yards down the road

CAVAN
CO CAVAN
MAP REF: H40

Just east of Lough Oughter, Cavan, its own county town, lies amongst gentle hills in good coarse fishing country. The bell-tower in Abbey Street is that of a Franciscan friary founded in 1300 by Giolla Iosa Ruadh O'Reilly. A drunk friar burned the friary down in 1451. Indeed, the whole town, including the friary and the O'Reilly Castle which stood on Gallows Hill (Main Street), were burnt down in 1576 by one of the O'Reilly ladies in a fit of jealousy. At the old prison at the top of Farnham Street, local genealogical workers are compiling a database useful to those tracing their ancestors from the area.

Cloughoughter Castle, to the west on an inlet of Lough Oughter, was an O'Reilly stronghold and dates from the 13th century. The Reillys, if not the O'Reilly's, surface again at Ballyjamesduff (10 miles south-east), named in a song in which one, Paddy, is urged to come back to the town. Ballyhaise House (18th century), four miles north, was designed by the famous architect Richard Cassels. Finn MacCool's Fingers, a group of prehistoric standing stones, can be seen on Shantemon Hill *en route*.

CEANANNUS MOR (KELLS)
CO MEATH
MAP REF: N77

Best known as Kells, an anglicisation of the first part of its Gaelic name, this was once one of the great centres of Celtic Christianity. The building by the round tower (1076), now called St Columcille's House, is all that is left of the several churches of the Columban monastery which was founded in 804. It resembles St Kevin's Church in Glendalough, has 4ft thick walls and measures 24ft by 21ft by 38ft. It is inside this 'house', possibly the monastic library, that the *Book of Kells*, that wonderful illuminated Latin manuscript of the four gospels (now on display in Trinity College, Dublin) was probably written. The monastery was a favourite target of the Vikings, and the 100ft capless round tower's five windows – an unusual number – watched over the five approaches.

There are five crosses in the town; the oldest, the Cross of St Patrick and St Columcille, is opposite the round tower. The cross in the market place was used as a gallows during the 1798 rebellion. At Creeve Lough, 10 miles west, are a crannog (an artificial island) and a fascinating souterrain.

CLAREMORRIS
CO MAYO
MAP REF: M37

Once an important rail junction, Claremorris might have faded away with the decline of rail traffic had it not been for the growth of Knock (seven miles north-east on the N17) as the Irish Lourdes. Apparitions of the Blessed Virgin Mary recorded there in 1879 were at first treated cautiously by the Church. Today, Knock is a major centre of pilgrimage and has its own international airport. Two miles north-east of Claremorris are the ruins of 13th-century Ballinasmalla Abbey. Just west of Ballyhaunis, off the little road to Island Lake, is the Bracklaghboy Ogham Stone.

CLIFDEN
CO GALWAY
MAP REF: L65

The 'capital' of Connemara, Clifden nestles to the west of the Twelve Pins (or Bens) in a little inlet of the Atlantic Ocean, by the tumbling Owenglin River, and is both a market town and holiday resort. Built to a T plan in the early 18th century by Thomas D'Arcy, the local landowner, the town gives equal prominence to the spires of the Catholic and Protestant churches.

▲ River stepping stones, *an clochán* in Irish, gave Clifden its English name

There are good beaches on its outskirts, whilst Derrygimlagh, Legaun and Mannin strands are just a few miles further on. The Sky Road around the peninsula passes the ruins of Clifden Castle (1815), the old D'Arcy house.

Inland from Mannin out on the moors, an unusual monument which suggests an aircraft's tail fin marks the spot where John Alcock and Arthur Whitten Brown landed after the first transatlantic flight in 1919.

The Connemara National Park (north-east of Clifden) consists of 5,000 acres of natural beauty running south of the Quaker village of Letterfrack and sweeping across four of the Twelve Pins. It is natural country for the well prepared and experienced hill walker. Two nature trails are signposted from the visitor centre – one runs through Ellis Wood, while the other, tougher route is the Sruffaunboy Trail.

THE VOYAGE OF ST BRENDAN

Navigatio Sancti Brendanni Abbatis, the story of the voyages of St Brendan the Navigator (circa 484–577), Abbot of Clonfert, Co Galway, was one of the most popular works of medieval times. Expansionist and adventurous, it echoed the spirit of the 15th century. St Brendan himself was born at

Admire the boat which rode Atlantic storms to reach America under sail ▼

Fenit, Co Kerry, and it was from there that he is believed to have set sail westwards more than 1,400 years ago, nine centuries before Columbus. The detailed descriptions of his experiences, which can now be recognised as the sighting of whales, passing between ice floes and sailing past volcanic islands (though couched often in fanciful terms), have the ring of authenticity and recognisable geographical certainties about them. So much so that, in 1977, the writer and explorer Tim Severin, after huge and detailed preparations, completed an ash wood and hide boat made to Brendan's description, and solely from substances which would have been available to the saintly navigator and his companions. Like the saint, he set sail from Fenit, his own and his crew's lives dependent on the prepared hides of 49 oxen.

Severin and his crew witnessed sights just as Brendan had done, their journal echoing his. They reached Newfoundland. Their tale is recounted in *The Brendan Voyage* (1979) and the boat is in the Craggaunowen Project near Shannon Airport.

superb passage-grave with slabs carved in elegant swirls and spirals reminiscent of those at Newgrange, Co Meath. At Dergina, just north-west of Ballygawley, stands the ancestral home of Ulysses Simpson Grant, 18th President of the United States.

CLONFERT
CO GALWAY
MAP REF: M92

Clonfert grew up around the monastery which was founded in AD563 by St Brendan the Navigator – who may well have discovered America centuries before Columbus. Destroyed five times, the monastery was completely rebuilt in 1200 and the cathedral ruins which survive today are part of that 12th-century construction. Of exceptional beauty is the rounded arch of the west doorway with its pediment of carved figures, ornaments and animals in the Irish Romanesque style. One is a smiling mermaid holding a mirror, perhaps in memory of a sailor, perhaps for St Brendan. The saint died in the arms of his sister, St Brigid, and is buried here by the Protestant cathedral, still in regular use.

The Sky Road, a scenic route, runs from Clifden to Streamstown Bay ▼

CLOGHER
CO TYRONE
MAP REF: H55

Augher, Clogher and Fivemiletown, a trio of quiet little market villages, used to be linked by the Clogher Valley Railway which ran along their main streets. Railway mementos may be found in the Fivemiletown Display Centre. Clogher itself is dominated by the Protestant cathedral (rebuilt in 1744) atop the hilly main street. It claims to be the oldest bishopric in Ireland, dating from the 5th century.

Downhill of the cathedral stands the former Bishop's Palace, now a home for the aged. The Iron Age fort behind the cathedral was the seat of the local kings of Oriel.

Brackenridge's Folly (two miles south) is the conspicuous mausoleum of George Brackenridge, getting his own back in death on those of the local gentry who shunned him in life.

Just outside Augher is a little thatched cottage, preserved as the birthplace of novelist William Carleton, author of *Traits of the Irish Peasantry*. On Knockmany Hill, just north of Augher, is a

CLONMACNOISE
CO OFFALY
MAP REF: N03

Clonmacnoise's monastic site on the left bank of the Shannon is one of Ireland's finest. Founded by St Ciaran in AD545 in a meadow (or *cluain*), it flourished for 600 years as a centre for religious learning. Amongst the treasures it produced is the earliest known manuscript in the Irish language, *The Book of the Dun Cow*, named after one of the saint's brown kine and dating from the 11th century.

The site has a cathedral, three high crosses, the remains of two round towers, castle ruins, evidence of eight churches and 200 monumental slabs, making it the most extensive monastic site in Ireland. It survived many Viking raids, but was razed by the English in 1552.

The Nun's Church is a simple 12th-century Irish Romanesque construction, built in 1167 by Dervorgilla who was referred to as the Irish Helen of Troy. Her abduction by the King of Leinster, Dermot MacMurrough, led inexorably to the Anglo-Norman invasion.

The Cross of the Scriptures (also called Flann's Cross) by the west door of the cathedral dates from the 10th century. Its richly carved surfaces depict scenes from the Last Judgement and the Crucifixion. A translation of an inscription on it reads 'A prayer for Colman who made this cross for King Flann'. The South Cross (11th century) depicts the Crucifixion, and the partly destroyed North Cross is carved

Clonmacnoise, best visited by boat ▼

with now weathered, almost abstract, human and animal figures. Very little of the 62ft long cathedral is the AD904 original. The Crozier of Clonmacnoise, the inlaid metal handle for the saint's wooden staff, is intricate and beautiful in its execution and is one of the treasures in the National Museum in Dublin.

CLONMEL
CO TIPPERARY
MAP REF: S22

Tipperary's county town, Clonmel lies within its old walls and has all the charm you might expect from a town whose name in Irish means 'honey-meadow'. Standing on the trout-filled River Suir, the well laid out town still has gates at each end of its main street. The West Gate is an imaginative reconstruction dating only from 1831, but the Main Guard (often erroneously attributed to Christopher Wren) was begun by the Duke of Ormonde in 1674 as a court-house.

On the Main Guard's west front are three greyhounds, the town's coat of arms, and indeed the town has an active greyhound track and popular horse-race meetings. Racing is an old tradition, for, so the legend goes, it was here that Finn MacCool promised to marry the first girl to reach the top of Slievenamon (2,368ft), the 'mountain of the women', seven miles to the north-east.

Sections of the old town walls – used for defensive purposes up until the 1798 rebellion – can be seen here and there, and form a corner of the churchyard of St Mary's Old Church which dates from the 13th century. The church's east and west windows are 15th century. The Franciscan friary dates from 1269 and contains the effigies of a knight and his lady on a tomb bearing an inscription to the Butlers, Lords of Caher.

COBH
CO CORK
MAP REF: W86

Once called Queenstown, after Queen Victoria, who first set foot on Irish soil here in 1849 when its fine natural harbour was one of Britain's major naval bases (a situation which continued until Ireland's neutral stance in the Second World War), Cobh (pronounced 'cove') means haven in Irish. The steep, narrow streets lead to the harbour below St Colman's granite Protestant cathedral. There is also the

Maritime Museum in a deconsecrated church, and the Royal Cork Yacht Club, based in Cobh, is the oldest in the British Isles.

COLERAINE
CO ANTRIM
MAP REF: C83

A mile to the south of the quiet riverside market town of Coleraine – with its River Bann cruises and Riverside Theatre, based in the University of Ulster – is a 200ft grassy mound, Mount Sandel. Once a Norman fort, it was previously the site of Ireland's oldest known human settlement, with mesolithic hearths dating from 7000BC. The Wilson Daffodil Garden is Ireland's finest. West of Ballymena (to the south) lies Gracehill, a pretty 18th-century Moravian blackstone settlement, recognised for conservation by Europa Nostra, where men and women are still buried on separate sides of the village church. Slemish, where St Patrick herded sheep, rises to 1,437ft to the east of Ballymena.

CONG
CO MAYO
MAP REF: M15

The Cross of Cong, 30in tall and 19in wide, was once reputed to have enshrined a fragment of the true Cross and is one of Ireland's treasures. Now in the National Museum in Dublin, the processional cross was fashioned in 1123 for Turlough O'Conor, then High King of Ireland. Over an oak base, its gilt bronze panels are interlaced with animals and serpents in a unique blend of Norse

West of this pretty Galway-border village of Cong is the picturesque land known as Joyce's Country ▼

▲ Ashford Castle Hotel, Cong, once home to the Guinness family, was built in 1870

▲ The view of Cork City, south down St Patrick's Street, from St Patrick's Hill

and Celtic styles. Cong Abbey, dating from the 13th century, was home to the cross but survives today only as pretty ruins by the river. The town is situated on an isthmus between loughs Mask and Corrib, and is a centre for fishing and other field sports.

COOLEY PENINSULA
CO LOUTH
MAP REF: J11

The *Táin Bó Cuailgne* (the Cattle Raid of Cooley), one of the great heroic tales of Ireland, is set amongst these lovely mountains which rise above Carlingford Lough. Slieve Foye (1,935ft) complements Slieve Donard in the Mournes across the sea lough.

Queen Maeve's Stepping Stones is the name given to rocks at Giles's Quay, a little coastal resort. Queen Maeve's envy is central to the Táin Bó legend. Covetous of her husband Ailill's white-horned bull, she sought the brown bull of Cooley by fair means or foul.

CORK
CO CORK
MAP REF: W67

Cork, Ireland's second city, has come a long way since the founding of St Finbar's monastery on the marshland by the banks of the River Lee. Norsemen came as raiders and

stayed on as merchants. Today, the heart of the city is still on an island in the middle of the Lee, and its total is a bustling profusion and confusion of bridges and spires, hills and waterscapes, quays and Georgian houses, old markets and old bars, and narrow alleys and wide riverside walks.

The Butter Exchange, in Shandon on the north bank, was founded in the 18th century to regulate the export of Cork and Kerry salted butter around the world, thus setting the pace for much of the city's expansion. Officially closed in 1924, it has now re-opened as a craft centre. Near by, a gilded salmon weather vane stands above St Anne's Church, a reminder of Ireland's salmon-rich waters. In the tower below the peal of eight bells known as the Bells of Shandon may be heard. For a small fee, visitors can play the bells by pulling on the ropes.

Cork City Museum, in Fitzgerald Park on the island, lies off tree-lined, riverside Mardyke Walk and has many fascinating exhibits relating to local history. Near by are the Tudor Gothic buildings of University College, Cork, making this amongst Ireland's most pleasant campuses. The three-spired St Finbar's Cathedral was built in 1865–80 to designs by William Burges in the French Gothic style.

The Red Abbey Tower (nearer the city centre) is all that remains of a 14th-century Augustinian friary. Curiously, the tower is of grey limestone, not sandstone as might be expected from its name. Christ Church, in South Main Street, was founded by the Norsemen in 1050 and Edmund Spenser, author of *The Faerie Queene* and Shakespeare's contemporary, was married there. Elizabeth Fort stands off Barrack Street, erected on the Queen's orders as a defence against a possible Spanish invasion.

Beside Cork Opera House stands the Crawford Gallery in Emmet Place where John Hogan's (1800–58) sculptures can be admired. Cork has international jazz, choral and film festivals.

Six miles north-west of Cork, atop the tower of the 15th-century McCarthy Castle, is the tourist Mecca – the Blarney Stone;

...a stone that whoever kisses
O he never misses
To grow eloquent.

◀The *bodhrán* ('boh-ran'), from which this Cork pub takes its name, is a traditional open-ended goatskin drum

COURTOWN HARBOUR
CO WEXFORD
MAP REF: T15

Claimed to have the lightest annual rainfall in Ireland, Courtown's pretty harbour, built by the Earl of Courtown in 1847 and thus helping with famine relief work, has obvious claims on the holiday-maker. The Owenavorragh River enters the sea at the harbour and there are fine golden beaches to the north and south. There is trout fishing in the Owenavorragh and golf near by. Courtown House, in a wooded demesne north of the town, has an ancient high cross in its grounds.

CRAIGAVON
CO ARMAGH
MAP REF: J05

Craigavon is a new town still waiting for many of its citizens to arrive. Devised as a focus for new industry and as an outlet from Belfast's then overcrowded artisan districts, it almost joins the old linen towns of Lurgan and Portadown off the M1. The famous greyhound, Master McGrath, lies in a grave in Lord Lurgan Park, named after his owner. The dog is also commemorated in Lurgan town's coat of arms. At Oxford (from 'oxford') Island, a nature reserve complete with hides offers close-ups of a range of waterfowl. There is world-class coarse fishing in the River Bann at Portadown.

Peatlands Park (west along the M1) has a fine information centre relating both the history of turf and turf-cutting as a source of Irish domestic and commercial fuel, and the environmental importance of bogland in a changing world.

Ardress House and The Argory, two National Trust houses south of Peatlands Park, give fascinating intimate insights into the life-styles of gentlemen farmers in the 17th, 18th and 19th centuries. Ardress House has dazzling plasterwork, while the riverside Argory has its own acetylene gas lighting system. Moira and Waringstown villages, 'blackstone villages' from their use of local stone, are typical of the well laid out planters' weavers' villages of the area.

CRAWFORDSBURN
CO DOWN
MAP REF: J48

The thatched, white-washed Old Inn (1614) in Crawfordsburn promotes itself as the oldest coaching inn in Ireland. Crawfordsburn Country Park has streams and glens running down to Belfast Lough and a wonderful, elegant railway viaduct. A coastal footpath, running along the borders of the Lough from Holywood past Helen's Bay, continues through Crawfordsburn and on to Bangor – a total of 10 miles.

CREESLOUGH
CO DONEGAL
MAP REF: C03

Creeslough, overlooking Sheep Haven in Donegal's far north, is a good base for climbing Muckish Mountain (2,197ft). There is a pretty waterfall at Duntally Bridge just outside the village, and picturesque Glen Lough is just four miles south-west. Massive Doe Castle (15th century), once a pirate stronghold of the McSweeney's, fell to the Cromwellians in 1650. Greatly altered since then, it was lived in until recent times. Dunfanaghy (to the north-west, see Walk 6) is a favourite resort for people from Belfast.

CROAGH PATRICK
CO MAYO
MAP REF: L98

Climbing Croagh Patrick in AD441, and spending 40 days and 40 nights there in the biblical tradition, St Patrick, it is said, took time off to banish all the snakes from Ireland. This is now a mountain of pilgrimage, situated south of the R335 between Westport and Louisburgh. Thousands climb the rock-strewn slopes every last Sunday in July to the oratory constructed on top of its 2,510ft peak, many completing the journey

 Elegant and holy Croagh Patrick

THE GAELTACHTS

There were a number of languages in ancient Ireland, but now, apart from English, only one – Gaelic – survives. Its name comes from the 7th-century Welsh word for Irish, *Gwyddel*. Since the formation of the Irish Free State, special efforts have been made to ensure the survival of the language and therefore the culture which goes with it. The Gaeltachts, or Gaelic-speaking districts, are located (with a few exceptions) in the far west, where a lack of communications has left more isolated communities. The Gaeltacht peoples receive grants to help them maintain their traditional culture, there is a state-run radio station operating wholly in Gaelic and there are a number barefoot. Traditionally, the climb was made at night, starting from the seashore ruins of Murrisk's 14th-century Augustinian abbey, but these night climbs are now discouraged.

CROOKHAVEN
CO CORK
MAP REF: V82

Crookhaven, off the R591 on the way to the 700ft cliffs on Mizen Head, the most south-westerly point in Ireland, is tucked into the natural shelter of Streek Head. Spanish Cove lies to the east and fashionable Barley Cove to the west. On Three Castle Head stands one castle, an O'Mahony stronghold called Dunlough Castle, with three square tower houses. There are the ruins of further O'Mahony forts at Dunmanus and Dunbeacon (near Durrus) in Dunmanus Bay.

Schull, or Skull (eastwards on the R592), is a yachtsman's harbour like Crookhaven. It nestles below the 1,339ft of Mount Gabriel and

▲ Note the restaurant sign, tribute to Dingle's resident dolphin, Fungi

▲ Cornish-style houses in Cushendun

of programmes on Radio Telefís Eireann transmitted partly or wholly in Irish. The BBC in Northern Ireland also has a small but significant Gaelic output.

There are summer schools, mostly directed at Irish schoolchildren but now increasingly attractive to Continental Europeans, in the Gaeltacht areas. The Dingle Peninsula, Connemara, the Aran Islands, northern Donegal around Gortahork, Falcarragh, Derrybeg and Macroom in Co Cork are areas where Gaeltachts and scenic tourism obviously converge. Less well known, perhaps, are An Rinn in Co Waterford and Gibbstown in Co Meath. There is also a very tiny Gaelic-speaking enclave in Belfast.

has a single, colourful main street and the Republic's only planetarium.

CUSHENDUN
CO ANTRIM
MAP REF: D23

Lord Cushendun had Clough Williams-Ellis, the architect who designed Portmeirion in Wales, devise Cushendun's (NT) white-washed cottages in a Cornish style in memory of his Cornish-born wife Maud. The village sits on the edge of ancient woodland by a fine stone bridge over the River Dun, flowing down to the sea from Glendun, one of the nine Glens of Antrim. A long sandy beach stretches north. The poet John Masefield often visited Cave House, approached only through a 60ft long red sandstone

cave, for he married a daughter of the Crommelin's who lived there.

The Gloonan Stone opposite the Catholic church has two hollows which were made, it is said, by St Patrick's knees. Tornamony Cashel (castle), dating perhaps from AD500 (off the road to Torr Head), has walls which are 20ft thick and 10ft high.

DINGLE
CO KERRY
MAP REF: Q40

Perhaps the most westerly, and certainly the prettiest town on the edge of the old world, Dingle is a cheerful jumble of little streets tumbling down to its harbour in Dingle Bay towards the furthest end of the scenic Dingle Peninsula. Deep in a Gaeltacht area, in earlier centuries it was the centre both of Kerry's thriving smuggling enterprise and for trade with Spain and France. On the corner of Main and Green streets there was once a house made ready to receive Marie Antoinette should its owner, Count Rice, have been successful in rescuing the imprisoned lady; unfortunately, according to Rice, she refused to travel.

To the north, Brandon Mountain (3,127ft), Gerhane and Ballysitteragh (both 2,050ft) dominate the horizon. There is one 10ft standing stone (or *gallan*) in a guest-house garden in Milltown and another two in an adjacent field.

▲ Until 1865 Donaghadee's fine harbour, built between 1821 and 1837, was a packet station

DONAGHADEE
CO DOWN
MAP REF: J58

Once the regular port of call for ferry boats from Scotland, Donaghadee eventually lost its importance to Belfast. Its fine harbour, complete with lighthouse, was designed by Sir John Rennie who also designed the Eddystone Light. Grace Neill's Inn, claiming to be the oldest in Ireland, has welcomed Peter the Great, Daniel Defoe, Franz Liszt, William Wordsworth, John Keats and Brendan Behan (when he was painting the lighthouse) over the years. During the summer a pleasure-boat service runs to the uninhabited Copeland islands, which have a lighthouse and a bird observatory. Ballycopeland Windmill (DOE), one of the only two working mills in Ireland, is open to the public.

DONEGAL
CO DONEGAL
MAP REF: G97

North-west of Donegal town is the wild and windy Barnesmore Gap. To the west is St Patrick's Purgatory, or Lough Derg, where the most strict of penances – a three-day pilgrimage on the lake's Station Island – takes place. Once the seat of the O'Donnells, their 1505 castle was added to in the Jacobean style by planter Basil Brooke. Not much is to be seen of the Franciscan friary which was founded in 1474, although it was in this abbey that work began on *The Annals of the Four Masters*, dating from the early 17th century, a massive history of Ireland from the time of Noah's grandmother. An obelisk in the Diamond commemorates the four authors.

DOWNPATRICK
CO DOWN
MAP REF: J44

A massive granite boulder carved simply with his name and with a cross marks the spot in the graveyard of Downpatrick's Protestant cathedral graveyard where it is agreed that St Patrick is probably buried, interred with the bones of St Brigid and St Columba. The plain 19th-century cathedral stands where its various

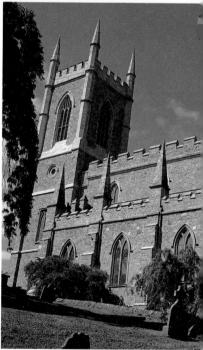

predecessors have stood for up to 14 centuries, atop one of the market town's two hills. In 1245 an earthquake destroyed a previous cathedral, the choir being the only remaining medieval remnant. The street leading up to the cathedral, English Street, has been declared an area of architectural significance with its former gaol and governor's residence and the elegant houses built to cater for judge and jury. The gaol is now the Down County Museum, part of which is devoted to telling St Patrick's story, the rest to local history. The cell block, built for 100 prisoners, is refurbished to re-create the conditions the prisoners experienced. Opposite the gaol and across the Mall stand the fine red-brick buildings of the Southwell Charity School, built in 1773 for the reception of 'decayed tenants of the family and other pious uses'.

Behind the Cathedral, the Mound of Down (a massive earthwork) overlooks the River Quoile and the picturesque ruins of Inch Abbey on the other side. Further down river, at peaceful Quoile Pondage (DOE), there is a small interpretive centre, picnic sites and angling stands. A small modern church, a replica of past ages, stands at Saul (to the north-west) and marks Patrick's landing place in Ireland. Across a valley, a granite statue on Slieve Patrick also commemorates him. By the Butterfly Garden in Seaforde, six miles west of Downpatrick, there is a fine mature hornbeam maze in the grounds of Seaforde House.

ST PATRICK

St Patrick, who was born in south Wales in AD389, was captured by pirates and sold into slavery to Miliuc, who set him to tending sheep on the slopes of Slemish, an isolated volcanic peak on the Antrim Plateau west of Ballymena. Escaping after six hard years, he made his way back to Britain (or possibly Brittany), trained as a missionary and then came back to Ireland, landing near the mouth of the Slaney River at Downpatrick in either AD432 or AD456. There is some evidence that he baptised Alphin MacEochaidh, Dublin's city king, in AD448 at a well south of the city in a place now generally associated with the park beside St Patrick's Cathedral. Ireland has many similar St Patrick's Wells.

The generally accepted version of his story is that Patrick began his mission, lighting a beacon on Slane Hill in order to challenge the druids of King Leary on nearby Tara, thus winning a permit from the authorities. From there he proceeded to Armagh where he founded his diocese.

St Patrick's Day (17 March), although a holiday in Ireland, has never been associated with the kind of green beer revelry encountered across the Atlantic. However, the shamrock, which Patrick is said to have used to illustrate the Trinity, is widely worn. A solemn religious procession follows the route from the tiny commemorative church at Saul to St Patrick's grave at Downpatrick each year on the saint's day.

(2000BC) in the Boyne Valley, south of the N51 and east of Slane, is one of the country's largest. The 1847 excavations found stone slabs decorated with spirals and concentric circles, animal bones, decorative copper pins and glass beads. A passage between stone slabs leads for 27ft to an almost circular chamber which is 11ft high and roughly 8ft wide. Side chambers give it a cruciform shape.

DROGHEDA
CO LOUTH
MAP REF: O07

Once two towns on either side of the mouth of the River Boyne, and made one by the Anglo-Norman Hugh de Lacy to form the largest English town in Ireland in 1412, Drogheda is a busy commercial centre due to its river bank position on the main Dublin–Belfast route. Medieval traces survive, particularly St Laurence's Gate with its two four-storey drum towers, the only one of the town's ten original tower gates. Magdalene Tower, dating from 1224 and to the north of the town, has a two-storey tower rising over a Gothic arch and was the belfry tower of a Dominican priory founded by Lucas de Netterville in 1224.

Millmount, a vast circular grassy mound topped by a Martello tower, was raised first by the Celts, was used by the Vikings for ceremonies and was then fortified by the Normans. Millmount Museum, once a barracks, has a display of the tools of past trades.

Inside St Peter's Roman Catholic Church, a shrine contains the embalmed head of St Oliver Plunkett, Archbishop of Armagh, who was disembowelled, beheaded and burnt in London in 1681. Drogheda was also the scene of one of the most brutal of Cromwell's massacres.

Drogheda, in the Boyne valley ▼

DROMAHAIR
CO LEITRIM
MAP REF: G83

St Patrick settled in the River Bonet's valley, founding a church, a monastery and a nunnery by its waterfalls and rapids. Few stones remain by this neat village whose chief claim to fame is that it is the place from which Dervorgilla, wife of the great O'Rourke, was abducted by – or eloped with (interpretations vary) – Dermot McMurrough, King of Leinster, whilst O'Rourke was on a self-imposed pilgrimage for whipping her. Years later and in revenge, O'Rourke dethroned Leinster, who appealed to England for help. Richard de Clare ('Strongbow'), lured by promises of land and of marriage with Dermot's eldest daughter, agreed to help, and thus began the Anglo-Norman invasion of Ireland. Ireland's Helen became Dervorgilla's soubriquet.

▲ Holy Trinity Cathedral, Downpatrick

DOWTH
CO MEATH
MAP REF: O07

Plundered by the Vikings in 861 (as was Newgrange), Dowth's prehistoric burial chamber

DUBLIN
CO DUBLIN
MAP REF: O13

With a logic which may seem particularly Irish, Dubh Linn (which translates as 'the dark pool') is now called Baile Atha Cliath ('the town of the hurdle ford'), although both names originate from early settlements on the banks of the

▲ Christchurch (CI) Cathedral, Dublin

River Liffey on which the capital city so elegantly stands at the mouth of wide Dublin Bay. The Norsemen came and settled here in the 9th century, the Danes

On the Liffey's left bank, the Four Courts houses the High Court and the Supreme Court of the Republic ▼

following them. Brian Boru, the great Irish king, broke Scandinavian rule in 1014 but 'Strongbow', the Anglo-Norman, stormed the place in 1170, beginning 750 years of English rule.

The oldest settled part of the city is around Christ Church Cathedral, on the Hill of Dublin, which once marked the division of the old Ireland into the fiefdoms of what were to become the provinces of the Kings of Munster and Connaught. King Sitric Silkbeard built a wooden church here in 1038, but the present cathedral only began to take shape in 1172. The crypt and transepts are fine examples of the Gothic style. In the nave is a tomb said to be that of Richard de Clare (Strongbow), who died in 1176. In a metal box is the heart of the Archbishop of Dublin in Strongbow's day, St Lawrence O'Toole. Down in the crypt are a preserved cat and mouse, recorded

as having been caught in the 1870s in full chase around the organ's pipes. Some claim that St Audoen's Church, near by, dates from AD650.

The Record Tower of Dublin Castle (east along Lord Edward Street) is all that is left of the key to Dublin's defence in the mid-13th century. It was the power centre of British administration in Ireland until 1920. Today, Irish presidents are inaugurated in the huge St Patrick's Hall and the Throne Room, whose massive throne (which was presented to the city by William of Orange) was used by visiting English royalty for state occasions. There are rumoured to be underground passages connecting Christ Church and the Castle.

The 300ft-long St Patrick's Cathedral, the largest in Ireland and situated to the south on Patrick Street, dates from 1190. It was erected on a site traditionally associated with St Patrick's baptismal conversions in the 5th century. The present building, although altered many times, dates mostly from 1225. From 1713 until 1745, Jonathan Swift, author of *Gulliver's Travels*, was Dean at the Cathedral and his pulpit, chair, writing table, portrait and death mask are still there. His tomb and that of his 'Stella' (Esther Johnson) are in the south aisle. His splendid epitaph reads 'he lies where furious indignation can no longer rend his heart'. The hole in the medieval chapter house door was cut so that two feuding chiefs, the earls of Ormonde and Kildare, could shake hands and make peace.

Handel first performed his Messiah in 1742 in a music hall in Fishamble Street, near by. The organ which he used is reckoned by many to be that in St Michan's Church, across the Liffey in Church Street. Down in the crypt of the church, itself a 1686 construction

▲ Christchurch Cathedral; here Lambert Simnel was crowned Edward VI in 1487

on the site of the original 1095 Danish church, corpses preserved in a state of mummification intrigue visitors.

By Temple Bar, on the Liffey's right bank and up river from Trinity College, the city's new 'Left Bank' area of bistros, art galleries and experimental theatres is emerging from the warehouses, cobbled streets and second-hand bookshops.

Trinity College, founded by Elizabeth I in 1592, lies at the base of Dame Street and is most elegantly laid out in lawns, cricket pitches and cobbled squares. It looks out on College Green where two of Dublin University's most famous alumni, orator Edmund Burke (1729–97) and Oliver Goldsmith (1728–74) are

The Chapel, Trinity College, built 1787, contains great stucco and fine wood ▼

THE BOOK OF KELLS

▲ The Long Room of Thomas Burgh's library, begun 1712, completed 1732

Ireland's monasteries, which had begun in the 6th and 7th centuries as simple wood or wattle and daub buildings for small groups of the faithful, in a few centuries became known throughout Europe as centres of study, artistic endeavour and worship. Here the gospels were recorded around the 9th century in Latin, in the most lavishly illuminated forms. These were the origins of many now famous books: the *Book of Durrow,* the *Book of Dimma*, the *Book of Armagh* and, most famously, the *Book of Kells*. Each of these books has its own adventurous history, having been hidden, lost, stolen and strayed. Some have

never been recovered. Of those which survive, that of Kells is the most sumptuous, although each is now priceless. Started in Iona, Scotland, the *Book of Kells* was completed at Kells by a team of specialist monks, working on a grand plan to unite all four gospels in the story of the life of Christ. All but two of the pages are coloured, the initial letters being worked in complex, intertwined designs of human and animal forms, often with touches of wit and individual cunning. The *Book of Kells* and the *Book of Durrow* are on display in Trinity College Library, Dublin, illustrated above.

commemorated in statues. Other famous graduates of the college include Jonathan Swift, Oscar Wilde, Bram Stoker (creator of Dracula) and Samuel Beckett. The Long Room in Trinity Library, 210ft by 41ft by 40ft houses many treasures including the *Book of Durrow* and the *Book of Kells*.

Across from the entrance to the College, the splendid windowless curve of what is now the Bank of Ireland building (dating from 1729–39) once housed Grattan's Parliament and Europe's oldest House of Lords. Guided tours are provided.

The city has many imposing public buildings, many being the work in whole or in part of the architect James Gandon. His masterpieces include additions to the Bank of Ireland, the Four Courts (1802) and the Custom House (1781). The port below the Custom House was designed in part by Captain Bligh, later famous for the mutiny on the *Bounty*. The nearby Halfpenny Bridge (pedestrians only) crosses the Liffey and is a lover's delight. Gandon also made adjustments to the design of the Rotunda, a Doric complex at the north end of O'Connell Street, completed in 1750 as Europe's first purpose-built maternity hospital. Beside it is the Gate Theatre, almost as famous as the Abbey, the state's National Theatre in Abbey Street a few hundred yards south. The General Post Office in O'Connell Street was designed by Francis Johnston who designed many of Dublin's and Armagh's Georgian houses. Leinster House (1748), now the seat of Parliament, is by Richard Cassels, architect of many of Ireland's great country houses.

The country's most innovative art gallery, the Irish Museum of

▲ St Michan's, Church Street, houses more than mummified corpses

GUINNESS

Originally called porter since it was devised in the 18th century for the tastes of porters in London's Billingsgate Market, stout, a beer which is dark because the barley from which it is made is roasted, was brought to Ireland by the Cork brewers Beamish and Crawford. Guinness, founded by Arthur Guinness in 1759 at St James's Gate on the Liffey, has since become synonymous with this dark brew throughout the world, although Murphy's and Beamish (still brewed in Cork) can also be found in many Irish pubs.

Guinness grew quickly in popularity. The first export orders left the brewery in 1769 and by the early 19th century the dark brew was on sale around the world. Later, in a recession following the Napoleonic Wars, Guinness made one of its characteristically shrewd marketing decisions. Other brewers lowered the alcoholic strength of their brews to make savings, but St James's Gate increased theirs, producing a new product sold first as 'extra stout porter'. Thus the name stout became synonymous with dark beers even, one presumes, in

▲ The solid gateway to the original Guinness brewery speaks of the strength of the dark stout within

Samoa where Robert Louis Stevenson took his own supplies and to the Poles where explorers also took theirs.

The Dublin brewery produces up to 2½ million pints of Guinness a day, still using the same strain of yeast selected by the original Arthur. Until 1939 this was the largest brewery in the world, covering over 60 acres and having taken over many rival firms on accompanying sites near by in its process of expansion. One of these was the Phoenix Brewery, owned by the son of Daniel 'The Liberator' O'Connell. The

Modern Art, is housed in the old Royal Kilmainham Hospital to the south-west of the city out past the massive Guinness Brewery. Kilmainham Jail, near by, held many of Ireland's revolutionary leaders. Refurbished, it is a rather grim reminder of darker days. The National Gallery, the National Museum and the Natural History Museum are close to Merrion Square, one of Dublin's most elegant squares which was home at different times to Oscar Wilde, Sheridan Le Fanu, the ghost story writer, WB Yeats and Daniel O'Connell, 'The Liberator'. The Irish Architectural Archive is also in this square. The houses where many of Dublin's famous writers lived are marked with blue plaques. The Dublin Writer's Museum, in Parnell Square, is a useful source of further information. There are guided tours to literary Dublin, the most notable being a literary 'pub crawl' which takes in, amongst other establishments, both Davy Byrne's in Duke Street and Mulligan's in Poolbeg Street. Other atmospheric pubs include Doheny and Nesbitt's in Baggot Street, the Brazen Head (reckoned to be

Dublin's oldest) in Lower Bridge Street and Ryan's in Parkgate Street out near the spacious (1,752 acres) Phoenix Park with its zoological gardens, racecourse and polo matches.

St Stephen's Square, 'the Green' to most Dubliners, is Europe's largest

CANALS

The Newry Canal, predating England's first (the Bridgewater), was finished in 1742 thereby opening the way for sailing barges to bring coal from the Coalisland mines via the Coalisland Canal to Lough Neagh, and thence by sea to an expanding Dublin. Although the possibilities of using Ireland's rivers for commercial navigation had been considered in the early 17th century – and indeed, in 1498 an attempt was made to connect Lough Corrib to the sea by opening up the course of the Terryland River – the canal age did not start until the building of the Grand Canal, joining Dublin to the Shannon 79 miles away. A southern branch opened up the traditional Irish harp on Guinness labels and cans is derived from the Brian Boru Harp, secure in Trinity College, Dublin.

Aficionados will insist that, whilst there is much to be said for the taste of a pint of stout poured anywhere, those brewed in Dublin and drunk there in a judiciously selected number of pubs, where the barmen pour the pints carefully and slowly with a fine head, cannot be equalled for creamy bitterness. In some pubs a barman will devise the pattern of a shamrock at the top of the head, although this will mark the recipient as a tourist. Others favour bottled stout, which is slightly more bitter and is made by a slightly differing process. In winter, a bottle is often accompanied by a glass ('a half 'un') of Irish whiskey. The original porter, a thinner drink which is often referred to in Irish literature – particularly in the magical realism of the work of Myles na Gopaleen (Flann O'Brien) – as ' a pint of plain' is no longer brewed.

Although now on sale in over 120 countries, Guinness is made in just 31 of these, but the brewery in St James's Gate has a visitor centre explaining how the famous stout is made.

▲ 'In Dublin's fair city, where the girls are so pretty...'

square. Mountjoy Square is, mathematically, precisely a square. Fitzwilliam Square is almost as elegant as Merrion, but the city's oldest Georgian houses, built around 1720, can be found in Henrietta Street. O'Connell Street is a wide and impressive looking thoroughfare from a distance; close up it is less interesting. The main visitor shopping and browsing district is bounded by St Stephen's Green, complete with pony and traps, pedestrianised Grafton Street and all the streets off it to the east and west, right down to the River Liffey. A life-size statue at the Trinity College end of Grafton Street commemorates 'sweet Molly Malone', although the city's street markets are located around Moore Street, off O'Connell Street. Bewley's Oriental Cafés are as much a part of the capital's literary and social life as any of the multiplicity of pubs.

waterways via the Barrow Navigation to Waterford. Work began in 1756 and was not completed until 1834.

The Royal Canal, unwisely built to rival the Grand, follows a mostly parallel course west from Dublin, then taking a more northerly route through Mullingar and reaching the Shannon near Longford. It was completed in 1817. The Ulster Canal joined the great Erne system in Co Fermanagh to Lough Neagh. The Lagan Canal linked Lough Neagh to Belfast, the River Bann linking the lough to the sea at Coleraine. The Erne canalisation linked Belturbet in Co Cavan to Belleek on the Donegal border with the sea just a few miles west. The Newry system gave Dublin access to Lough Neagh. Only one gap in the picture remained, and a project was put forward to join the Erne and the Shannon, so that in practice a boat could make the journey from Dublin to the Shannon, proceed north to join the Erne, go east to Lough Neagh and then on to Coleraine, Belfast or back to Dublin again via Newry. Thus the ill-advised Ballinamore–Ballyconnell Canal was begun. Badly managed, poorly built and too late for the canal age, only a score or so of boats ever completed the journey.

Recently, however, with the growth in popularity of canal and lake cruising holidays on the Shannon and the Erne systems, the idea has been revived, leading to the reopening of the Ballinamore–Ballyconnell Canal in the early 1990s. It is expected that the renovation of the canal will prove more successful since hire cruisers take much less draught than barges and, having their own power, are not dependent on sail to traverse awkward lakes where horse's tow paths could not run.

Hire cruisers are available principally on the Shannon and the Erne, but also on the Grand Canal at Tullamore. There are waterbuses on the Shannon, Erne, Barrow, Suir, Lough Neagh, Lough Corrib, the Lower Bann and the Grand Canal. In Dublin, the Grand Canal can be seen at its best by Baggot Street, home of Bord Failte (Irish Tourist Board). A seat by the lock commemorates the poet Patrick Kavanagh.

▲ The strong walls of Dundrum's Castle, which nevertheless fell to Cromwell

DRUMCLIFF
CO SLIGO
MAP REF: G64

*'Cast a cold eye
On life, on death,
Horseman, pass by!'*

So runs the inscription on the grave of the poet WB Yeats in the tiny graveyard of Drumcliff Church by the little village and the stream which takes Glencar Lough's waters to the sea under Benbulben Mountain's flat-topped head (1,722ft). There are two crannogs in Glencar and splashing waterfalls. There is also a 13ft 10th-century high cross by the poet's grave, all that remains of an AD575 monastery.

Lissadell House (further west), home to the Gore-Booth family, is a late Georgian mansion which was designed by Frances Goodwin. Yeats was a frequent visitor. The life-size murals of domestic staff are by Count Markievicz who married Constance, a daughter of the house and heroine of the 1916 rising.

At Carney (east of Lissadell) there is a bird reserve which is noted for Ireland's largest colony of barnacle geese.

DUNDALK
CO LOUTH
MAP REF: J00

Just half-way from Dublin to Belfast on the N1, busy Dundalk, with its port, quays, breweries and cigarette factories, has the air of a small crowded provincial city. It takes its name from an old Norman fort, or motte, evidence of which can still be seen on the western outskirts.

Its court-house, designed in the Doric style and built between 1813 and 1818, copies its proportions exactly from the Temple of Theseus in Athens. St Patrick's Mourne granite church is in the perpendicular style by Thomas Duffy of Newry, and dates from 1835 to 1840. It shows the influences of King's College Chapel, Cambridge. The 'Green Church', the Protestant St Nicholas's, dates from 1207 and has the remains of Agnes Galt, sister of the Scots poet Robert Burns, buried in its graveyard. Both brother and sister are commemorated in an 1859 monument.

Inland, just south of where the R177 meets the border, stands the romantic ruin of Castle Roche. Built in the 13th century, it has a castellated curtain wall and a murder window from which Rohesia de Verdun, the castle's original owner, had its builder thrown to his death.

DUNDRUM
CO DOWN
MAP REF: J43

For 400 years the great stone walls of Dundrum's castle withstood all-comers until, like so many others, they fell to Cromwell's forces in 1652. Built by de Courcy, the castle still gives views right up and down the coast – of little Dundrum clustered by its tidal harbour and of the great sweep of Dundrum Bay. The castle is in an excellent state of preservation.

Murlough Nature Reserve (NT), Ireland's first such reserve, runs across dunes and heathland to beach and estuary. It is favoured by birdwatchers, botanists and nature-lovers. Evidence of Stone Age settlements have been found – the big dolmen opposite the entrance is called the Slidderyford Dolmen. The car-park by the many-arched bridge gives excellent views of Slieve Donard, the highest peak in the Mourne Mountains. Maghera (two miles inland) has the stump of a round tower, the remnant of a 6th-century monastery which was founded by St Donard, after whom Slieve Donard is named.

DUNGARVAN
CO WATERFORD
MAP REF: X29

Dungarvan, a market town and industrious sea port, stands either side of the River Colligan as it enters Dungarvan Harbour. A motte and bailey at Gallowshill marks the Norman presence which brought the town its first prosperity in the 1170s, although St Garvan had first founded a monastery here in the 7th century. A causeway connects the town to Abbeyside and the ruins of the 1290 Augustinian abbey. The ruins by the river are those of Prince John's castle, while the 'Dead Walk' has remnants of the old town walls. The ruins of a McGrath Castle in Abbeyside explain the memorial outside town to Master McGrath, the greyhound which won the Waterloo Coursing Cup in 1868, 1869 and 1871. Off Gratton Square in Parnell Street is the Old Market House, now a museum.

DUNGLOW
CO DONEGAL
MAP REF: B71

Capital town of The Rosses, 60,000 acres of rough rock landscape sprinkled with 130 trout-filled lakes, Dunglow (also spelt Dungloe) is a tiny place with one fine looking hotel devoted to an angler's needs. South-west of the town is a geological curiosity, a 12ft-wide chasm running for almost ¼ mile. It is called Talamh Briste which translates as 'broken earth'. There are impressive cliffs at Crohy Head, the caves at their base being accessible only by boat. Burtonport (to the north) is the port of departure for Aran Island. To the north-west is the Poisoned Glen, so named because God, it is said, poisoned the area and deprived it of birdsong for ever.

The Glenveagh National Park (10,000 acres) mixes wild natural scenery with the formal gardens of Glenveagh House. Glebe House, by Gartan Lough and now owned by the nation, contains fine primitive paintings from Tory Island plus works by Degas, Renoir and Picasso. A flagstone at Church Hill pinpoints St Columba's birthplace and the Colmcille Heritage Centre chronicles his life.

DUN LAOGHAIRE
CO DUBLIN
MAP REF: O22

Pronounced 'Dunleery', this cheery seaside resort just nine miles south-east of Dublin is the terminal for

▲ Trafalgar Square, Dun Laoghaire

Ireland is located in Haigh Terrace in the former Mariners' Church. Three yacht clubs – the Royal Irish, the National and the Royal St George – have their bases in the town, now Ireland's major yachting centre. Two other clubs, the Royal Alfred and the Dublin Bay Sailing Club, also sail from here.

The Martello tower at Sandycove, featured in James Joyce's *Ulysses*, is now a small but fascinating museum of Joyce memorabilia. Joyce stayed there for a week in 1904, and Bloomsday (16 June) is the day to go. The Forty-Foot, a rocky bathing spot near by, also features in *Ulysses* and was once reserved for naked male bathers.

DUNMORE EAST
CO WATERFORD
MAP REF: S60

On the western head of Waterford Harbour, Dunmore East has a 600ft pier, and a reputation both as a resort and a base for sea fishing. To the south stands Black Knob promontory with Merlin's Cave. The town's name derives from the huge earth fort (or *dún*) which can still be seen. There is a cairn at Harristown, two miles north, with a megalithic tomb.

Across the bay is Hook Head, and north of Dunmore East past Woodstown Strand lies the small village of Crooke. Cromwell, heading for Waterford, vowed he would take it 'by Hook or by Crooke' – that is, either up the east or west side of the estuary.

the Holyhead ferries.

The original harbour's engineer was Sir John Rennie, who designed the Eddystone Light, and Donaghadee Harbour and lighthouse in Co Down. The lighthouse (on the East Pier) looks best in the setting sun. George Bernard Shaw's family, like many of Dublin's middle classes, had a summer home nearby at Dalkey, immortalised in a novel by the cult author Flann O'Brien (Myles na Gopaleen) and the plays of popular Irish author Hugh Leonard. Dun Laoghaire's Victorian architecture – for example, its bandstand on the pier – are pointers to its heyday, when it was called Kingstown. The National Maritime Museum of

Peaceful Dunmore East harbour ▼

MUSICAL TRADITIONS

The Chieftains, U2 and Van Morrison represent different strands of popular Irish music, while in the 1960s, Aran-sweatered groups such as The Dubliners drew on an old tradition to revive different threads of Irish music. Much of this tradition dates back to the great Belfast Harp Festival of 1792 when musicologist Edward Bunting first set down tunes played by the great harpers of the day.

In truth, much of the popular music heard in Irish pubs today owes more to the sentimentality of Country and Western than anything else – a curious situation when these songs of infidelity, divorce and infanticide are sung in a country where the old Catholic values have been enshrined in the constitution. In the meantime, much Irish music has travelled abroad, has influenced the Appalachian and the Blue Grass fiddlers, and has come back home again. The instruments of Irish music are the fiddle, the *bodhrán* (single-headed drum), the *uileann* pipes (fairly similar to Scottish bagpipes) the guitar, the banjo, the accordion and the human voice in *sean nós* (a cappella singing). The harp is confined to banquets.

A *ceilidh* (pronounced 'kaylee') is a music session in a pub, a *fleadh* ('flah') is a summer music festival and a *feis* ('faysh') is a competitive version of a *fleadh*. Step-dancing (distantly akin to Scottish country dancing) is also currently undergoing a fashionable revival.

▲ Daniel O'Connell and his square; Ennis

ENNIS
CO CLARE
MAP REF: R37

The town centre of Ennis is distinguished by intriguing narrow winding streets, known locally as 'twisters', and curiously 'un-square' O'Connell Square with its imposing statue of Daniel O'Connell on a plinth of Tuscan limestone. A friend of O'Connell's, 'Honest' Tom Steele, once an MP for the area in the early 19th century, is commemorated in a style befitting this eccentric town on the River Fergus. On a rock in the middle of the Fergus there are three painted shields and a carved lion. This is known as Steele's Rock for, from there, he expressed his unrequited love for a Miss Crow, whose home can still be seen from this viewpoint.

The Franciscan friary (dating from 1242) has not been much improved by its 'improvements', although the rich medieval carvings have not been affected. The De Valera Museum and Library, housed in a former Presbyterian church, commemorates Eamon De Valera (1882–1975), once MP for East Clare and both *Taoiseach* (Prime Minister) and President of Ireland during his long political career.

ENNISCORTHY
CO WEXFORD
MAP REF: S93

At the limit of River Slaney navigation, Enniscorthy, Co Wexford's cathedral town, has a triangular square and splendid steep streets with traditional shop-fronts running down to the river banks beyond Abbey Square. There are two elegant spires, that of St Aidan's Cathedral and that of St Mary's Church. St Aidan's was designed by Augustus Pugin and was completed in the 1840s.

At the top of Castle Hill stands a Norman fortress, begun in 1205 but rebuilt 400 years later and added to in the early 20th century. It now houses the County Wexford Historical and Folk Museum. In the 16th century it was owned by the poet and statesman Edmund Spenser, given to him by Good Queen Bess who was flattered by his poem to her, *The Faerie Queene*.

Vinegar Hill (on the east bank of the Slaney) was the location of one of the bloodiest battles of the 1798 rebellion. The Cotton Tree, beside the pleasant six-arch bridge, is claimed to be where the English soldiers tied up their horses after the battle. If you mount the hill on a summer's evening and listen at the site of the old windmill (now a National Monument) where the rebels made their last stand, holding out for several weeks, locals say you can still hear the sounds of battle.

St Senan's Hospital, with its imposing 300ft red-brick front, would look well on India's North-West Frontier. The story goes that its plans, like those of Ennis's court-house, were mixed up with those bound for the Indian subcontinent by frolicsome, bored or inefficient bureaucrats. There are massive 12th-century castle and cathedral ruins at Ferns, eight miles north.

From Daniel Robertson's fine terraces (1843-75) Powerscourt's gardens seem to stretch to the distant Sugar Loaf ▼

▲ Beside the newest of Enniskillen's two west bridges, the twin towers of the Watergate look out over the River Erne

ENNISCRONE
CO SLIGO
MAP REF: G23

Facing Killala across the bay of that name, Enniscrone (on the R297) was once noted for its sulphur baths. There is excellent surfing off the three-mile strand, and the island offshore is Bartragh Island. The *Book of Lecan* (1416), now in the Royal Irish Academy in Dublin, was compiled by a MacFirbis of Castle Firbis, near by.

ENNISKERRY
CO WICKLOW
MAP REF: O21

Powerscourt, one of the great gardens of Europe which extends over 34,000 acres, is Enniskerry's main attraction. Up the hill and through the gates, a long avenue of mature 200-year-old beech trees leads to the once great house, designed by Richard Cassels and completed by Richard Wingfield (later Viscount Powerscourt) in 1740, but gutted by fire in 1974. Pebbled steps lead down to the Triton Pool with its 100ft fountain, its grottoes, and its bronze winged horses of Fame and Victory.

The gardens were planted in 1745, being well established by 1767. There are areas in the English, Italian and Japanese styles, and the view from the great terrace over Triton Pool to Sugar Loaf Mountain is one of the most splendid and breath-taking in Ireland. There is also a 400ft waterfall in the grounds.

ENNISKILLEN
CO FERMANAGH
MAP REF: H24

Meaning 'Kathleen's or Ceithlinn's Island', Enniskillen began its life as a strategic settlement on an island in the narrows between Upper and Lower Lough Ernes. At the time of the Plantation it was heavily fortified, but before that Hugh 'The Hospitable' Maguire built a castle in the 15th century beside which the West Bridges now stand, and Captain Cole (an officer of the King's Long Boats) developed the site in the 17th century. The Watergate, with its fairytale turrets, now houses both military and civil museums, the former devoted to two famous regiments, the Royal Inniskilling Fusiliers and the Inniskilling Dragoons (both now disbanded).

Across the river, on a hilltop and dating back to the early 17th century, stands Portora Royal School, whose old boys include Oscar Wilde, Samuel Beckett and Francis Lyte, composer of the 'Wembley Anthem' and King George V's favourite hymn, 'Abide With Me'. Portora Castle, by the lock gates behind the school, was blown up by schoolboys experimenting with gunpowder.

On another hill, this time across the East Bridge, in a tidy park and on a tall pedestal, is the statue of General Sir Galbraith Lowry Cole, hero of the Peninsular Wars, who married Wellington's unwanted betrothed.

On the island itself, the main street winds its way up and down two hills, and around gentle bends between solid houses and shop-fronts, changing names several times as it does. On one hill, St McCartan's Protestant Cathedral (1841) stands opposite the Catholic and Methodist churches by Peg o' the Bull Lane. The old Butter Market has been re-opened as a craft centre where products include skilfully dressed trout and salmon flies, and full-size reproductions of the enigmatic stone heads and figures found on the Erne's many islands.

ENNISTYMON
CO CLARE
MAP REF: R18

A picturesque little town at the meeting point of the N67 and the N85, and well south of the Burren, Ennistymon is a typical combination of market town and tourist angling centre. Built around the Cullenagh River just above a waterfall called the Cascades, a pleasant walk follows the river bank.

The Midnight Court, an uncharacteristically rumbustious (for Ireland) satirical poem was written by Bryan Merriman, born in Ennistymon around 1747. It relates a dream in which the women of Ireland put Irish men on trial and charge them with having low sex drive and marrying late in life, thus keeping nubile women in frustrated harness or domestic slavery.

At Corrofin (to the east, where the R460 crosses the R476) the old Protestant church is now the location for the Clare Heritage Centre, with displays relating to the Great Famine and a T-shaped (Tan) Cross dating from the 12th century. Across the road is a genealogical centre, and there is an Archaeological Centre in Dysert O'Dea's restored tower house.

▲ This fissure was caused by the Grey Man's legendary passing by rugged Fair Head

FAIR HEAD
CO ANTRIM
MAP REF: D14

Herds of wild goats scrabble over the almost vertical 400ft slopes of Fair Head, a headland known to Ptolemy, the Alexandrian geographer. Almost the last refuge for Ireland's choughs, this wild headland is broken by the light shining on three dark lakes – Lough Doo, Lough na Crannagh and Lough Fadden. A great fissure, the Grey Man's Path, in legend created by the passage of some great mysterious kraken-like figure, leads careful walkers down the headland. Waymarked paths lead from the forbidding yet beautiful plateau to the total contrast of the natural amphitheatre of Murlough Bay (NT).

FERMOY
CO CORK
MAP REF: W89

Planned by Scots merchant John Anderson in 1791, this well laid out market town lies astride the salmon-rich Blackwater River. It betrays its origins as a military centre on the main coach route from Dublin to Cork in handsome

Pearse Square, with its well-built market house and the coaching stable yards of 18th-century Grand Hotel on Ashe Quay. From Barnane Walk there are views of Castlehyde House, the ancestral home of Douglas Hyde, first President of the Republic.

Two miles south-east on a small hill is Labbacallee Cairn, dating from 3,500 years ago and one of the

▲ In spring, the salmon run the weir on the River Blackwater at Fermoy

best preserved wedge-tombs in Ireland. Doneraile Court, with its 400-strong herd of Irish red deer, once witnessed the only recorded instance of a woman being initiated as a Freemason, when a daughter of the house was discovered spying on the Lodge.

FORE
CO WESTMEATH
MAP REF: N57

Fore, between Lough Lene, Lough Glore and White Lough, and north of the R395, is traditionally famed for its seven wonders. Wonder No. 5 concerns a feat of faith performed by St Feichin who is said to have raised the great 2-ton stone lintel above the west doorway of St Feichin's Church by the power of prayer alone. St Feichin founded a monastery here in AD630, and died of the plague in AD665. The monastery was burnt down 12 times and the current church of St Feichin dates only from two periods, the 11th and the 13th centuries. There is a tiny anchorite's or hermit's chapel (wonder No. 7) on the hill above. There are also extensive 13th-century and 15th-century remains of a large Benedictine abbey (wonder No. 3) built on marshy bogland and endowed by the de Lacy family. The first two wonders, non-combustible wood and unboilable water, turn out to be a branch so studded with the copper of votive coins that it will not burn, and the apparent curious chemical composition of the water in a well near by. Wonder No. 4, a mill without a mill-race, is elusive. From certain angles, the water flowing out of Lough Lene reputedly appears to be flowing uphill; wonder No. 6. The details are perhaps best recorded, in murals, in the Abbey, Fore's nearby pub.

Gallarus Oratory's perfect beauty ▼

TE Lawrence (Lawrence of Arabia) was the illegitimate son of Thomas Robert Chapman, the ruins of whose 18th-century house, Killua Castle, stand off the N52 to the west. Boats for fishing on Lough Sheelin may be hired at Finea, while the fine castellated greystone Tullynally Castle, home of the Earls of Longford and situated outside pretty Castlepollard, is occasionally open to the public.

FOATY ISLAND
CO CORK
MAP REF: W77

Foaty Island (or Fota Island), surrounded by mudflats teeming with wildfowl, lies in Cork Harbour. It has an arboretum, established in 1820, and a wildlife reserve (owned by the Royal Zoological Society of Ireland). Fota House, once an 18th-century hunting lodge and later remodelled in the Regency style, is not open to the public.

GALLARUS ORATORY
CO KERRY
MAP REF: Q30

Reminiscent of an upturned stone boat and at least 1,200 years old, the Gallarus Oratory is, in its simplicity, the most perfect early Christian building in Ireland. It is well signposted just a mile inland from Smerwick Harbour, north-west of Dingle. It measures just 10ft by 15ft inside, and 18ft by 22ft outside, with a narrow low doorway to the west and a tiny window in its east wall. Its maximum height is just 16ft. Neither window nor doorway have perpendiculars. At each gable's summit the sockets in the stones would have held crosses.

No mortar was used in its still waterproof construction, and an interesting modern realisation of this style of building, echoed down to the smallest detail, can be found in the Ulster History Park, near Omagh in Co Tyrone.

CRANNOGS

For defensive reasons, crannogs (artificial islands) were built in a huge number of Ireland's tiny loughs from Neolithic times right up to the 17th century.

A layer of turf (peat), logs and stones was laid first to create the island, and then the crannogs were finished with whatever suitable materials were at hand. At Lough na Crannagh, on Fair Head in Co Antrim, well-built drystone walls rising to 7ft above the waterline may be seen clearly.

Crannogs have provided a great number of artefacts since water, cutting off oxygen, has acted as a preservative on wood and leather materials which otherwise would not have survived. Today, there are a number of crannog interpretive centres – for instance, at Lough Gur in Co Limerick, at the Irish National Heritage Park at Ferrycarrig in Co Wexford, and at the Ulster History Park in Co Tyrone – which present rather clean and tidy, but historically accurate, examples of reconstructed crannog buildings.

GALTEE MOUNTAINS
CO TIPPERARY
MAP REF: R92

Galtymore (3,018ft) is the highest point in the Galtees (or Galtys), Ireland's most important inland mountain range. Most of Ireland's other ranges are coastal, making the island a vast oval geological saucer. The Galtees run parallel to the N8 from Cahir to Mitchelstown, several access roads leading up the southern slopes to the peaks. The northern approaches, from the Glen of Aherlow, along the valley of the River Aherlow and past tiny corrie lakes, are steeper and more challenging, and are therefore more suitable for the rock climber than the walker. Lyracappul (2,712ft) is west of Galtymore, while Sturrakeen (2,004ft) is to the east. The Mitchelstown Caves lie south of the N8.

GALWAY
CO GALWAY
MAP REF: M32

The River Corrib rushes through Galway city, the sluices, weirs and great stone structures of the old abandoned waterside mills on both its banks giving evidence of one past source of the city's wealth. Spring-run salmon still mass below the weirs, attracting anglers and idlers on the riverside walks. Down by the quays and next to Galway City Museum, the Spanish Arch marks the old fish market. On the river's right bank, opposite, stands the Claddagh, once the base of a fiercely independent fishing community, now known for Bing Crosby's version of Galway Bay and for the ring named after it.

Here and there amongst the restored warehouses and new shopping centres in the Republic's fastest growing city, traces of the past times abound. Lynch's Castle in Shop Street, now incorporated in a bank, is an early 16th-century tower house with archery slit windows. Set in a wall in the graveyard of the Collegiate Church of St Nicholas of Myra is a skull and crossbones – the restored Lynch Memorial, dating from 1493. The church itself dates from 1320, its tower dating from 1500. Its triple nave is the second largest in Ireland. It is said that Christopher Columbus worshipped here, wishing to learn more of the voyages of St Brendan before he set out himself to find the Americas. Rice de Culvy, a Galway man, went with him when he left in 1492. Norah Barnacle's Cottage (near St Nicholas's Church) is a little museum commemorating James Joyce's wife, who lived there.

The city's most prominent building, the Cathedral of our Lady Assumed into Heaven and St Nicholas, dates only from 1965. Its

Galway city's great stone mills, now restored, finding a new life ▼

THE SPANISH CONNECTION

Brown-eyed and olive-skinned west Irelanders are evidence, perhaps, in Galway city of centuries of trade with the Iberian peninsula, long before the Armada's doomed ships were storm-wrecked off Donegal and Kerry. The Kerry blue, a terrier, is also said to have Spanish antecedents.

More concrete evidence of the Spanish connection can be seen in Galway's buildings, particularly in the style of the Browne doorway, now standing alone in the city's main square, the sole remnant of a big city mansion owned by one Martin Browne. Another reminder near the old fish docks is the Spanish Arch.

The Lynch Memorial by St Nicholas's Church relates to a sadder Iberian connection. James Lynch Fitzstephen, Mayor of Galway city in 1493, was forced to hang his own son Walter, convicted of killing a Spanish wine merchant called Gomez. Gomez, son of the Mayor's business contact in Cadiz, had taken a shine to Walter's girlfriend Agnes. No one else would perform the execution, and to sustain the city's honour – and, it must be said, his own business connections – the Mayor hanged his own son from his window bars. According to one theory, it was this event that added the phrase 'lynch law' and the word lynching to our vocabulary.

demonstrative appearance has led to it being called the 'Taj Michael' after the then Bishop of Galway, Michael (pronounced 'Mee-hawl') Brown.

Galway's beginnings go back 1,000 years. By 1240 the Anglo-Norman de Burgo family had a strong castle here, commanding this natural trading post which soon established sea links with both France and Spain. Today, the city prospers. There are interesting bookshops, art galleries, theatre companies with international reputations – Druid, Punchbag and An Taibhdhearc – plus an International Arts Festival, an exciting race week and two famous oyster festivals.

GIANT'S CAUSEWAY
CO ANTRIM
MAP REF: C94

Stretching for four miles and sometimes reaching up 300ft cliffs, this fantastical series of 40,000 tall and many-sided basalt columns is lapped by the swirling seas. Their shapes, mostly hexagonal in cross-section and as geometrical as if they had been machined, inspired the legend of Finn MacCool. Warring with a Scottish giant, he began to build a causeway to Scotland (and indeed there is a smaller manifestation on the Scottish shore opposite at Staffa). Finn retreated when he saw the size of the Scots giant, built himself a giant cradle and had his wife wrap him in swaddling clothes. The Scot advanced triumphantly until, noting the size of the 'baby', he calculated the father's size and cannily backed away.

The reality, now listed as a World Heritage Site, is no less fascinating. Sixty thousand years ago cooling lava from a vast undersea volcano formed into crystalline shapes on contact with the cold sea water. Victorian guides gave the natural formations their current labels: the Wishing Chair, the Giant's (musical) Organ and the Giant's Foot. A bus is available to take visitors from the modern Interpretive Centre with its replicas of Causeway trams and explanatory audio-visual displays to the most popular parts of the Causeway. However, a walk along the majestic and towering headlands will reveal the true glory of the Causeway and provide romantic views to Rathlin Island and Scotland beyond over a sea dotted with sport fishing boats.

GLENCOLUMBKILLE
CO DONEGAL
MAP REF: G58

Once the retreat of St Columcille, or St Columba, and hideaway for Bonnie Prince Charlie, this secluded little village sits at the head of Glen Bay and almost in the shadow of Slieve League (1,972ft). It was first noted as a co-operative, formed by the local priest in an effort to find a way to stem emigration from the isolated glens. Reconstructed cottages in the Folk Museum Village illustrate the life-styles of different periods in the history of such villages. Near St Columba's Oratory are reputed relics of the saint's life.

Susanna Drury's two paintings of the Giant's Causeway, completed in 1740 and now in the Ulster Museum, Belfast, encouraged scientists and tourists ▶

GLENDALOUGH
CO WICKLOW
MAP REF: T19

Spread around Gleann dhá Loch ('Glen Two Lakes'), nestling between 2,000ft mountains, are the extensive remains of the monastic settlement (now a National Monument) which was founded by St Kevin in the 6th century. He chose this splendid setting, retreating from the advances of a beautiful redhead with 'un-holy eyes'. Various stories state that he rolled both himself and his putative lover in stinging nettles to distract them both from the lusts of the flesh, or that he threw the lady off a cliff into a cold lake to cool her ardour.

and the reconstruction of Teampull-na-Skellig, the Rock Church.

Russborough House (open to the public), south of Blessington, houses one of the most remarkable private art collections in Ireland, and includes works by Murillo, Goya and Velázquez.

GLENGARRIFF
CO CORK
MAP REF: V95

Surprisingly, the name of this lush, almost subtropical valley dotted with oaks, arbutus, holly, yew and great pine trees, means 'rough glen' in Irish. There are scattered boulders, but there are also palm trees and tropical flowers down by

▲ In wild Glenmalure, the road up the valley is fine until Barravore ford. Then, only a track leads to the top at 686m, and the Glen of Imaal beyond

▲ George Bernard Shaw wrote *St Joan* in the calm of Garinish Island. Rowland, son of John Allan Bryce, the gardens' original owner, gave them to the nation

By the 12th century there was an important diocese here despite Viking raids in the 9th century, but its decline started after a great fire in 1398. Restoration began in the 19th century, and today the visitor centre provides useful information on the general layout. St Kevin's simple church, known locally as St Kevin's Kitchen from its chimney-like tower, is well preserved. The round tower, 100ft high, dates from the 10th century, while the Priests' House dates from the 12th century. Near by is St Kevin's Cross, 11ft high and also from 12th century. The Cathedral of St Peter and St Paul is 10th century. Further up the valley, near the Upper Lake and approached only by boat, are St Kevin's Bed (a stone slab in a cave)

the edges of small streams, for the warm waters of the Gulf Stream have brought a Mediterranean microclimate to this valley, and to the little island of Garinish in Glengarriff Harbour, which opens into bigger Bantry Bay beyond. The northern woodland species, nearer the shoreline, form the basis of Glengarriff Forest Park which is noted for its nature trails.

Garinish (or Ilnacullin) is connected to the mainland by regular ferry boats which leave from a little shaded cove near Glengarriff's main street. The island has a Martello tower and superb Italian-style gardens which were devised by John Annan Bryce – who once owned the island – with help from Harold Peto. The gardens

were laid out in the 1920s when Annan Bryce, a Scottish MP who had bought the island for his wife, sought the help of Peto, a noted architect and garden designer of the day. The centre-piece is the lily pond with its paved surround. Plants include rare conifers, scented mahonias, camellias, exotic bamboos and New Zealand privet. There is a miniature Japanese garden with an overhanging rockery, and a replica of a Greek temple, shaded walks and wonderful views over the Martello tower.

GLENMALURE
CO WICKLOW
MAP REF: T09

Somber and forbidding to some, yet the most alluring of Wicklow's glens to others, Glenmalure, with the Avonbeg River running along it, opens into a high-sided steep amphitheatre above Drumgoff, near Baravore. The Military Road here, running across the valley from Aghavannagh to Laragh, is so named as it was built to enable soldiers to get into the hills in order to seek out and destroy rebels from the 1798 rebellion. A ruined military barracks stands forlornly on guard at Drumgoff, where the Military Road crosses the valley road running down to Rathdrum on the R755.

GLENS OF ANTRIM
CO ANTRIM
MAP REF: D12

The nine glens of Antrim follow the courses of sparkling streams rushing from the Antrim Plateau to the sea. The plateau itself can seem haunting and wind blown, empty but for distant cropping moorland sheep, but the wooded glens shelter tiny farms and small green fields, often located by white waterfalls. Until the construction of the Antrim Coast Road, from which the mouths of many of them can be seen, the glens and their people were isolated.

Driving north, Glenarm (the 'glen of the army') comes first, reaching the sea at the village of the same name, seat of the McDonnells, Earls of Antrim. Next comes Glencloy ('glen of the hedges'), running down to pretty Carnlough with its white limestone harbour, then Glenarriff (the 'ploughman's glen') with beautiful Glenarriff Forest Park and its waterfalls meeting the sea at Red Bay. Further north are Glen Ballyemon (the 'glen of Eamon's town'), Glenaan (the 'glen of rush lights') and Glencorp (the 'glen of the slaughter'), all meeting to run down to Cushendall with its beach and red-sandstone Curfew Tower. Glendun (the 'brown glen') runs down to Cushendun. Glenshesk ('glen of the sedges') and Glentaisie ('Taisie's glen', named after Taisie, Princess of Rathlin Island, who escaped from the clutches of a Norse king when her betrothed, Congal of the Long Nails, arrived by boat in the nick of time in 200BC) run north, rather than east, to meet the sea at Ballycastle.

GLIN
CO LIMERICK
MAP REF: R14

Glin Castle was the 18th-century home of the Knights of Glin, the Fitzgeralds, and stands on the edge of this Shannonside village. There is also the ruined keep of an older, 16th-century castle here. Desmond Fitzgerald (the present and 29th Knight of Glin) was once a curator at London's Victoria and Albert Museum, and in a series of rooms leading off the Corinthian-pillared hall of the castle is a splendid collection of Victorian (and earlier) furniture, ceramics and paintings. The plasterwork ceilings are masterpieces.

The present Georgian castle, with its unique double flying staircase, is open to the public only during the month of May. It was constructed in the 1780s by the 24th Knight, Colonel John Fitzgerald. The purely decorative castellations date only from the 1820s.

GOREY
CO WEXFORD
MAP REF: T15

Gorey's grid of wide streets attests to its importance in times gone by. It was built by the Ram family – one of whom, Bishop Thomas Ram, is buried in the old cemetery in Market Square – in the early 17th century. The town's arms – a cross, a lion, a rose and a swan – are symbolic of religion, fortitude, unanimity and industriousness are displayed on the Market Hall in Main Street. St Michael's Catholic Church is by Augustus Pugin, and its graveyard has always been associated with the travelling people or 'tinkers'. Some of stained-glass artist Harry Clarke's work can be found in Protestant Christ Church.

The Celtic Cross on Gorey Hill (418ft) commemorates the role of local insurgents in the rising of 1798. To the north, Tara Hill (833ft) has splendid views of Courtown Strand, while to the south along the N11, is Ferns with the ruins of an Augustinian abbey and its odd square tower with its conical roof.

To the west and just off the N80 near Clonegall, Huntington Castle, built in 1625 by Lord Esmond, stands down a leafy drive. Stanley Kubrick used it as the setting for his film *Barry Lyndon*. A vine in the conservatory was grown from a cutting presented by Cardinal Wolsey to Anne Boleyn. The current owner of the castle, the Reverend Durdin-Robertson (who founded the Fellowship of Isis in 1976), has set up shrines to this Egyptian goddess in the cellars. Guided tours are available from March to October.

GORT
CO GALWAY
MAP REF: M40

Thoor Ballylee, the tower house purchased and restored by poet WB Yeats in 1917, stands close to the spot where Coole House once stood in Coole Park, north of the little town of Gort on the main Galway–Ennis road (N18). Home of Lady Gregory who was noted for her patronage of young Irish poets and playwrights, Coole House was demolished in 1941. However, the sparsely furnished 16th-century Thoor Ballylee, where Yeats wrote many of his poems and with its views of the Slieve Aughty Mountains and the Burren, is open to the public.

Gort, a typical Galway market town ▼

GOUGANE BARRA LAKE
CO CORK
MAP REF: W06

The ruins on the little island in Gougane Barra Lake unfortunately date from the 18th century rather than the 6th century when St Finbar, patron Saint of Cork, built his monastery here in perhaps Ireland's most beautiful setting. This mountain lake near the source of the River Lee draws many visitors seeking solace by the lakeside or strolling between the birch and conifers of Gougane Barra Forest Park, the Republic of Ireland's first such park.

Keimaneigh (from the Gaelic for 'deer') Pass, steep sided and lush with greenery, is as romantic a spot as one could wish for. Downstream at Ballingeary, an ancient stone slab footbridge crosses the Lee.

▲ 'I met Murder in the way – He had a mask like Castlereagh,' wrote Shelley

most famous equestrian portrait hangs in Mount Stewart (NT) two miles north, the home of the Marquess of Londonderry. The gardens, with their Italian, Spanish, Irish and other national themes, were laid out by the 11th Marchioness in the 1920s. A stone carved menagerie of animals relates to private nicknames she had for prominent politicians of the day. The house was designed by George Dance, architect of Newgate Prison, and contains memorabilia of a previous member of the family, Robert Viscount Castlereagh, Minister for War and Foreign Secretary during the Napoleonic Wars. In Ireland he is more likely to be remembered as the creator of the Act of Union in 1800 and is thus one of the most hated men in Irish history.

GRIANAN OF AILEACH
CO DONEGAL
MAP REF: C31

Seven miles south-east of Fahan, this great circular stone fort which crowns 750ft Grianán Mountain, its terraced walls built 17ft high and 13ft thick, forms an enclosure 77ft in diameter. The wall is cut by an entrance giving access to two passages inside the walls. Outside there is evidence of other circular embankments. Built around 1700BC and later taken over as a power base by the O'Neills, Kings of Ulster, it was unsubtly restored in 1870. Not surprisingly, archaeologists argue about its purpose.

HEADFORD
CO GALWAY
MAP REF: M24

Ross Errilly Abbey, on the banks of the Black River and off the Cong road to the north-west of the little town of Headford, was founded in the 14th century by the de Burgo family. It was largely rebuilt in the 15th century when the castellated tower with its first-floor gallery was added. Its state of preservation affords interesting insights into everyday Franciscan monastic life, and a bakehouse, kitchen, fish tank and refectory have been identified. There are excellent views over Lough Corrib from Moyne Castle near by.

GREYABBEY
CO DOWN
MAP REF: J56

Affreca (daughter of Godfred, King of the Isle of Man, and wife to John de Courcy) had the holy body, now presumed to be that of St Patrick, moved for reasons of politics to its final resting place by Downpatrick Cathedral. She also founded the Cistercian Grey Abbey (DOE) here in 1193 on the tranquil shores of Strangford Lough. It sits in a hollow in mature parkland surrounded by a fine stand of trees on the edge of the picturesque little village. Due to its use as parish church up to the 18th century, the buildings are in a much better state of preservation than many others of similar age. Its focal point now is the multi-arched west door.

Hambletonian, George Stubbs'

HILLSBOROUGH
CO DOWN
MAP REF: J25

Built on a hill and by a Hill, Hillsborough, a pretty and quite English-looking town of antique

The Grianán of Aileach, Bronze or Iron Age, dominates a country it once ruled ▼

▲ Hillsborough, a village of trees; here the avenue leads to the fort

shops and Georgian houses, was once the home of the Governor of Northern Ireland. His official residence, Hillsborough Castle, is now only used for Government receptions and meetings. The castle's fine wrought-iron gates can be seen behind the 1760 Tholsel (toll house).

Off the square on the opposite side is Hillsborough Fort, built for Colonel Arthur Hill in 1650 to command the Dublin–Carrickfergus road. The curious original gatehouse was remodelled with an added gazebo in the 1850s for family amusements. A superb star fort with artillery positions, towers and ramparts stands behind the gatehouse, and beyond the star fort is Hillsborough Forest Park with its peaceful walks and trout lake. St Malachy's Church, at the bottom of the hill, was rebuilt from 1760 to 1774, and is the finest example of Georgian Gothic Revival in the country.

HOLYCROSS
CO TIPPERARY
MAP REF: S05

South-west of Thurles on the R660, in a wonderfully peaceful setting by the banks of the River Suir, Holy Cross Abbey (now a National Monument) was founded for the Cistercians in 1180. It underwent a massive restoration in 1975, but unfortunately little of the original remains apart from the entrance at the south-east angle of the cloister – although the sheer bulk of the squat building with its battlemented tower impresses. It housed two relics reputed to be

from the true Cross on which Christ died, hence the Abbey's name.

HOWTH
CO DUBLIN
MAP REF: O23

Howth Head, rising to 560ft, is a landmark on the northern tip of the great sweep of Dublin Bay. Beauty spot, resort and suburb all in one, and with a cairn atop the Ben of Howth, the little village of Howth is still one of Ireland's major fishing ports. The Bailey Lighthouse dates from 1814 and the pier is recommended for buying fresh fish. Howth Castle, west of the harbour, dates from the 14th century but was remodelled in 1910 by Sir Edwin Lutyens. There is a massive dolmen in the grounds, a fine display of 2,000 species of rhododendrons, 30ft-high beech hedges and the oldest known introduced tree in Ireland – an elm planted in 1585. From the Ben of Howth there are fine views to the Mournes in the north (see Walk 11).

About seven miles north-west lies the picturesque village of Malahide. The castle, dating from the 14th century, has a remarkable great hall with minstrel's gallery, as well as 20 acres of botanic gardens, including a notable collection of Australasian species.

INIS CEALTRA
CO CLARE
MAP REF: R68

Holy Island (or Inis Cealtra) is a solitary uninhabited 49-acre island

set in a bay in Lough Derg, north of Killaloe and reached by ferry from Mountshannon on the R352. The island has the remains of no less than five churches, a 10th-century, 79ft round tower, a hermit's cell and a graveyard whose stone slabs date back to the 12th century. St Caimin founded his monastery here in the 7th century.

INISHOWEN
CO DONEGAL
MAP REF: C43

With Lough Foyle on its east and Lough Swilly on its west, the mountainous diamond-shaped Inishowen peninsula points north to end in precipitous Malin Head, Ireland's most northerly promontory which will be familiar to anyone who listens to the shipping forecasts. From Baba's Crown (362ft), near the old Martello tower on Malin Head, there are good views of the Scottish islands of Jura and Islay on a clear day. Buncrana is the peninsula's largest town and Slieve Snaght (2,019ft) is its highest point. At Carndonagh stands Donagh Cross, Ireland's oldest such remain. The cliffs at Malin Head reach 200ft, while those at Glengad, to the east, reach 800ft.

Bonnie Prince Charlie hid at Culdaff after the 1745 rebellion failed. Fort Dunree on Dunree Head, once an important gunnery post in the Napoleonic Wars, later kept a watchful eye on British convoys gathering for the Atlantic run in the First World War. It is now a military museum.

JERPOINT ABBEY
CO KILKENNY
MAP REF: S54

Founded by the Cistercians in 1180, probably on an earlier (1158) Benedictine site, Jerpoint Abbey combines awe for its size and presence with enough domestic detail to lend it a purely human scale. It towers above a curve in the N9 south of Thomastown. The chancel and the transepts, the oldest parts, are Irish Romanesque. The east window is 14th century and the splendid tower dates from the 15th century. On the walls of the chancel are faded paintings of benefactors. An effigy of Bishop O'Dulany who died in 1202, his crozier being chewed by a serpent, is also to be found here, and there are amusing carvings on the restored cloister piers, many of them echoing drawings from medieval manuscripts.

KANTURK
CO CORK
MAP REF: R30

The poet Edmund Spenser, who lived at Kilcolman Castle outside Buttevant near by on the R780, mentions both the Duala and the Mallow rivers, whose meeting point marks the attractive town of Kanturk ('boar's head' in Irish), in his poem *The Faerie Queene*. The town was developed by the Earls of Egmont who gained the lands hereabouts after the 1641 rebellion. Before that, MacDonagh MacCarthy began building the ambitious five-storey Jacobean Kanturk Castle in 1609, but the English were suspicious of its battlemented towers and possibly jealous of its size, and ordered him to stop. Enraged, MacCarthy smashed the glass tiles ordered for his roof and abandoned the castle.

KENMARE
CO KERRY
MAP REF: V97

Kenmare, a most colourful market town almost at the head of the Kenmare River estuary, gives easy access to two excellent drives, the Ring of Kerry and the Ring of Beara. It was laid out in the shape of an X in 1670 by Sir William Petty, Cromwell's Surveyor-General. A stone circle at the Shrubberies on the banks of the River Finnihy is at least 3,000 years old, and is known locally as the Druid's Circle. It consists of 15 stones in a 50ft-diameter ring with a four-stone burial dolmen in the centre. The dry-stone Cromwell's Bridge near by is named in a curious mistranslation from the Irish *crombheal*, meaning 'moustache', a reference to the bridge's drooping shape. Kenmare lace, famous in the late 19th century, is enjoying something of a revival. Cnoc an Cappeen (two miles east) is a vast mushroom-like stone which was left behind in the last Ice Age.

KILDARE
CO KILDARE
MAP REF: N71

Kildare, deep in the heart of horse-breeding country beside the Curragh plain, has a solid, affluent air about it due to its linked connections with horse-racing and the long-established military barracks near by. The Protestant cathedral, begun in 1223 and reconstructed many times since, is probably built on the site of St Brigid's AD490 monastery. The

round tower, 105ft high with its doorway 12ft up the wall (and unnecessary modern battlements) may date from the 10th century. Dan Donnelly's Footprints in Donnelly's Hollow mark the steps taken in 1815 by this celebrated Irish boxer after he had beaten the English champion George Cooper. Monasterevin (east) and Robertstown (north) are both on

Kildare's surprising Japanese Gardens ▼

the Grand Canal and are of interest to canal enthusiasts. Monasterevin was the home of the poet Gerald Manley Hopkins and the tenor Count John McCormack.

KILKEE
CO CLARE
MAP REF: Q85

Kilkee is one of those old-fashioned 'family' resorts of long beaches and tall Victorian guest-houses,

Jonathan Swift, George Farquhar and William Congreve were pupils. The castle's stables are now a focal point for locally designed crafts.

The Rothe House, built by a merchant called John Rothe in 1594 and restored in 1966, is now a museum, archive and library. The court-house lies across the street and dates from 1794. Kilkenny Tourist Office is housed in what was a Tudor almshouse, built by lawyer Sir Richard Shee in 1584. City Hall, once the Tholsel (toll-house), has a fine octagonal clock dating from 1761 and the city mace dating from 1677. Kyteler's Inn has associations with the beautiful and possibly murderous Dame Alice Kyteler, charged by Bishop Ledrede of consorting with demons and killing her four husbands. Sentenced, she escaped, leaving her maid Petronilla to burn in her place outside the Tholsel opposite Butler Slip. It is said that Petronilla still haunts the inn.

The 13th-century St Mary's Church, connected to the almshouse by St Mary's Steps, displays the heraldic crests of a number of Kilkenny families including those of the Archers and the Shees. George Archer-Shee's court case was the basis for Terence Rattigan's famous play, *The Winslow Boy*. St Canice's Cathedral dates from 1251, while St Mary's Cathedral dates from 1843. The Black Abbey (still occupied by Dominicans, the 'Black Friars') dates from 1225, the ruined St John's Priory dates from 1250 and St Francis's Friary dates from 1232.

although Moore Bay now attracts as many scuba divers as paddlers to its clear waters. A blow hole to the south and rock pools for bathing in at low tide, known locally as the 'Pollock Pools', complete the resort's picture. The ferry from Killimer (east on the N67) to Tarbert across the Shannon estuary avoids a 100-mile detour via Limerick.

KILKENNY
CO KILKENNY
MAP REF: S55

Kilkenny once rivalled Dublin's claims to be capital city, and numerous Irish Parliaments sat there. Its castle, built between 1192 and 1207 for Strongbow's son William, mixes the Gothic and Classical styles, and inevitably its three conical-roofed drum towers recall the chateaux of the Loire in France. The fourth tower and much else was destroyed in a Cromwellian bombardment in 1659, leaving the castle open to acres of parkland. Over the years the castle – home to the Ormondes from 1391 until 1936 – changed from medieval to Victorian. There are splendid views over the River Nore from its walls, and also of Kilkenny College where

▲ At Gurteen, near Kenmare, the stone circle is known (as usual) as the Druid's Circle. In the centre are four boulders, known (as usual) as the Giant's Grave

Kilkenny Castle, seat of the Butler earls; guided tours can be arranged ▼

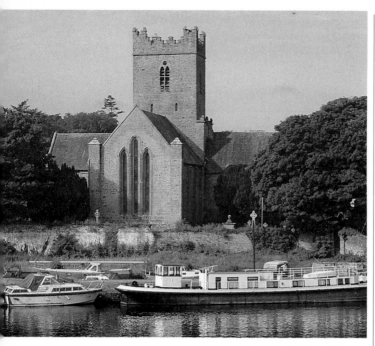

grounds and another, rescued from Friar's Island, drowned when the Shannon was dammed for hyrdroelectricity, has been re-erected next to the modern Catholic church.

KILLARNEY
CO KERRY
MAP REF:V99

Killarney is Ireland's tourist honeypot, and the business which was started by Lord Kenmare in 1750 is now a huge money-spinner. Killarney is a town of hotels, bars and shops, and of jarveys and jaunting cars. To the south-west of the town lie the lakes of Lough Leane, Muckross Lake and Upper Lake. To the west beyond them lie Killarney National Park, Purple

In Killarney, be prepared to surrender your individuality, in the nicest possible way, for this is serious tourist territory ▼

▲ Attributed to King Donal Mor O'Brien, who died in 1194, St Flannan's (CI) Cathedral, on the west bank of the peaceful Shannon, presides over pretty Killaloe

KILLALA
CO MAYO
MAP REF: G23

Eleven hundred French troops under General Humbert landed on Kilcummin Strand in Killala Bay in August 1798 in an abortive attempt to help the rebellious Irish; theirs was the spirit of their own 1789 revolution. Pretty little Killala was the first town to fall to them, Ballina the second and Castlebar the third. However, the few Irish who joined them were ill-equipped and untrained, and Humbert surrendered in September of the same year. His French troops were treated as prisoners of war, the Irish being hanged as traitors.

A 12th-century round tower, complete with stone cap, stands 84ft high on the skyline. The spire of the Cathedral of St Patrick (Church of Ireland) is almost as prominent. Built in 1680, its box pews are a fascinating reminder of the days of privilege. Two miles south, the ruins of the 15th-century Rosserk Abbey are well preserved. Rathfran Abbey, in ruins four miles north-west, is Dominican and dates from the 13th century.

KILLALOE
CO CLARE
MAP REF: R67

A 13-arch bridge across the Shannon, south of Lough Derg, connects the village of Ballina in Co Tipperary with Killaloe, sheltered by the forests of the Slieve Bernagh

Mountains in Co Clare. At 1,746ft, Moylussa is their highest peak. Although there is now no trace of Kincora, the royal palace of King Brian Boru, it was once here; the large Béal Boru fort, a wooded mound to the north of Killaloe, is the place from which his title comes. Another fort stands at Greenaunlaghna – Grianán Lachtna – on Craglea.

St Flannan's Cathedral, dating from the 13th century, has a splendid carved Romanesque doorway. Outside this door is an inscription in granite in both Ogham and runes (Viking script), noting the conversion of one Thorgrim. There is a small 12th-century oratory in the cathedral

Muckross 'Abbey' friary was founded for the Observantine Franciscans ▼

Mountain (2,739ft), Tomies Mountain (2,413ft) and the Gap of Dunloe, then Macgillycuddy's Reeks with Carrantuohill, at 3,414ft, their highest peak. With its 30 islands, Lough Leane covers 5,000 acres; Muckross covers 680 acres and has four islands, as has Upper Lake which covers 430 acres. There are two further small lakes: Black Lake and Auger Lake further along the Gap of Dunloe which bears west at Upper Lake.

The fine limestone cathedral in the town is St Mary's, designed by Augustus Pugin in the Early English style and completed in 1855. The Franciscan friary was finished in 1860. There is a Transport Museum in the town, but most visitors opt for the jaunting car to Kate Kearney's Cottage – Kate Kearney was a local temptress and poteen maker. From there, take a pony and trap through the Gap of Dunloe, return by boat down the river, shooting the rapids and then crossing the lake to 14th-century Ross Castle, inspiration for Tennyson's *The Princess*, and head back. Inisfallen Island in Lough Leane bears the ruins of a monastery where Brian Boru, it is said, was educated in the 10th century. Alternative trips run by jaunting car to Muckross House, near Wild Deer Woods and by the 15th-century Muckross friary. Muckross House, built in the Tudor style in 1843, now houses the Kerry Folklife Museum

The elusive native Irish red deer roam Killarney National Park, 25,000 acres of woodland and lake. There are also tamer Japanese sika deer and wild goats, and a multitude of other wild mammals and birds. The best view in Killarney is that from signposted Ladies' View on the Killarney–Kenmare road. The town's two golf courses have excellent reputations, and there is good fishing locally.

KILLORGLIN
CO KERRY
MAP REF: V79

Following the Ring of Kerry route (R562) west from Killarney, the visitor joins the N70 at Killorglin on the River Laune, noted, like many in the area, for its salmon. Built on a steep slope, Killorglin is famous both as the gateway to the beautiful Iveragh peninsula and for its Puck Fair. The latter is held over three days in August and includes the crowning of a goat, subsequently to reign as king over all on a raised platform.

▲ Killorglin, without its Puck Fair

KILLYBEGS
CO DONEGAL
MAP REF: G77

With its steep streets roughened by the passage of heavy lorries bearing away fish and its sky whirling with seagulls, Killybegs, one of Ireland's major fishing ports, has the air of a frontier town despite its Victorian houses. On a wall inside spacious St Catherine's Church is the 16th-century tomb slab of one Niall Mór of the local MacSweeney family, showing him in remarkable effigy as a galloglass, or Scottish mercenary. There is a similar slab in the old graveyard in Creeslough. The views from Drumanoo Head to the south are spectacular, and the beach at Fintragh is a noted bathing spot.

KILLYLEAGH
CO DOWN
MAP REF: J55

Killyleagh's fairy-tale castle, all turrets and battlements, is surrounded by mature trees and blends easily into this hilly little seashore port. The castle was begun in 1625 and was remodelled until 1850. In its library a local boy, Hans Sloane, was encouraged by the then owner, the Earl of Clanbrassil (1660–1753), to educate himself. He went on to become physician to George II, and founded Kew Gardens and the British Museum. His own eclectic collection of books, manuscripts and eccentricities were the original basis for the British Museum. A stone near the castle's gatehouse commemorates him, and a plaque notes his birthplace in Frederick Street in the town in 1666. The castle is not open to the public.

Sketrick Castle, to the north and also on the lough's shores, is situated on a causeway linking Sketrick Island to the mainland and dates from the 15th century. The large 'room' on the ground floor was originally a boat house. There are commercial oyster and mussel beds in the sea near by.

KILRUSH
CO CLARE
MAP REF: Q95

Kilrush is one of those well laid out towns which was devised by the local landlords – in this case the Vandeleurs, whose house was burnt out in the troubles of the 1920s. There are broad streets, a market square and a pier at Cappagh on the Shannon estuary. Offshore is Scattery Island with its round tower, at 122ft reputedly the tallest and most ancient in Ireland, and its five ruined churches. A monastery on the island was founded by St Senan, whose curse condemns any woman who walks on the island to childless years. Until well after the turn of the 20th century, women would come here hoping that the misogynist's curse might affect their family planning without offending the church.

Kilrush was the departure point of Ellen Hanley, Lieutenant John Scanlan and Scanlan's servant, Sullivan, in June 1819. Hanley, aged only 15, was a peasant betrothed to an officer. She was never seen again, and eventually Scanlan was convicted and hanged for murder, although Sullivan later confessed to having acted on Scanlan's orders. The story was the basis of Dion Boucicault's play, *The Colleen Bawn*.

Kilrush Heritage Centre provides a useful briefing for those visiting Scattery Island.

KINSALE
CO CORK
MAP REF: W85

With its yacht-filled harbour, the Georgian houses in its streets decked with hanging flower baskets, its fashionable pubs and restaurants, and its gourmet festival, Kinsale has become a tourist Mecca.

In the year 1601 the English defeated a joint Irish and Spanish force at the Battle of Kinsale, sealing the fate of the old Gaelic Ireland. Kinsale saw history passing by again when James II, fleeing from his defeat at the hands of William III, took sail from this small harbour for France. The early 18th-century house James lodged in, in Lower O'Connell Street, is marked with a plaque. History touched yet again in 1703 when the 90-ton *Cinque Ports* sailed out from the little harbour with Alexander Selkirk (whose story inspired Defoe to write *Robinson Crusoe*) on board. Yet more recently, a German U-Boat sank the liner *Lusitania* in 1915 off the Old Head of Kinsale.

St Multose's Church, dating from 1190 but later extensively modified, retains its original north transept and font. Desmond Castle – sometimes called the French Prison – held French prisoners during the Napoleonic Wars. The original building dates from the 15th century. The Dutch-gabled 18th-century court-house is now the Kinsale Regional Museum. At Summercove (two miles south-east) are the 40ft-high walls of 1677 Charles Fort, overseeing the entrance to the Bandon estuary. It is one of the best preserved star forts (so called because of their star shape) in the world. Downdaniel Castle ruins beside Innishannon village, further up the estuary, date from the 15th century.

KNAPPOGUE CASTLE
CO CLARE
MAP REF: R47

Knappogue, like Bunratty, was built by the MacConmaras, or MacNamaras – the former by the son John in 1467, the latter by Sioda, the father. Like Bunratty, Knappogue is the venue for medieval banquets on summer evenings. The first castle was completed here in 1467, but suffered additions and adaptations as government offices until secured exactly 500 years later by the then Assistant Secretary to the US Navy, Mark Edwin Andrews. He turned the stone shell into this setting for

▲ Knappogue Castle, where pageantry and splendour can still be had

twice-nightly pageants, with dinner and tales of the history of the women of Ireland.

KYLEMORE ABBEY
CO GALWAY
MAP REF: L75

Kylemore Abbey, exotic and 'medieval', sits in an enchanted setting in deep woodlands on the shores of Fannon Pool, one of a trio of tiny lakes on the escarpment slopes of 1,736ft Doughruagh. Benedictine nuns who came here from Ypres in Flanders after the First World War now run it as a girl's school. It was built by Liverpudlian magnate Mitchell Henry, who, the story goes, came to this spot on his honeymoon in the 1860s and liked it so much that he knew that this was the place for his mansion. He had scrubland cleared, the castle built, and a Gothic chapel with Connemara marble interior pillars created, designed as a miniature version of Norwich Cathedral.

LAGAN VALLEY
CO DOWN/CO ANTRIM
MAP REF: J26

The Lagan Valley Regional Park now encompasses much of an area which was once, with its canal and linen factories, one of the busiest in Ulster. Now it is an area of quiet riverside walks, open parkland, rose gardens, canoe slaloms and fascinating glimpses of the old Lagan Navigation which ran from Lough Neagh to Belfast. With linen came real wealth for some, and so grand houses and great demesnes grew beyond the white-washed cottages and the lock keepers' houses. International Rose Trials are held at Sir Thomas and Lady Dixon Park. Barnett's Park, with its

rolling acres and Georgian mansion is a weekend escape for city dwellers. Edenderry, upstream, is a pretty mill village. Above it is the Giants's Ring, a vast circular enclosure with a central dolmen, once an ancient fort and place of ritual which has been used in more recent times as a two-mile racecourse. Going from Edenderry to Lisburn, the river negotiates nine miles of old locks. There are fine stands of mature beech at Minnowburn near Shaw's Bridge, where canoeists often compete.

LAHINCH
CO CLARE
MAP REF: R08

Lahinch, or Lehinch as it is often spelt, lies behind a walled promenade on a mile-long beach looking out across Liscannor Bay. Beach resort town though it is, Lahinch's fame comes from its two golf courses, the Old Course and the Castle Course. Both have 18 holes, but the Old Course is the more famous, known throughout the world.

The Cliffs of Moher are four miles to the north-west, and on the road at Liscannor are the ruins of an O'Connor Castle. Still in Liscannor, in Castle Street is the birthplace of

Edward III of England gave pretty Kinsale its Royal Charter in 1334 or 1335, but it was a town of little consequence until the arrival of the Spanish in 1601 ▼

John P Holland, the man largely credited with the invention of the submarine. Holland's motives were, in part, originally political. His research was financed by Irish Americans who hoped his devices could be used against the Royal Navy. Eventually both the US and the British governments built submersibles to his designs.

Nearer Lahinch, but also to the west at O'Brien's Bridge over the Cullenagh River, are the ruins of 15th-century Kilmacreevy Church and of Dough Castle.

LARNE
CO ANTRIM
MAP REF: D30

Larne, at the mouth of Lough Larne, is the disembarkation port for the car and passenger sea ferries from Cairnryan and Stranraer. It is also the starting point for a drive up the stunning Antrim Coast Road, passing the nine green Glens of Antrim on the way.

The Vikings landed at Olderfleet in the 10th century, and Edward, brother of Robert the Bruce, landed at the same spot in 1315 to begin his fruitless mission to become High King of Ireland. Three years later he was dead, killed in battle. Olderfleet Castle was built a century later, but is now in ruins. The round tower, standing 92ft high, is a comparatively modern replica (1888) commemorating local MP James Chaine who was buried, at his own request, upright in a niche in the cliffs near by. The tower doubles as a lighthouse.

Larne and District Historical Centre in Victoria Road has artefacts relating to domestic rural life in the 18th century. St Cedma's Church dates from the 16th century, and the First Larne Presbyterian Church was built in 1626. There is a maze in Carnfunnock Country Park to the north.

LEENANE
CO GALWAY
MAP REF: L86

The striking little resort of Leenane (or Leenaun) is in a beautiful setting on Killary Harbour. If Ireland has a real fjord, then Killary Harbour is it, an arm of the sea stretching 10 miles between the Mweelrea and Maumturk mountains, deep into Joyce's Country on Galway's western coast. The Mweelreas reach to a height of 2,688ft, and in past times the bay was a natural shelter for warships. The waterfall at Aasleagh, near by, is impressive. There are some fine walks in Derreen Wood, and the exposed gravels on the sides of Killary Harbour will be of interest to geologists.

LEITRIM
CO LEITRIM
MAP REF: G90

An air of other-worldliness blankets the quiet village of Leitrim, once important enough to give the county its name, but now just containing a village pump, a spreading chestnut tree and a crumbling castle wall. The castle is all that is left of the stronghold of the once-powerful O'Rourke chieftains. The refurbished Ballinamore–Ballyconnell Canal, joining the River Shannon by the little bridge, may bring back some of its lost glory.

Ballinamore's Heritage Centre and Museum, in the village 14 miles to the north-east, houses farm and kitchen implements and the collar of a shirt worn by patriot Seán MacDiarmuid at the time he was executed during the 1916 rebellion. Drumshanbo, a beautiful little village on the banks of Lough Allen, is a Mecca for pike fishermen. North at Barnameenagh is a rock said to have been thrown by the legendary giant Finn MacCool of Giant's Causeway fame. Its grooves are supposed to have been made by his fingers. If yours fit, you will gain great strength and stamina – perhaps allowing you to take monster pike from the lake! The Poor Clare Convent (also north of the town) attracts pilgrims from all over the world who come to join the nuns in prayer. The countryside hereabouts is dotted with old stone sweathouses – Irish saunas. One stands just off the R207, going north from Drumshanbo.

LEIXLIP
CO KILDARE
MAP REF: O03

Leixlip Castle's 13th-century battlemented towers once watched over King John as he set out on his hunts for red deer and wolves. Now it is the headquarters of the Irish Georgian Society, but is not open to the public.

The Gothic Revival Celbridge Abbey in the very pretty village of the same name on the River Liffey (to the south) was home in the 18th century to Esther Vanhomrigh, Jonathan Swift's Vanessa. Many places in the village commemorate her. Castletown House at the end of the village's main street dates from 1772. It is one of the country's most imposing houses, having been modelled on an Italian palace. It is noted for its stucco and is open to the public. There is the splendid 80ft-long Pompeian Gallery and the Great Hall, its two black-and-white chequered floors connected by a grand, sweeping staircase. Connolly's Folly, an arched obelisk two miles north-west, was constructed to provide work during the severe winter of 1739. Just a few years later, the building that is known as the Wonderful Barn (south-west of Leixlip) was also commissioned by Lady Connolly of Castletown House in order to provide famine relief work. Unfortunately, its five storeys with their vaulted ceilings are not open to the public.

▲ King John's Castle on Shannon's bank, once vital to the town's defences

LETTERKENNY
CO DONEGAL
MAP REF: C11

Almost bypassed by huge road developments, Letterkenny has a long, narrow, winding main street and sits on a little hill overlooking the River Swilly just above the point where it flows into broad Lough Swilly. The 215ft of the spire of St Eunan's Cathedral, claimed to be one of the tallest in the country, towers over what is claimed to be the longest main street in the country. The cathedral is a late 19th-century construction in late, and rather freely interpreted, Gothic style. The Protestant church, across the square, dates from the 17th century and has some intriguing old slabs in its graveyard. There are further interesting old gravestones in Conwal Cemetery, west of the town, beside the ancient stone fort of Conwal Dun.

The County Museum is housed in the recently restored workhouse on the corner of New Line and High Roads. Swilly, originally written Suileach, was a man-eating monster which was killed, it is claimed, by St Columba, although not before the various pieces he had cut it into had continued to attack him many times.

Glenveagh National Park (to the west) is much recommended for its walks, gardens and loughs.

LIMERICK
CO LIMERICK
MAP REF: R55

Limerick, now the Republic's third city, is an industrial and manufacturing base due to its situation on the River Shannon and proximity to Shannon Airport. It began in AD922 as a Viking settlement on a bare hilly island, now called King's Island, between the Shannon and its tributary, the Abbey. The oldest parts of the city are still sometimes referred to as English Town (on King's Island), Irish Town (on the mainland to the south-east) and Newtown Pery (west of Irish Town). Although the Irish under Brian Boru took the town, the Norsemen stayed on as traders, even after Limerick's conquest by the English Prince John in 1197. It was the site of many battles between the Irish and English, the most notable being Patrick Sarsfield's daring defence against William III's forces in 1690, leading eventually to the Peace Treaty of Limerick.

Limerick's most important historical sites are on King's Island:

St Mary's Protestant Cathedral (probably AD1170), and the great solid waterside bulk of King John's Castle by Thomond Bridge, with its five heavy drum towers dating from 1200. There is an archaeological museum in the Castle courtyard, and there are fragments of the original town walls by St Murchin's Protestant Church. The cathedral has been much altered over the years, but contains many interesting tombs and a fine Romanesque doorway. The 'leper's squint' is a slot in the north wall of the Chapel of the Holy Spirit through which lepers were allowed, unseen, to receive communion. The black oak choir stools have wonderful carvings of human heads.

The Gerald Griffin School near the Cathedral is named after the eponymous novelist whose most famous work, *The Collegians*, was the inspiration for Boucicault's play, *The Colleen Bawn*.

The Hunt Museum (in the riverside University of Limerick) was established by the man who devised the Craggaunowen Project, while the Limerick Museum (on John's Square) also contains Stone, Bronze and Iron Age artefacts as well as the 'nail' (a pedestal) on which city merchants settled their debts – the origin of the saying 'paying on the nail'. The City Art Gallery near People's Park has works by Jack Yeats, amongst others.

On another pedestal across the river from the Castle stands the Treaty Stone, on which it is said the Treaty of Limerick was signed. The next bridge down river, Sarsfield Bridge, was named after Limerick's dashing defender and has ironworks modelled on those of the Pont de Neuilly in Paris. There are fine Georgian houses in St John's Square beside the tall-spired St John's Catholic Cathedral in the Newtown Pery section of the city. The style of witty doggerel poem called the limerick was reputedly devised in a long-gone pub in the city's Limerick Street.

LISDOONVARNA
CO CLARE
MAP REF: R19

Lisdoonvarna's first fame came to it in Victorian times when its sulphur-, magnesium- and iron-rich waters were reckoned to have therapeutic properties. It became a

spa town around the turn of the century, and many of the older buildings still have a distinctive class about them. The spa wells are still active, making this Ireland's only spa resort. However, the town has had a separate claim to fame since the 1970s, when the old late August hiring fair match-making traditions had a revival at autumnal hotel dances in the town. The traditions originally grew partly out of the isolation of rural communities, partly out of the church's strict attitude to the segregation of the sexes in rural parts, and partly from a heritage of large families growing up on smaller and smaller farms, thus leading to emigration, poor dowries and late marriages. This match-making phenomenon has now grown into a well publicised tourist event, much examined by the media and sociologists.

There is sea bathing at Doolin Point and Fisherstreet to the west, and the Burren, with all its walks, rare botanical delights and archaeological wealth, is all about.

LISMORE
CO WATERFORD
MAP REF: X09

Massive and square, Lismore Castle was rebuilt in the 19th century by the sixth Duke of Devonshire. Standing on a commanding cliff-top site overlooking the River Blackwater, it was originally an 1185 castle constructed for Prince (later King) John, Henry II's youngest son. The Devonshires still occupy the house, and the seven-acre garden is laid out with camellias, rhododendrons and magnolias. The garden is open to the public during the summer, but the house is not.

St Carthach's Cathedral with its tower and elegant spire dates from the 17th century, although the saint first founded a double monastery here in AD633 – one for monks and the other for nuns. The village at one time was known throughout Europe as a university town, and had 20 churches. As usual, however, the monastery was sacked and pillaged by the Vikings and Anglo-Normans, and was finally razed in 1173 by Raymond Le Gros.

Ballyduff Castle (further upstream on the River Blackwater) was built by the Earl of Cork in 1628, but is not open to the public. Strancally Castle (downstream) was built in the Gothic Revival style in the 1820s. Further downstream is Old Strancally Castle where the Fitzgeralds invited landowners to dinner, cut their throats, and dumped them in the river in a succession of medieval take-over bids.

LISNASKEA
CO FERMANAGH
MAP REF: H33

Castle Balfour, approached through the Church of Ireland churchyard, dominates one side of Lisnaskea. Built in 1618 for Sir Thomas Balfour, a Scots planter, the castle, with its corbelled turrets and pitched gables, was burnt down in 1803 but later much restored. The town's market cross was erected in 1841 on the instructions of the second Earl of Erne, and sits on a carved shaft depicting Adam and Eve having a jolly time. It was moved there from Galloon Island, whose churchyard has grave slabs bearing skull, crossbones, coffin, sand timer and the tolling bell. The grounds (NT) of the current private Crom Castle (19th century) include the romantic lakeside 1611 ruins of its predecessor. There is a circle of huge stones, called locally the Druid's Stones, at Annaghmore Glebe four miles south of Newtownbutler.

◄Joseph Paxton, who built the Crystal Palace, also built Lismore Castle. Robert Boyle (1627–91), formulator of Boyle's Law, lived there with brother Roger

LONDONDERRY
CO LONDONDERRY
MAP REF: C41

Built on a hill overlooking the estuary of the River Foyle, Londonderry, now Northern Ireland's second city, was always going to be a settlement of such obvious practical and strategic significance that its future would rarely be left in the hands of its own citizens. Thus, from St Columba founding his first abbey here in AD546, the city witnessed over 1,000 years of war and pillage until the end of the last great siege. On 26 April 1689, William III's forces broke this final 105-day siege in one of the most politically significant battles in Irish history.

Columba's monastery took its name from *doire*, the Irish word for the oak grove which surrounded it. Norsemen then raided it and a new abbey was built in 1162. The English took the medieval city in the mid-16th century, inadvertently blowing most of it up in a munitions explosion. Only the Long Tower of the Cathedral was left standing, but the rubble was used to make new defences. The City of London Guilds (later to become the Honourable the Irish Society) unwillingly were forced by the Crown to develop the town, and added the prefix London to its name. Today some use it, but many do not.

The walls, still the most complete of any city walls in Europe, were built as a copy of those of the French riverside town of Vitry-le-François on the Marne, themselves built to the plan of a Roman military fort. Streets converge from four gates on a central square, or Diamond, 'a Diamond as big as a square' in Ulster parlance. A complete walk around the circuit of the walls, partly at street level and partly on top of the broad walls, provides an understanding of the city plan. From the walls, graffiti reflecting the city's more recent past are visible.

St Columb's Protestant Cathedral, built in Planter's Gothic, has stained glass dedicated to Cecil Francis Alexander, composer of 'There is a Green Hill Far Away' and 'All Things Bright and Beautiful'. A 1663 inscribed stone in the porch reads:

IF • STONES • COVLD • SPEAKE THEN • LONDONS • PRAYSE SHOVLD • SOVNDE • WHO BVILT • THIS • CHVRCH • AND CITTIE • FROM • THE • GROVNDE

St Eugene's Cathedral, with its 256ft spire (65ft taller than St Columb's) was designed by JJ McCarthy.

There are many Georgian-fronted houses – including those of the Irish Society near the Diamond – on hilly streets inside and outside the walls, and a fine red-sandstone City Guildhall just outside Shipquay Gate.

The recent and architecturally uncertain O'Doherty Tower is to be the location for a genealogical databank, specialising in records of emigration to America from the city's quays. Beside the Tower, off Shipquay Street, is the Craft Village.

Across the river from the modern rail terminus is the Foyle Valley Railway Centre, with a museum and a short stretch of line. Just north of the city on the west bank of the Foyle at Ballyarnet, a small cottage museum commemorates the spot where Amelia Earhart, the first woman to fly the Atlantic solo, landed in May 1932. Near by is Culmore Fort, a gun emplacement dating from 1610. Ornithologists – as well as thousands of waterfowl – flock to the east bank of the Foyle (RSPB). It is said that Princess Macha founded Ireland's first hospital in the 3rd century BC, and a sculpture of her by the celebrated Irish sculptor, FE McWilliam, stands outside Altnagelvin Hospital off the A6. The Roe Valley Country Park lies west on the A2 past Eglinton, the city's small airport, and has pretty woodland walks.

Not St Mel's Cathedral, Longford, copied from St Pancras, London, but St John's, typically Anglican in style ▼

LONGFORD
CO LONGFORD
MAP REF: N17

The county town of its namesake county, Longford grew up around a Dominican friary and a castle, both built by the then powerful O'Farrell family in the 15th century. No trace of either remains, and there are but scant traces of a subsequent stronghold built by the Earl of Longford in 1641. The wide streets have attractive houses, many dating from the 18th century, and are dominated by the pepper-pot tower of St Mel's Cathedral which was begun in 1840 and completed after the famine years in 1893. There is a small museum with a range of antiquities behind the Cathedral. Another museum, in the post office, recalls the Republican battles of the 1920s. Longford was also once the terminal for the ill-fated Royal Canal.

Richmond Harbour, at Cloondara to the west, is a delightful spot. Carriglas Manor, Ireland's first Victorian country house, sits in a 650-acre estate and is open to the public.

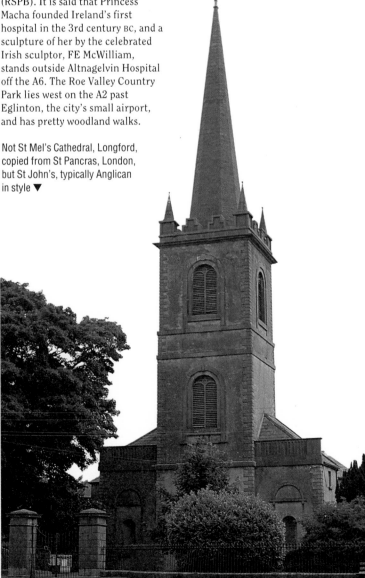

CASTLES

Motte and bailey castles were the first Anglo-Norman castles built in Ireland. The motte, many of which can still easily be distinguished today overlooking towns and villages, was a flat-topped earth mound which was surrounded at its base by a ditch. A circular keep, usually a wooden defensive wall, topped the flat surface. The bailey adjoined the motte and was less strongly defended, giving some security to cattle, herdsmen and camp followers. It was made up of a ditch, an earth bank and a palisade. These forts were often built on top of ready-made prehistoric burial mounds.

The motte and bailey was replaced by the stone castle. At first simple, these became immense, heavy structures designed as much to impress and spread terror as to withstand actual assault. The years between 1190 and 1215 were years which saw the arrival of many of the great city castles, such as those which can now be seen in Dublin and Limerick, and of the coastal defence castles such as those at Carrickfergus, Co Antrim and Dundrum in Co Down. Smaller castles – really

▲ Kanturk has three castles, Magner, Lohort and this, Kanturk (1609), another of the MacCarthy family's strongly fortified houses

fortified square stone houses, again with defence towers at each corner – were built in strategically significant towns such as Enniscorthy in Co Wexford.

By the 15th century, the great surviving Irish families were building strong castles too. This was the era which gave us today's most popular castles, including that of the MacCarthys at Blarney in Co Cork, of the MacNamaras at Knappogue in Co Clare, and of the MacConmaras at Bunratty, also in Co Clare. Two centuries later, in relatively more settled times, the great houses became houses of style and sometimes folly, the need for defence having gone.

LOUGH CORRIB AND LOUGH MASK

CO GALWAY/CO MAYO
MAP REF: M14/M16

Linked both by canal and underground river, these two loughs are amongst Ireland's prime trout lakes (Lower Lough Erne, to the north, is another) and are known to anglers the world over. Lough Mask is triangular in shape and, 10 miles long by 4 miles wide, it covers 20,000 acres. Corrib is vast, covering some 68 square miles (27,000 acres).

On one of Lough Corrib's many islands, Inchagoill, stand the ruins of ancient Teampull na Naomh and Templepatrick. There are ruins of a 15th-century cathedral, a 15th-century priory and an 11th-century church at Annaghdown on Corrib's east shore, and splendid gargoyles on the well-preserved 13th-century Franciscan ruins at Claregalway on the N17 further east.

Casting with mayfly, tied to hooks at the end of a billowing silk floss line, in order to catch Lough Corrib's wild brown trout is an angler's delight ▶

▲ White Island bishop, Lough Erne

LOUGH ERNE
CO FERMANAGH
MAP REF: H15/H23

Although the two Lough Ernes – which run north and west for over 50 miles from Leitrim, through Co Fermanagh to Donegal and the sea – were never a major commercial waterway, there are water bus excursions from Enniskillen and Lisnaskea. Other companies also hire out rowing boats, hire cruisers and day boats with outboard engines.

By road, the A47 and A46 hug the shores of the Lower (most northerly) Lough, and there is an excellent cliff-top panorama from the 900ft Mahoo Cliffs on the west shore. This lough broadens into a wide lake north of Devenish Island. Devenish, with its well-presented 6th-century monastic settlement, has a 10th-century 81ft round tower, St Molaise's 12th-century church, the Teampull Mór (a 13th-century church), plus the remains of 15th-century St Mary's Augustinian Priory and a small museum. On White Island there is a remarkable series of eight carved stone figures, representing bishops and biblical figures, and a *sheila-na-gig* (fertility figure). Castle Archdale Country Park has jetties, a caravan site and nature trails.

More stone figures on Boa Island (on the A47) include a two-faced Janus figure, one side of which is proudly male. Another two-faced idol near by is plumply female. Further towards Belleek village – famous for its Parian china pottery which is open to visitors – Castle Caldwell Forest lies off the A47.

South of Belleek, on the shores of Lough Melvin, known to anglers for its spring-run salmon, charr and five species of trout (the sonaghan, the gillaroo and the ferox, as well as brown and sea trout), is the little village of Garrison with its outdoor pursuits centre. Tully Castle, a cross between a tower house and Scots castle, was built in 1613 and was never lived in again after its defenders were slaughtered by the Maguires on Christmas Day in 1641. Monea Castle, complete with musket loops, barrel towers and corbelling, is well preserved and stands at the end of an impressive avenue of beech trees.

Upper Lough Erne, stretching back from Enniskillen to the Republic, is a maze of water and reedy islands with narrow farm roads leading to the calm water's edge. The Olde Barn Family Museum (near Tamlaght, south-west of Enniskillen) tells the story of the Carrothers family who have farmed here for over 200 years, having come as planters from Scotland. There are the remains of a medieval church on the site of a 6th-century monastery close by.

LOUGH GUR
CO LIMERICK
MAP REF: R64

Prehistoric artefacts from both the Stone and Bronze Ages found around Lough Gur are amongst the most significant in Ireland. Over 20 stone circles, tombs, forts, lakeside dwellings and hut foundations have been excavated here, making it a site of European significance. There is a visitor centre, complete with audio-visual displays to explain the Lough Gur story. Best known is Grange Stone Circle, made up of 100 stones and with a

Even the information centre seems to echo the structures from Lough Gur's mysterious Stone and Bronze Age past ▼

diameter of approximately 50yd. It dates from 2000BC. There is also a Bronze Age tomb, two crannogs, an early Christian earthen fort, two stone Viking forts and the 15th-century Bourchier's Castle.

LOUGH NEAGH
MAP REF: J07

According to legend, Lough Neagh was formed when Finn MacCool, rowing with a Scots giant, scooped up a great handful of earth and threw it short, thus also forming the Isle of Man. Lough Neagh is the largest lake in the British Isles, with an area of 153 square miles and a maximum depth of 45ft. The Lough provides the basis for the biggest commercial eel fishery in Europe, and the pollan, a member

of the whitefish family which looks rather like a freshwater herring, is also fished commercially. The waters have other properties:

Lough Neagh hones, Lough Neagh hones.
You put 'em in sticks and you take 'em out stones.

Thus goes the old Belfast rhyme referring to pieces of petrified wood found on the lake shore and looking and feeling rather like hones, traditional stones used for sharpening knives and sickles. There is a high cross, one of the finest in Ireland, at Ardboe on the west shore, and marinas at Antrim, Ballyronan and Oxford Island. A waterbus tour of the lake departs from Antrim.

patterns in what is known as the La Tène style.

MACROOM
CO CORK
MAP REF: W37

The old market town of Macroom stands on a slope on the banks of the River Sullane where it flows down to meet the Lee. Macroom Castle entrance, which dominates the big market square, once led to the castle of Sir William Penn, father of the William who founded the US state of Pennsylvania. There is a small local museum near the castle entrance.

Above Macroom's shop fronts evidence of the original late Georgian architecture of this Co Cork town survives ▼

Carrigaphooca Castle, three miles west of Macroom, is built on a rock, as the first part of its name signifies. The second part, *púca*, refers to the goblin or puck which haunts the rock. Carrigadrohid Castle (east of Macroom), now just a ruin overlooking a wonderful stretch of the Lee as it widens out to become almost a lake, in 1650 witnessed one of the grimmest moments from the Cromwellian wars.

MALLOW
CO CORK
MAP REF: W59

Like Lisdoonvarna, Mallow was a spa town, and was once so fashionable that it was known as 'the Irish Bath'. Like the Lisdoonvarna of more recent times, it was also known in those days for the high spirits of its visitors whose behaviour gave rise to the popular song 'The Rakes of Mallow'. Now, more prosaically, it is the centre of Ireland's sugar-beet industry, although fine buildings from its heyday still survive. The 1850s neo-Tudor Clock House replaced an earlier Georgian building where the rakes of the song used to gather.

There are white fallow deer, descendants of a pair given by Queen Elizabeth I, in the parkland of the town's Elizabethan castle. Kilcolman Castle, where Edmund Spenser wrote much of *The Faerie Queene*, is now in ruins and can be found to the north, off the R522 at Twopothouse Crossroads, between Doneraile and Buttevant. At Buttevant on the River Awbeg (which becomes the River Mole in *The Faerie Queene*) are the ruins of 13th-century Ballybeg Abbey and the modernised building of Buttevant Castle. On 12 July each year, Ireland's horse-traders gather in Buttevant for the Cahirmee Horse Fair.

LOUGHREA
CO GALWAY
MAP REF: M61

Loughrea, on the edge of Lough Rea (the 'grey lough'), was founded by the de Burgos family who began a Carmelite friary here in the 13th century. Ruins of the old priory stand beside its 19th-century successor. Much more impressive, however, is the artistic interior of St Brendan's Cathedral, which was built between 1879 and 1903. The Turoe Stone at Bullaun (north by the R350) dates from pre-Christian times, and has elegant incised

MANORHAMILTON
CO LEITRIM
MAP REF: G83

The Hamiltons came as planters from Scotland in 1630, persuaded by Charles II's gift of 5,000 acres of pasture, and 10,000 acres of bog, wood and mountain. Thus Manorhamilton was born. The Hamilton Castle, once a fine 17th-century construction, is now but a roofless ruin. The mountains around the town rise to 1,500ft and are rich in alpine plants.

◄ Macroom Castle's imposing gateway now dominates the quiet main square

MARBLE ARCH
CO FERMANAGH
MAP REF: H13

The Cladagh River ran (and still does) through caverns measureless to man, from the collapsed natural limestone Marble Arch through the vast system of the Marble Arch Caves, some only accessible to trained speleologists, but much now open to guided public tours. Taking place well over 100ft beneath the Cuilcagh Mountains, the cave trip includes an underground lake crossing by boat, and reveals a fairy-tale world of stalactites and stalagmites, many given anthropomorphic, if banal, names by the guides.

Florence Court (NT) near by, once the home of the Earls of Enniskillen, is a mixture of grandeur and homely charm, and was built in the early 1700s. The Florence Court yew, *Taxus baccata fastiagata*, is 220 years old and can be propagated only by cuttings. The mother of all Irish yew trees, it grows in the Forest Park.

MELLIFONT ABBEY
CO LOUTH
MAP REF: O07

Inspired by his experiences at the French Cistercian abbey at Clairvaux in south-west France, St Malachy, the Bishop of Armagh, decided to found Mellifont in a similar riverside setting by the Mattock, a tributary of the River Boyne. The first of 35 Cistercian abbeys in Ireland, founded in 1142, it was suppressed 397 years later. The imposing doorway, gatehouse and the octagonal lavabo, or washing area, with its Romanesque arches, survive amongst other fragmentary remains. The Mellifont Abbey in Collon, with its 1,000-acre wildlife sanctuary to which visitors are welcomed, is a 1930s replacement. Tours of medieval Smarmore Castle (to the west) can be arranged.

MIDLETON
CO CORK
MAP REF: W87

The world's largest pot still, a great copper flask which holds 33,333 gallons and which was used in the manufacture of Irish whiskey, stands in Midleton's modern distillery which today also produces vodka and gin. The distillery, now Ireland's largest, was begun by the Murphy family (who later left for nearby Cork to become brewers of stout) in 1826. It has a heritage centre telling the story of Irish whiskey.

MITCHELSTOWN
CO CORK
MAP REF: R81

Deep in the Golden Vale, Ireland's prime dairy country, the market town of Michelstown was laid out in the 19th century by the Earls of Kingston and is now known to the Irish people for its industrialised cheese making. The creamery was built where the Earl's Gothic Revival castle (burnt down in 1922) once stood, in the midst of still

attractive gardens. Ballyporeen, from where former President Ronald Reagan's great great grandfather probably hailed, is on the R665.

Three miles north of Ballyporeen, at Coolagarronroe in Co Tipperary, are the Michelstown Caves with the biggest known single chamber in the British Isles. The Old (or Desmond) Caves were used by the Earl of Desmond when a £1,000 price was put on his head in 1601. Nearby Burncourt was a 17th-century castle, destroyed not long after its construction by Cromwell in 1650.

MOHER CLIFFS
CO CLARE
MAP REF: R09

South of the wondrous Burren, running south-west for six miles to Hag's Head on the Co Clare coast and plunging almost 700ft into the tossing Atlantic, the Cliffs of Moher are one of Ireland's most impressive, disturbing and majestic natural features. The approach on foot is from Liscannor (three miles east) or from Doolin (five miles north). There is a visitor centre which can be reached by car near O'Brien's Tower, built as a look-out by Cornelius O'Brien in 1835. Doolin is an embarkation port for the Aran Islands.

Majestic in the calm, Moher's cliffs can be different in winter's storms as winds hurl up pebbles from the beach below ▼

MONAGHAN
CO MONAGHAN
MAP REF: H3

Monaghan's County Museum, in the 1829 court-house building, has won awards for excellence, and there is a 14th-century crannog in a lake in the grounds of the St Louis Convent girls' school. The elegant classical 1792 Market House (now the Tourist Office) stands in the Diamond, one of the town's three wide interconnected squares. Also in the Diamond is the Rossmore Memorial drinking fountain, with its marble columns supporting a sandstone canopied roof. To erect the fountain, the 17th-century market cross (in reality a sundial) was moved to Old Cross Square and re-assembled to little purpose with its dial upside-down. The central obelisk commemorates a local worthy, Thomas Dawson, who died in the Crimean War. St Macartan's Cathedral in French Revival Gothic style is by JJ McCarthy, referred to as the Irish Pugin. Rossmore Forest Park and Dartrey Forest, both south of the town, have pleasant walks. The Scots baronial Glaslough House (or Castle Leslie), north on the R185, and its gardens can be visited. At Annaghmakerrig, near Newbliss (eight miles south-west) is the Tyrone Guthrie Centre, a haven for artists, writers and film-makers.

MOURNE MOUNTAINS
CO DOWN
MAP REF: J32

As Percy French wrote in his eponymous song, 'The Mountains of Mourne sweep down to the sea'. Slieve Donard (2,796ft), the highest peak in the range and Northern Ireland's highest mountain, stands just 1½ miles back from the coast, with Newcastle – the chief resort of south Co Down – in its shadow. From Slieve Donard, almost all the other Mourne peaks sweep around in a grand curve, running roughly south-west towards Rostrevor. Within this 15-mile arc, ranging over 80 square miles, 15 summits rise to over 2,000ft. Young as mountains go, Mourne rock (all granite) ranges from pink to grey. In winter and in early spring snow can turn the tops white. Just one road, the B27, cuts across the arc as it climbs up the valley of the Aughrim River between the valleys of the White Water and the Kilkeel River. From the sea at the busy fishing port of Kilkeel, the road reaches 1,200ft by Spelga Dam (which holds much of Belfast's water supply), then nips west and down to Hilltown and the road to Newry. There are many walks (see Walk 3) tracking across the mountains, and the patchwork of sheep-cropped fields which are enclosed by the tracery of dry-stone walls is best seen silhouetted against the sun.

Though roads are few, smuggler's tracks (such as the aptly named Brandy Pad) run from the coast to Hilltown through valleys between Mourne peaks ▼

MONASTERBOICE
CO LOUTH
MAP REF: O08

Monasterboice lies off the N1 and is one of Ireland's best known Christian sites. It comprises a 10th-century 95ft round tower, three high crosses, the ruins of two churches, a pre-Gothic sundial and a decorated grave slab, all in a walled graveyard. It was founded by St Buite (also called St Boyce) in the 6th century.

The round tower, which was originally taller than average, has had an exterior staircase and interior floors added in its restoration. The most impressive cross, the South Cross (or Cross of Muiredach) is 1,000 years old and

▲ Muireadach's Cross, Monasterboice

stands 17ft 8in high. Cain can be seen slaying Abel in one panel. The West Cross (or Tall Cross), 4ft higher, is the tallest in Ireland. The North Cross is incomplete.

MOSTRIM (EDGEWORTHSTOWN)
CO LONGFORD
MAP REF: N27

Once always called Mostrim, the town was recently renamed Edgeworthstown after Maria Edgeworth (1767–1849) whose satirical novels of provincial life – particularly *Castle Rackrent* – were much admired by Jane Austen, Sir Walter Scott, Ivan Turgenev and William Wordsworth. The convent school in Ardagh village near by (then a school) was mistaken by Oliver Goldsmith for an inn, thus giving him inspiration for *She Stoops to Conquer*.

MULLINGAR
CO WESTMEATH
MAP REF: N45

The twin 140ft towers of the 1939 Cathedral of Christ the King dominate Mullingar, a cattle town on the N4 and the Royal Canal, and at the junction of the Dublin–Sligo and Dublin–Galway railway lines. In the cathedral, an ecclesiastical museum has as its prized possession the 17th-century vestments of the Bishop of Armagh, St Oliver Plunkett, who was hanged for treason in 1681 and whose head rests in Drogheda's cathedral. Killucan (to the west) is a pretty canalside hamlet. Loughs Owel and Ennell have good stocks of pike and a unique species of charr, named Sharff's charr after its discoverer, RF Sharff.

MULRANY
CO MAYO
MAP REF: L89

Appearing on many maps and signposts as Mallaranny or An Mhala Raithni, the seashore town of Mulrany at the neck of the Corraun Peninsula is where drivers must decide whether to go north on the N59 to Ballycroy and Belmullet, or west on the R319 to Achill Island. There is a fine sandy beach and golf course in the town.

Carrigahowley Castle (also referred to as Rockfleet Castle) was once the home of Grace O'Malley, 'the Pirate Queen', who dominated the seas around Clew Bay and Achill in the mid-16th century. The tiny stone tower has been restored sympathetically. Burrishoole Dominican Priory, beautifully situated on the estuary of the Shramore River, dates from the

Christ the King Cathedral, Mullingar ▼

15th century. Newport, on the Newport River, is a noted angling centre with activities focused on 17th-century Newport House, now a hotel.

NAAS
CO KILDARE
MAP REF: N81

Kildare's county town, Naas has interesting signposted walks taking in both what is left of the 13th-century Norman castle in the grounds of St David's Protestant church, and the Naas Canal Harbour on the Grand Canal with its towpaths. The town's fortunes are tied to the business of horse-racing, and there are frequent meetings at both Naas and Punchestown, near by.

The North Motte was the site of the palace of the Kings of Leinster. Jigginstown House, a mile to the south-west, was conceived in 1632 as a palace for another king, Charles I, by Thomas Wentworth, Earl of Strafford, who, like his patron, was later beheaded in London.

The 676ft Hill of Allen (to the north-west) was, according to legend, the home of the 3rd-century hero Finn MacCool. The Long Stone of Punchestown marks a Bronze Age burial ground.

NAVAN FORT
CO ARMAGH
MAP REF: H84

The great palace of Queen Macha, Emain Mhacha, and her hospice which sheltered those in sorrow (both built in the 3rd century BC) stood on this 16-acre hill, now known as Navan Fort, just over two miles west of Armagh. It became the home for the Red Branch Knights, their champion being Cú Chulainn, and they held reign from 700BC until AD332. Later, a great circular temple, 120ft in diameter and rising to 36ft at its centre, was erected on the spot. In 94BC it consisted of five concentric circles of timber uprights, their height increasing towards the centre. It was burnt to the ground in, possibly, some great ceremony. Limestone cobbles were piled 6ft deep over the ashes and the lot grassed over.

Four bronze trumpets, skulls and bones were found in Lough na Shade near by, and at the King's Stables to the north-west there is evidence of a Bronze Age fort. All these, combined with Haughey's Fort to the west and other tombs in the surrounding hills, point to an area of great political and religious significance.

NENAGH
CO TIPPERARY
MAP REF: R87

Nenagh's Norman castle was built by Theobald Fitzwalter, a cousin of Thomas à Becket, in the early 13th century and has a massive round tower 100ft high with walls 20ft thick. The crenellations are 19th-century additions. In the town there are ruins of a 13th-century Franciscan friary founded by the Kennedy family, an elegant 19th-century Town Hall and an impressive court-house built in 1843. Near the court-house stands the grim jail and the accompanying Governor's House, now the Nenagh Heritage Centre. Georgian Summerhill is a street of delightful Georgian houses.

NEWCASTLE
CO DOWN
MAP REF: J33

A fountain on Newcastle's promenade, sweeping around the wide bay at the foot of Slieve Donard, the highest of the Mourne chain of mountains, commemorates

▲ Newgrange, site of world importance

composer Percy French who wrote that 'the Mountains of Mourne sweep down to the sea', thus bringing fame to this corner of Co Down.

The redstone Slieve Donard Hotel dominates the north end of the bay, and behind it stands the Royal County Down Golf links, voted among the top 12 in the world.

▲ Newcastle's harbour shelters leisure craft – out of herring season

There is a small harbour and lifeboat station at the other end of the bay. A boating lake, amusement parlours, ice-cream saloons and cake shops vie for the visitor's custom.

Donard Park, right in the town, leads up the Glen River into the Mournes. Tollymore Forest Park (see Walk 6), Northern Ireland's most popular, is dotted with follies, walks and a hermitage. South around the coast is Maggie's Leap, named for a local beauty who, being sexually harassed on her way to market, leapt the chasm and escaped. Bloody Bridge to the south was the scene of a 1641 massacre.

NEWGRANGE
CO MEATH
MAP REF: O07

Older than Stonehenge and older than the pyramids of Egypt, Europe's most important Stone Age tomb, part of a great area of cemeteries known as Brugh na Bóinne, stands at Newgrange. This passage-tomb and the tumulus above it are 4,000 years old. Ten miles south-east, a grassy mound marks another passage-tomb at Four Knocks. Inside, a 17ft passage leads to a chamber 21ft across, larger than Newgrange's and with further carvings.

The mound over the tomb at Newgrange is 36ft high and 300ft across. Its carvings, concentric circles and zigzag patterns remain an undeciphered mystery. Oldbridge, on the south bank of the River Boyne, marks the site of the Battle of the Boyne, where in 1690 the Protestant William III defeated the Catholic James II.

NEW ROSS
CO WEXFORD
MAP REF: S72

New Ross's grid of steep streets, with their brightly painted tall, narrow, terraced houses and traditional shop-fronts, range up the hill overlooking the River Barrow. Founded where Isabella de la Clare, daughter of Strongbow, had a bridge built across the river in the 13th century, New Ross is now a thriving inland port. The river cruise from the town, down the River Barrow to Waterford and then up the River Suir, takes in magnificent scenery.

In the town hall, once the Tholsel or toll-house, there are two magnificent maces: the Mace of King Edward III and the Mace of King Charles II. A tombstone in the ruined Gothic chancel of St Mary's Church, inscribed 'Isabel la Fem', is that of the town's and the church's founder, who died in 1220. Parts of the town walls, including Three-Bullet Gate which was hit by three Cromwellian cannonballs in 1649, still exist.

Seven miles south of New Ross is the John F Kennedy Arboretum.

NEWRY
CO DOWN
MAP REF: J02

Newry's town hall stands on arches built over the Newry River and Newry Canal which, although now out of use, runs through the town beside the river. It was finished in 1741, 20 years before the Bridgewater Canal became England's first. Newry Ship Canal, now an important coarse fishing venue, connects the town to Carlingford Lough and the sea. Part of the 1578 tower of St Patrick's Church is a survival from the first Protestant church to be built in Ireland. The Cathedral of St Patrick and St Colman (in Hill Street) was the first Catholic cathedral to be completed in Ireland after the Reformation.

OLDCASTLE
CO MEATH
MAP REF: N58

Three miles south-east of this neat town, at Loughcrew, is a remarkable group of 30 or more Neolithic chambered cairns. Many are decorated in the style of Newgrange, and they spread over the peaks of Slieve na Calliagh (904ft), Patrickstown Hill (885ft) and Carnbane (824ft). (See separate walk on this page.) Virginia, to the north, is one of Ireland's prettiest villages.

OMAGH
CO TYRONE
MAP REF: H47

Omagh, Tyrone's county town, grew up where the rivers Camowen and Drumragh join to form the Strule. King James's Bridge, dating from the 17th century, spans the Drumragh and the five-arched Bell's Bridge spans the Strule. The best view of the town is from Strule Bridge, with the unevenly sized spires of the Catholic Sacred Heart Church – the town's landmark – on one side and the meeting of the waters on the other.

Gortin Glen Forest Park (north), Seskinore Forest (south) and Baronscourt Forest Park (north-west) each have special attractions. At Camphill, north of the town, stands the Ulster American Folk Park which re-creates both the living conditions that Irish emigrants of the 18th and 19th centuries would have left behind, and those they created when they arrived in America. Towards the little village of Gortin, the Ulster History Park has re-created an even earlier Ireland in its 35-acre grounds.

WALK AROUND LOUGHCREW

The great megalithic passage-tombs on the grassy hilltops near Oldcastle give this walk more than a touch of the eerie and distant past. The walk is approximately 2½ miles long; allow 1½ hours. If it can be managed, these tombs are best seen by the early light of dawn. Remember to take a torch if you intend to go inside any of the tombs.

If in Oldcastle, take the R195 south to Millbrook and branch left here. If in Crossakeel, take the R154 north-west and branch left off it after three miles. In either case, take the narrow signposted road north-west to a car-park ¾ mile uphill. The keys to some of the graves may be obtained at the corner house (signposted) at the bottom of this narrow road.

From the car-park, cross the stile and take the path beyond. This is intermittent in places, although the route is at all times clearly uphill and the great stone mound on the summit, called Carnbane East, is unmistakable. Retrace your steps to the car-park, turn left, walk along the narrow road and cross the stile on the right after about 350yd. Follow the intermittent path across the fields to Carnbane West, again quite unmistakable. Retrace your steps to the start. To the south stand the ruins of Loughcrew House, where your torch may come in useful again: there is a splendid, but muddy, souterrain which can be visited (permission is required from the nearby large house).

OUGHTERARD
CO GALWAY
MAP REF: M14

Pretty Oughterard, with its Georgian houses, and its lines of mature beech trees and burgeoning gardens, sits a mile or so back from the shore of Lough Corrib on the banks of the River Owenriff. From

Omagh's four churches, Catholic, Church of Ireland, Methodist and Presbyterian all cluster close by one another on a hill crest ▼

Oughterard, the N59 turns west and heads into Connemara, the Maumturks and the Twelve Bens.

To the south-east lie Ross Lake and Ross Castle, home at one time to the pseudonymous Martin Ross (in real life Violet Martin) who, with her cousin Edith Sommerville, wrote the hilarious *Some Experiences of an Irish RM*. It was also home to 'Humanity Dick' Martin, founder of the RSPCA.

PARKNASILLA
CO KERRY
MAP REF: V76

George Bernard Shaw came to Parknasilla to draft his great play, *St Joan*, drawn by the subtropical climate in this idyllic resort on the east shore of the River Sneem estuary.

PORTAFERRY
CO DOWN
MAP REF: J55

Little white cottages strung out along the shoreline and elegant town houses pose over the ferry terminal by the broken tower of ruined 16th-century Portaferry Castle. The Northern Ireland Sea Aquarium (left of the ferry

terminal) houses 2,000-plus species of marine creatures whose natural habitat is Strangford Lough. Other Norman tower houses dot the shoreline on both sides of the Lough's entrance. Quintin Castle, on the Ards Penninsula's eastern shore, originally dates from the 15th century, but has been added to on many occasions. Portavogie, further north, is one of the north's main fishing ports. Kearney (NT) is a preserved fishing village with cottages for rent.

PORTARLINGTON
CO LAOIS/CO OFFALY
MAP REF: N51

One part lying in Co Laois (pronounced 'leesh') and the other in Co Offaly, Portarlington sits astride the River Barrow, having

▲ Warmed by the Gulf stream, Parknasilla's plants flourish by its manicured lawns

been founded by Sir Henry Bennett in 1666 on land confiscated from the Irish and settled with English immigrants. A Huguenot colony was added later, and indeed services in the Protestant Church of St Paul's were conducted in French until 1861. Lea Castle (two miles to the east) was a Fitzgerald stronghold which was torched by Edward Bruce.

Emo Court, designed in 1790 by James Gandon for the Earl of Portarlington in the Palladian style, is a few miles south. In Ballybrittas village a little thatched cottage behind the Old Pound is also a museum.

PORTRUSH
CO ANTRIM
MAP REF: C84

Portrush juts out into the sea and is surrounded on three sides by fine beaches. It has a sheltered harbour, traditional brightly painted Victorian guest-houses on

Landsdowne Crescent, plus amusement parlours and promenades. Coupled to these traditional attractions is Royal Portrush Golf links, one of the top dozen in the world. In addition, there is an indoor water-based recreation centre and the Portandoo Countryside Centre, where the locally abundant fossil ammonites are well explained.

To the east, the ruins of the 13th-century Dunluce Castle perch on the cliff's edge. Much of the castle fell into the sea, kitchens first, during a banquet in 1693. The Armada ship the *Girona*, many of whose treasures are in the Ulster Museum in Belfast, was wrecked near by, its captain having mistaken the rock formations at the Giant's Causeway for the Castle's chimneys.

PORTSTEWART
CO LONDONDERRY
MAP REF: C83

Counterbalancing Portrush's resort brashness, calm Portstewart is dominated by the bulk of a cliff-top Gothic pile, built in 1834 for local magnate Henry O'Hara. It is now a Dominican convent school. To the west, the town's three-mile strand (NT) sweeps westwards, forming a spit encroaching on the estuary of the River Bann.

RATHDRUM
CO WICKLOW
MAP REF: T18

High on the western side of the charming valley of the Avonmore, Rathdrum, meaning the 'rath (a ring fort) of the ridge', is close to Avondale, the residence (open to the public) of Charles Stewart Parnell, who was born there in 1846. Parnell's affair with Kitty O'Shea still divides the nation.

▲ By the Flight of the Earls Heritage Centre (Rathmullan) Wolfe Tone was imprisoned

RATHLIN ISLAND
CO ANTRIM
MAP REF: D15

This L-shaped island lies seven miles, and 45 minutes by boat, from Ballycastle's pier. On its east coast and close to a lighthouse is the cave where a demoralised Robert the Bruce hid from the English in 1306, having been vanquished at Perth. A spider, attempting to complete its web on the wet cave wall inspired him to try, try again. He returned to Scotland to win at Bannockburn. Man's history on Rathlin goes back further – flints found at Brockley are 6,000 years old, part of a stone-axe 'enterprise',which exported weapons and tools all over Europe.

At Bull Point stands another lighthouse, and on the 350ft cliffs the Keeble Nature Reserve (RSPB) is home to 175 species of bird in colonies numbering thousands. Guillemots, kittiwakes, razorbills and puffins perch and breed on the cliff ledges and sea stacks.

Fought over by the Vikings, the Irish, the Scots and the English, the island has had a bloody history, particularly in the 16th and 17th centuries. Sir Francis Drake had guns on the island in 1575 when the Earl of Essex, his commander-in-chief, massacred the inhabitants, whilst their chieftain Sorley Boy MacDonnell watched helplessly from the mainland. The MacDonnells were massacred again in 1642 when the Campbells, raiding from Scotland, threw the inhabitants over the cliffs. Another lengthy dispute as to whether the island belonged to Ireland or to Scotland (the Mull of Kintyre is but 12 miles away) was solved in the courts in 1617, Ireland's advocates having pointed out that St Patrick had banned all snakes from Ireland and that Rathlin had no snakes. Around 100 inhabitants now make a living there from farming, fishing and tourism.

RATHMULLAN
CO DONEGAL
MAP REF: C22

By the long concrete harbour jutting into Lough Swilly's western shore, a solid battery fort, built in 1810 by the English in anticipation of a Napoleonic invasion, now houses Rathmullan's Flight of the Earls Heritage Centre. Right in the centre of this little resort, with its white-washed cottages and solid harbour hotel, the Centre relates, with documents and tableaux, the traumatic story of the mass emigration of the last of the great Irish chieftains, the Earls of Tyrone and Tyrconnell, to continental Europe in 1607. There are also the remains of a 15th-century Carmelite friary in the town. A little beach north of the pier leads to a pleasant coastal walk, and sea fishermen flock to Rathmullan for summer tope fishing.

Rathmelton (to the south), a splendid old Plantation town with fine riverside Georgian houses and tree-lined riverside walks along the banks of the River Leannan, is now preserved as a town of architectural interest. The great warehouses, amongst them the Fish House on the quayside, attest to past times when the river was navigable and the pier witnessed exports of fish, grain, linen and iodine. The old 17th-century Presbyterian Meeting House, now called the Makemie Centre after the cleric who took that faith to North America, is being developed as a museum and heritage centre for the town. There is a splendid 12ft-high salmon weir on the Leannan, just north of the town.

RENVYLE
CO GALWAY
MAP REF: L66

Renvyle, or Rinvyle, Castle is a 14th-century O'Flaherty tower house right out at the point of the Renvyle peninsula, which has excellent beaches.

RING OF KERRY
CO KERRY

As with all magical roundabouts, visitors may join the Ring of Kerry where they will, but since the route is in essence designed to make the most of the Iveragh peninsula, it is best to begin in Killarney and go south to colourful Kenmare, at the head of the Kenmare estuary. Go west along the banks of the estuary through Parknasilla with its woodland walks to pretty Sneem. Swing south-west for nine miles to West Cove and the splendid stone

'The Liberator' O'Connell was born. On then north-east, past beautiful lakes to Glenbeigh's golden strands, and the beauty of Lough Caragh (to the east) and Dingle Bay (to the north and west). After that it is through Killorglin and back to Killarney.

ROBERTSTOWN
CO KILDARE
MAP REF: N72

In the mid-18th century, the Grand Canal once carried 100,000 passengers a year, and freight still ran until the 1960s. Now the Canal is a haven for coarse fishermen and visitors who hire canal cruising boats. Robertstown's waterfront, at the canal's highest point above sea level (279ft), has been restored to its former glory. The Grand Canal Company's brightly painted hotel is used for candlelit period dinners and as a centre for canoe training and canal barge trips. Castletown House, built in 1772, lies at Celbridge (to the north-east) and is most impressive.

ROE VALLEY
CO LONDONDERRY
MAP REF: C62

In Limavady, chief town of the valley of the Roe, many of the fine Georgian houses dating back to its prosperous linen manufacturing past have been restored. A house bears a plaque to Jane Ross who, on hearing a travelling fiddle player, transcribed the tune he played; it was 'The Londonderry Air', or 'Danny Boy'. In the Roe Valley Country Park, O'Cahan's Rock marks where an O'Cahan leapt the 80ft chasm on horseback. Limavady's name means 'the dog's leap' in Irish, referring to a cross-river leap an O'Cahan hound made through enemy lines.

▲ Bull Rock in Derrynane Bay marks the entrance to the Kingdom of Donn, God of the Dead. When the sun shines through a hole in the rock it opens a rich golden gate to the next world

fort at Staigue. It is another 13 winding miles north-west to Waterville with its beaches, fishing and golf, then on another 11 miles north to Cahirciveen where Daniel

PLACE NAMES

The names of many Irish cities, towns and villages were purely descriptive in their original Irish: Dublin comes from Dubh linn ('dark pool'); Cork comes from Corcaigh ('marshy place'); Derry comes from Doire ('oak grove'). Others received the poet's touch: Clonmel is from Cluain Meala ('honey-meadow'). Of the generic names, *dun* as a prefix means fort, *kil* means a church, and *slieve* means a mountain. *Bally* (or *baile*), perhaps the most frequent prefix, means homestead or town. *Knock* (or *cnoc*) means hill, *drum* (also *drom* or *droim*) a height, *ard* a hill, *ath* a ford, *inch* (also *inis*, *ennis* or *inish*) an island, and *carrick* (or *carraig*) a rock. Some suffixes are quite common: *beg* means small, *more* (or *mór*) great, *derg* (or *dearg*) is red, as is *roe* (or *rua*), *boy* (also *bui* or *bhui*) is yellow, and *glass* (or *glas*) is green. English soldiers, carrying out the first Ordnance Surveys, sometimes opted for translations and sometimes for rough phonetics. Brian Friel's marvellous play, *Translations*, offers an insight into the significance of Irish place-names.

ROSCOMMON
CO ROSCOMMON
MAP REF: M86

A place of learning 1,200 years ago, the buildings of Roscommon's past can today only be traced to the remains of the 1253 Dominican Friary of the Assumption beside the school. An effigy on a 15th-century tomb may be that of the town's founder, Felim O'Connor. The figures at the base are those of gallowglasses, mercenaries of the time. Roscommon Castle, by fields to the north of the town, dates from 1269 although the windows are 1580 additions. It fell to Cromwell in 1652.

A plaque on the old castellated jail in the main square commemorates the notorious 18th-century hangwoman, Lady Betty. At Castlestrange (to the south-west) stands a signposted boulder decorated in spirals in the La Tène style and dating from the Iron Age.

◀ Roger d'Ufford built Roscommon's Castle in the 13th century. Cromwell's men dismantled it in the year 1652, leaving just the fine twin-towered gate, a west gate and four great D-shaped corner towers

ROSCREA
CO TIPPERARY
MAP REF: S18

The Dublin–Limerick road runs right through 12th-century St Cronan's Abbey in Roscrea, one of the country's oldest towns. The figure carved by the doorway in the west façade is probably that of the founding saint. The 12th-century high cross also features the saint. Across the road stands a 60ft round tower, and right in the centre of the town is the solid Gate Tower of Roscrea Castle, built by the Normans in the 13th century. Damer House, inside the castle walls, was restored by the Irish Georgian Society. It has a splendid doorway and staircase and is now used as a heritage centre. In Rosemary Square the ornate 19th-century fountain, originally erected in Market Square, no longer plays, but there is a wealth of other interesting buildings in this little town, including the Temperance Hall, originally built as a prison in 1815, the bell-tower of a 1470 Franciscan friary, now the gateway to St Cronan's Church, and the 1920s Abbey Hall.

By Borris-in-Ossory (eight miles east), the great Fitzpatrick castle of Ballaghmore has recently been splendidly restored and is open to the public. Devil's Bit Mountain, supposedly serrated by the Devil's teeth marks, is to the south.

ROSSLARE
CO WEXFORD
MAP REF: T01

The ferry terminal for the French and Welsh ports, Rosslare benefited from Wexford silting up. There is a fine six-mile strand and a golf course. Connected by a causeway to the mainland, Lady's Island to the south lies in a salt marsh. With its Augustinian priory ruins and Norman castle, complete with leaning tower, it is a place of summer pilgrimage, many crawling across its 12 acres on their knees and others circling it with one foot in the water. Ring forts, or raths, abound and there are pagan shrines at Ballyrent and Carnsore Point. Hints of druidic customs still persist today in funerary practices; small wooden crosses are still placed in hawthorn bushes around the cemetery.

ROUNDSTONE
CO GALWAY
MAP REF: L74

North of the little Victorian resort of Roundstone and at the heart of western Connemara, Roundstone Bog stretches from 987ft Errisbeg to the Twelve Pins (Bens). Hundreds of tiny lakes catch the summer sun or mirror grey winter skies. Otters sport in the 10,000 acres of this unspoilt environment, and *Erica mediterrania* – a rare heather – grows on Errisbeg's slopes while *Erica mackaianna* grows by Craiggamore's lake shores. Just one, beautiful road weaves and winds its way from Toombeola to Ballinaboy, affording stunning views of the Twelve Pins east of Clifden. The 20th century barely intrudes on this wilderness.

ROUNDWOOD
CO WICKLOW
MAP REF: O10

Roundwood, a tiny village almost on the shores of Vartry Reservoir, is a focal point for fishermen fishing the Annamoe River and Loughs Dan and Tay. Laurence Sterne spent some of his childhood at Annamoe and claimed to have survived a fall through a mill-race there. Where

'White horses' ride the waves and seagulls follow fishing skiffs; in the distance is the little resort of Skerries, Co Dublin ▼

the Avonmore and Glenmacnass rivers meet at Laragh, there is a wonderful waterfall in a glen.

ST MULLIN'S
CO CARLOW
MAP REF: S73

St Moling, a Renaissance man of his day – poet, artist, engineer, prince and priest – founded a monastery here in the 7th century and dug a mile-long watercourse to power its watermill. The watercourse is still there, but the monastery has gone. A high cross stands outside the ruins of a later abbey. Situated on a little loop of a road off the R729, this River Barrow waterside village has four ancient churches, a holy well and an oratory. A Norman motte stands beside the churchyard, where people still come to worship at the penal altar used in the days when anti-Catholic laws forbade Mass. The little Protestant church, in whose graveyard Catholics and Protestants lie side by side, is to become a heritage centre. Barrow cruises pass the village, while the Blackstairs Mountains, with 2,610ft Mount Leinster, rise to the north-east and Brandon Hill (1,694ft) rises to the north-west.

SALTHILL
CO GALWAY
MAP REF: M22

Galway's seaside suburb, Salthill stretches west along Galway Bay, its promenade affording splendid views of Clare and the Aran Islands. There is an 18-hole golf course, and all the usual resort amenities amongst a wealth of seaside hotels and bed and breakfasts. There are *currach* races and sea-angling festivals in season. Spiddal (further west) is a charming little Irish-speaking enclave set back from the sea. Local crafts are available from the Spiddal Craft Centre and boats leave from the quay for the Aran Islands.

SHILLELAGH
CO WICKLOW
MAP REF: S96

The little village of Shillelagh on the R749 is where oaks, it is claimed, were once cut to help build Dublin's St Patrick's Cathedral and the Palace of Westminster in London. The village is more likely to be remembered for having given its name to the Irishman's cudgel. These were originally cut from oak and not the blackthorn used for the souvenir shop product of today.

▲ Medieval church and tower, Swords

SKERRIES
CO DUBLIN
MAP REF: O26

Its proximity to Dublin and to splendid strands makes Skerries the capital's most popular resort. The name (from the Norse) means 'offshore rocky islands', and many little groups of islands called 'the Skerries', will indeed be found off Ireland's coasts. This group comprises St Patrick's, Colt and Shenick's, the last island being accessible by causeway at low tide. St Patrick's, with its ancient church, is one of the several places where the patron saint is said to have begun his mission. His 'footsteps' are carved in the rock on Red Island, now part of the mainland.

Inland, there is a village with the strange name of Man o' War. Lambay Island, further out to sea, is a restricted-access bird reserve. There is a 75ft round tower and a 13th-century castle at Swords to the south, whilst at Donabate, Newbridge House (built for the Archbishop of Dublin) has a museum and other curiosities.

SKIBBEREEN
CO CORK
MAP REF: W13

On the River Illen and capital of a district called the Carberies, Skibbereen was founded inland after Baltimore was sacked by pirates from North Africa in 1631. The little market town had its

moment of fame when its weekly paper, *The Skibbereen Eagle* (now amalgamated), warned the Tsar of Russia that it had its eye on him! The Cathedral dates only from 1826, but to the west are ruins of the 14th-century Cistercian Abbeystrowry. Sherkin and Clear Islands stand out to sea, the former with 15th-century Franciscan friary ruins and the latter with its ruins of Fineen O'Driscoll's Dunamore Castle, which was destroyed in 1538 by Waterford seamen who had had enough of his piracy. The Fastnet Lighthouse, perched on a rock, stands further west. The Carbery Coast, as the land west is known, provided the settings for the Somerville and Ross novels.

CURRACHS

First fashioned by stretching hides, now canvas (which is later tarred) over a wood frame, the *currach* is superbly suited for the waters off the west. With its flat bottom, it can be man-handled up strands, and with its high prow, it can face the Atlantic swell and surf. The materials used to make it are also readily available. The oars, made of solid wood with little blades, have a block through which a thole pin, fixed to the thwarts, is slotted, so giving great manoeuvrability and fast retrieve near rocky landing places.

SLIGO
CO SLIGO
MAP REF: G63

Sligo is located where the waters from Lough Gill, with its lake isle of Inisfree immortalised by WB Yeats, flow down the River Garavogue into Sligo Bay. It is a town of splendid old shop-fronts, traditional pubs and places to buy woollens and tweeds. Although Yeats only came here to holiday with family friends, the Middletons and Pollexfens (who owned the Sligo Steam Navigation Company), this is the centre of Yeats Country. The Sligo County Museum and Art Gallery have mementoes of both poet William Butler and his brother Jack, painter of race meetings. Across from the worthy court-house, a solicitor's window bears the unlikely names of the partners Argue and Phibbs!

Once the gateway from Ulster to Connaught, only the remains of Sligo's Dominican 1252 abbey remind the traveller of the town's medieval past.

Coney Island (to the west) claims, amongst many in Ireland, to have been the inspiration for New York's beach of the same name. *Coney* (or *coinín*) means 'rabbit' in Irish. In the tideway stands the Metal Man, a navigation mark erected by the Steamship Company. At Carrowmore, two miles south of Sligo, are the largest group of Bronze Age megaliths in these islands.

STRABANE
CO TYRONE
MAP REF: H39

Gray's Printing Shop (NT), with its bow windows and now almost the only reminder of the town's past fame as a printing centre, is where John Dunlap learned his trade. He later printed the original American Declaration of Independence and published the *Pennsylvania Packet*. He was born in 1746 in Meeting House Street. James Wilson, grandfather of Woodrow Wilson, President of the United States, also learned his trade here. The white-washed, thatched Wilson family home, open to the public and still inhabited by members of the family, is at Dergalt two miles south-east.

Brian O'Nolan, who later achieved fame as surreal humorist Myles na Gopaleen/Flann O'Brien/Brian O' Nolan (he wrote under all three names), was born in Bowling Green. A plaque marks the house. The Sperrin Heritage Centre at Cranagh, near Sperrin village in the beautiful valley of the Glenelly (to

▲ From Strangford to Portaferry, the car ferry ploughs the narrows. At sunset on Strangford Lough, Scrabo's Tower, on Scrabo Hill, watches over Newtownards

the west),interprets local history. Harry Aimbreidh O'Neill offered his disadvantaged sister's suitors the choice of marriage or death by hanging; 19 chose the latter. Harry Avery's Castle at Newtownstewart, to the south-west, echoes his strength of purpose.

STRANGFORD
CO DOWN
MAP REF: J54

Ranged above its pretty old harbour and modern ferry slipway, Strangford sits on the water's edge and has fine, solid merchant's houses and pretty cottages. A 16th-century tower house stands amongst houses just up from the harbour. Castle Ward (NT), an 18th-century mansion built by Lord Bangor, has a classical front to his own taste, and a Gothick one to suit his wife's. Set in splendid 800-acre parklands with a tower house, saw-mill, corn-mill, Victorian laundry, old stone piers and information centre, its barn is used for an open-air opera season in June.

Audley's Castle (built in the 15th century) and Kilclief Castle (dating from 1413) were placed at strategic points. Audleystown Cairn, near the former, dates from the Stone Age.

STRANGFORD LOUGH
CO DOWN
MAP REF: J56/J55

Two-thirds of the world's population of Brent geese overwinter in Strangford, and there are excellent viewing points along the shores of this, one of the largest sea inlets in the British Isles. Up the lough there are 150 miles of coastline, while in it there are 120 islands, mostly of typical drumlin shape and locally called pladdies. The best overview is from Scrabo Tower in Scrabo Country Park (DOE) above Newtownards, with its wide main street, Georgian town hall and market cross, as well as the ruins of a 13th-century Dominican friary and 15th-century Movilla Abbey. Birdwatchers flock to Castle Espie, which has a bonus collection of exotic wildfowl and a café and art gallery, and which is run in association with the Wetlands and Wildfowl Trust, and to Ballyreagh (NT). The National Trust, which monitors the whole lough, organises boat trips for seal- and birdwatchers.

The Monastery of Nendrum on Mahee Island covers six acres of a low hill and was founded in the 5th century by St Mochaoi.

GAELIC GAMES

Hurling, Gaelic football and hand-ball are the games whose rules are governed by the Gaelic Athletic Association (GAA). Hurling, easy to identify as the oldest, goes back in some form or other to pre-Christian times, and a game very like it is described in the legends of the Red Branch Knights. A 15-a-side stick and ball game, it has a principle and team placings not unlike hockey. However, the ashwood sticks, or hurleys are broader, and the ball may be hand caught (although not thrown) and must be picked up from the ground with the stick. The ball, or *sliotar*, can be played on the ground or above the head. There is no offside rule.

To the uninitiated, Gaelic football looks like a mix between soccer and Rugby, using a small soccer ball. Its enthusiasts argue that it evolved naturally and separately. As in hurling, a point is scored by putting the ball between the goal posts, but this time over the bar. Three points make one real goal.

Camogie, played by 12-strong women's teams, resembles hurling but with shorter sticks. It is administered by a different governing body. Hand-ball, played in tall, three-sided and mostly outdoor courts, contains elements of squash and pelota.

TARA
CO MEATH
MAP REF: N95

Once Ireland's great acropolis, the Hill of Tara's heritage mixes fact and fantasy. For centuries it was the seat of Celtic kings, and by the 3rd century it had become Ireland's Camelot. Now nothing remains but a 300ft green hill, the outline of the perimeter ditch 300yd across, and inner earthworks, now named after different Celtic royals. Even before the Celts came, Stone Age people had used it as a burial site. A horned figure in the churchyard is that of Cernunnos, a god of the Celts. It was with the coming Christianity that Tara's importance waned.

THOMASTOWN
CO KILKENNY
MAP REF: S54

Thomastown's houses rise in a pleasing jumble up the banks of the lazy River Nore. Once the town walls (dating from the 13th century) had 14 towers, a house of religion and a castle. Another castle, called Grenan, stands in ruins along the river. Parts of the town walls still survive, and there is a pleasant water garden at the top of the town. George Berkeley (1685–1753), philosopher and Protestant Bishop of Cloyne, was born at Dysart Castle. California's Berkeley University is named after him.

THURLES
CO TIPPERARY
MAP REF: S15

Hayes Hotel in Liberty Square in Thurles was the birthplace in 1884 of the Gaelic Athletic Association (GAA), the governing body for all Gaelic games. The market town sits by the trout-rich River Suir, and is dominated by all that is left of a 15th-century tower by the old bridge and by Black Castle, dating from the same era. There is both a racecourse and a golf course.

▲ Holy Cross Abbey, by the Suir south of Thurles, dates from the 12th century

Brittas Castle, two miles north, was modelled on England's Warwick Castle.

TIPPERARY
CO TIPPERARY
MAP REF: R83

Jack Judge and Harry Williams – who wrote 'It's a long way to Tipperary' in 1914 – had never been there, but the town's other memories are darker or more exotic. Red Kelly, the father of the Australian bushman Ned, came from this town. So did financier John Sadleir, whose affair with dancing girl Clara Morton led him into fraud and suicide on London's Hampstead Heath. A park commemorates Sean Treacy who fired the first shots in the War of Irish Independence (1918–22).

One statue commemorates Charles Kickham (1828–82), the novelist, poet and revolutionary who spent four years in London's Pentonville Prison. Another commemorates the Manchester Martyrs, executed in 1867 for killing a policeman whilst trying to liberate a Fenian prisoner.

◀ Tipperary's rich pasturelands have understandably earned this valley the soubriquet 'Golden Vale'

THE IRISH COTTAGE

Clay, rubble and stone made the walls, and ox-blood helped to hold them together. Lime, made locally, helped plaster the walls, then whitened them with wash. Tree boughs formed the roof frame, while sods of earth or thatch from straw or reeds covered it.

The Irish cottage, nestling in a clump of sycamore out of the wind in a hollow by a stream, was an organic entity. Turf cut from the peat bog heated it; wood made the furniture; wool from sheep reared on the hillside, dyed with lichens from the rocks, clothed its

walls, it is well preserved. The ruins of St Mary's Augustinian Abbey across the river date from the 13th century. Talbot's Castle (1415) in High Street is also confusingly known as St Mary's Abbey. It became a school, with Arthur Wellesley, later Duke of Wellington and who once lived in Emmet Street, as one of its pupils. Behind the real St Mary's atop the slope stands the Yellow Steeple, the 125ft ruin of a 14th-century bell-tower, partially destroyed by Cromwell.

At the opposite (eastern) end of the town are the ruins of the medieval cathedral of St Peter and St Paul, and an accompanying church. In the church are the effigies of Sir Lucas and Lady Jane Dillon, separated primly in death by a sword. To the south is the ruined abbey of the Canons Regular of St Victor, founded in about 1200. Downstream is 15th-century St Peter's Bridge. Trim Pony Races, in June, includes one reserved for nuns. Another Derby, the Irish one, takes place at Fairyhouse (to the south-east) at Easter.

South-east Ireland's coast from Dungarvan to Tramore is filled with rocky bays, strands, cliffs and quiet coves, all Mecca to the traveller▼

TRALEE
CO KERRY
MAP REF: Q81

Sources differ as to who wrote 'The Rose of Tralee', the song associated with Tralee's talent and beauty contest which is promoted the world over. Some say it was C Mordaunt Spencer, and some say it was local man William Mulchinock. Whoever it was, good looking Tralee, which grew up around the fortified 13th-century Desmond Castle (long since gone), deserves its many visitors. There are fine 18th-century houses in Castle and Denny streets and a splendid 19th-century court-house, designed by Sir Richard Morrison and flanked by cannons commemorating Kerrymen who died in the Crimean War and the Indian Mutiny. St John's Church, built in 1870, claims to have the tallest spire in Ireland, and Holy Cross Dominican Church was designed by Pugin. Siamsa Tíre Theatre presents folk theatre and traditional music. The town is the gateway to the Dingle Peninsula, and has a racecourse and golf links.

At Blennerville, to the south-west, is the country's only commercially-run working windmill, complete with a coffee shop and gift shop.

TRAMORE
CO WATERFORD
MAP REF: S50

Tramore, in sweeping Tramore Bay, is known throughout Ireland as a

▲ Castle Street in trim Trim town

seaside resort, complete with pier, beach and 50-acre leisure complex with the multi-media CeltWorld experience, a boating lake, miniature golf, a miniature railway, plus a golf course and racecourse and well-developed windsurfing and angling facilities. A 'Metal Man' rivalling Sligo's, on Great Newtown Head on Doneraile Cliffs, acts as a marker for seafarers. Hopping around it three times non-stop, so say locals, guarantees marriage within the year.

TRIM
CO MEATH
MAP REF: N85

Now a rather ordinary market town, Trim once vied to be the capital of Ireland. De Lacy's Castle, on the Boyne's banks, was built in 1172 but battered by Cromwell in 1649. With its 16-sided, 75ft-high keep

inhabitants; milk from their cow, mixed with mashed potatoes grown in their small dry-stone walled fields, fed them; and another field grew corn for bread. A small bed by the open turf fire sheltered the very young and the very old. A cooking pot hung over the turf fire which was never allowed to go out. The half-door was 'borrowed' from a big house's stable.

The Ulster Folk and Transport Museum at Cultra in Co Down and Bunratty's Folk Park, near Shannon Airport, preserve the memory.

TULLAMORE
CO OFFALY
MAP REF: N32

The explosion of a hot-air balloon and the subsequent fire in 1785 cleared old Tullamore's centre and led to the building of wide Patrick Street. Only the fine market house and another restored bow-fronted house pre-date the fire. Thirteen years later the Grand Canal came along, bringing further progress, flour mills, and brewing and distilling. Tullamore Dew, now called Irish Mist Liqueur, can be sampled after a tour of the distilling process, or sampled from the deck of a hired canal cruiser. The fine church on Hop Hill is by

include simple one-room thatched cottages, a substantial 1717 rectory, a water-powered spade mill, mill houses from Belfast's Tea Lane, a church, a school, a court-house, a forge and a linen bleach-green watch-tower. Across the road is the transport section, to be augmented by the displays from Belfast's Witham Street Transport Museum, but already including schooners and monoplanes.

VALENTIA ISLAND
CO KERRY
MAP REF: V37

Just a side-step off the Ring of Kerry drive, Valentia Island is reached by a modern bridge which

▲ Lismacloskey House (1717), now the Ulster Folk and Transport Museum

TUAM
CO GALWAY
MAP REF: M45

Tuam, established around St Jarlath's 6th-century monastery (of which only 14th-century ruins remain), is a centre for church affairs, having two cathedrals. The 1878 Protestant Cathedral incorporates a splendid 16ft-high, 22½ ft-wide red sandstone Irish Romanesque chancel arch, possibly dating from 1184. Tuam's high cross (now in the cathedral) dates in parts from the 12th century. The town's industrial past is demonstrated in the Mill Museum, which has a functioning corn-mill.

the noted architect Francis Johnston, who also designed much of Georgian Armagh.

ULSTER FOLK AND TRANSPORT MUSEUM
CO DOWN
MAP REF: J48

Over the rolling hills of 136 acres, the award-winning open-air Ulster Folk and Transport Museum re-creates the wide vernacular of the province's architecture – domestic, commercial, industrial and religious. Buildings which have been painstakingly recorded, taken down and reassembled in a topography echoing their original

spans the 120yd channel at Portmagee. It is now a popular resort, although it was named by Spanish traders in past centuries. Attractions include Geokaun Mountain and Bray Head cliffs, the former rising around 800ft and the latter dropping around 800ft. There is a grotto in a dark slate quarry to the west, and superb views of Great Blasket Island can be had from the cliff-top road. Knightstown has a natural history and heritage centre with details of the laying of the first transatlantic telegraph cable from here in 1866.

WATERFORD GLASS

The brothers George and William Penrose set up a glass-making factory in 1783, the quality and style of whose products, from their triumph at the 1851 Great Exhibition in London, was to become world famous. However, a year later they were hit by recession and closed. The heritage was revived, starting in a small way, in 1947. Now Waterford Lead Crystal, hand-blown and with its deep-cut traditional patterns, is one of Ireland's major exports. The modern factory at Kilbarry, south-west of the city, has a showroom and video presentation. In the Waterford tradition, Ireland now has a number of other glassworks, those at Cavan and Dungannon (Tyrone Crystal) being just two which also offer factory tours.

WATERFORD
CO WATERFORD
MAP REF: S61

Waterford's narrow streets lying above its busy container port are a reminder of its medieval past, as are the few surviving bits and pieces of the 9th-century Viking walls. The 73ft Reginald's Tower, built in 1003, was once part of the fortifications around the original 19-acre settlement. The tower, which has been a royal residence, military ordnance store, jail and mint over the centuries, is now the location for the Civic and Maritime Museum. It contains royal charters and city maces, for Waterford maintained a loyalty to the English crown long after others wavered. Near by is another tower, that of the French Church which was founded as a Franciscan friary in 1240 and later sponsored by Henry III. Its name comes from its use by Huguenot refugees.

Blackfriars Abbey, whose ruins date from 1226, making it one of Ireland's oldest Dominican institutions, incorporates the west wall of St Olaf's AD870 Viking church. Keyser Lane, near by, is a polite rendering of 'kiss arse', a throw-back to drunken sailors on shore leave. St Patrick's Catholic Church in Jenkin Lane was founded in 1750, but was used as a corn store in which Jesuits worshipped secretly during the time of the Penal Laws. It has been splendidly restored. Christ Church Anglican Cathedral, copied from the style of Christopher Wren by local architect John Roberts, was begun in 1770 on the site of the previous Viking cathedral. The most fascinating feature inside it is the Rice Sarcophagus, where the effigy of James Rice (who died in 1490) is adorned with worms which emerge from between his ribs. Roberts also designed the City Hall of 1788 (now the Theatre Royal) and the Chamber of Commerce building of 1795. Across Cathedral Square, the building which now contains the council offices was once the 1741 Bishop's Palace.

St Martin's Gate, by the Palace, was built in the 11th century as part of the city's walled defences.

Holy Trinity Catholic Cathedral in Barronstrand Street, also by Roberts, dates from 1793. Waterford Heritage Centre, in a 19th-century Methodist church building in Greyfriar's Street, houses an exhibition on the city's Viking past. The fine Georgian buildings in the Mall date from between 1780 and 1810, a period of great expansion for Waterford's glass manufacturing industry.

WATERVILLE
CO KERRY
MAP REF: V56

Waterville is a resort town whose attractions for celebrities – amongst them George Bernard Shaw and Charlie Chaplin – include its wonderful beach and excellent lake fishing. In Lough Currane, a 12th-century ruin and 6th-century anchorite's beehive hut stand on Church Island. Near Caherciveen, north on the N70, are the massive stone ramparts of Leacanabuaile Fort. Caherciveen (or Cahersiveen) itself is dominated by the Daniel O'Connell Memorial Church and the ruins of a British Army barracks which burnt down in 1922. Nine miles from Waterville, on Greater Skellig (Sceilig Mhicil) and at the top of a 500ft climb up 1,000-year-old stone steps, is a stunning AD800 monastic settlement of churches and beehive huts. Boats leave from Valentia Island. Little Skellig is a bird sanctuary and cannot be landed on.

WESTPORT
CO MAYO
MAP REF: M08

Laid out to complement the Marquis of Sligo's Westport House, with its fine James Wyatt dining room and Richard Cassells hall, Westport has elegant, lime-tree-shaded twin malls each side of the canalised River Carrowbeg. It also has a curious octagonal 'square' and is a town of some style. Once a port of some importance, its quays afford fine views of Clew Bay. Louisburgh (to the west) is the departure point for Clare Island, site of pirate chief Grace O'Malley's ruined castle.

WEXFORD
CO WEXFORD
MAP REF: T02

Wexford, like Waterford to whom it lost its maritime trade, has a Keyser's Lane – 'keyser' being a sailor's expression for 'kiss arse' – thus attesting to the town's lengthy association with commerce and the

Europe's oldest mortared stone tower, named after Reginald the Dane, Waterford ▼

sea. Commodore John Barry, a local man who founded the US Navy, is commemorated in a statue dominating the now quiet quays. Henry II spent six weeks in penance in 1172 for the murder of Thomas à Becket in 12th-century Selskar Abbey, whose sandstone tower still stands in Abbey Street. The Protestant St Iberius Church, in the town centre, dates from 1760. There is a portion of the old 13th-century wall in the Cornmarket, and many attractive old-world shop-fronts. The town is at its busiest during its autumn Opera Festival, although ornithologists are attracted all year round by the birds on Wexford Slobs.

Just outside the town at Ferrycarrig, on the banks of the River Slaney, is the Irish National Heritage Park which, with its open-air re-creations of Stone and Bronze Age dwellings, a Viking long ship, early Christian buildings and a towering Norman castle, evokes the hard grind of life and death in past centuries.

West of Youghal, beaches sweep west past Ballymadog, across the delta of the Womanagh river with its bird reserve, out towards the rocks on Knockadoon Head and Capel Island ▼

WICKLOW
CO WICKLOW
MAP REF: T39

The Vikings claimed it as Wykinglo (meaning 'the Viking's meadow'), then the early Christians came, and finally the Normans. There are scant remains of a 13th-century friary on Main Street and of Black Castle (1176) by the harbour. Today, Wicklow is a resort town with a sand and shingle beach and a promenade. There is a heritage centre and museum in the Old Jail.

YOUGHAL
CO CORK
MAP REF: X07

Coincidentally pronounced as in 'yawl', this town at the mouth of the River Blackwater has long associations with sea and sail. Norse pirates raided it in the 9th century, as did the Normans in the 13th century. Each night a dozen nuns from nearby St Anne's Convent scurried down an underground passage to where the predecessor of the current lighthouse stands, keeping its beacon burning. Then Edward I fortified the town in 1275. From 1588 until the following year its warden, or mayor, was Sir Walter Raleigh, who lived at Elizabethan Myrtle Grove (now open to the public) and grew the first potatoes there, having brought them from the New World. While he was smoking a pipe in its gardens, his maid thought her master's beard on fire and doused him with a pitcher of water. The pipe, but not the pitcher, has survived.

The well-preserved town walls, dating from the 15th-century, are amongst the best preserved in the island, and coupled with its other medieval buildings, this has led to the town's preservation and promotion in recent years. The Collegiate Church of St Mary, an Anglican church still in regular use, dates from the 13th century. In the holes in its chancel walls are earthenware jars, said to improve its acoustics. A monument to Catherine, Countess of Desmond, is notable in that she is said to have died at the age of 147, having fallen out of a cherry tree.

The Clock Gate, a four-storey red-sandstone structure on an arch spanning Main Street, was built in 1777. The town's old walls and defences are best examined from steps leading up the hill above the Clock Gate.

▲ With its extensive coastline and countless loughs, Ireland is ideal watersports territory. The 1985 European Surfing Championships were held in Co Donegal

FACT FILE

CONTENTS

Places to Visit
Stately homes, castles, gardens, museums and other attractions

Sports and Activities
Angling, canoeing, cycling, golf, equestrian pursuits, inland cruising, sailing, walking, watersports

Useful Information
Addresses, tourist information

Customs and Events
A calendar of festivals

PLACES TO VISIT

The following list is just a selection of the numerous places of interest in Ireland. Attractions are listed under their nearest town or village.

The details given here are intended to provide a rough guide only to opening times. Very often a place may be only open for part of a day or closed for lunch. Also, although stated as open all year, many places close over Christmas and New Year, and on some bank holidays. Full information should be obtained before a visit from the nearest tourist information centre (see pages 110–11).

Etr = Easter
BH = bank holiday
NT = National Trust
AM = Ancient Monument

ANNALONG

Corn Mill, Marine Park. *Restored working corn-mill. Guided tours and an exhibition.* Open Apr to Oct, weekends; Jul and Aug, daily.

ARMAGH

Ardress House (NT). *Elegant house with lovely grounds and a farmyard with animals and traditional implements.* Open Etr to Sep at varying times.

The Argory (NT). *Regency house by the Blackwater River. Many unusual features.* Open Apr to Sep at varying times.

Planetarium and Observatory, College Hill. *Star shows and space travel displays.* Open all year, Mon to Sat.

ASHFORD

Mount Usher Gardens. *Plants from all over the world and good views of Mount Usher.* Open Mar to Oct, Sun to Fri.

BANTRY

Bantry House. *Georgian mansion set in formal gardens. Armada centre in grounds.* Open all year, daily.

BEAUFORT

Dunloe Castle Hotel Gardens. *Plant rarities in lovely setting.* Open May to Oct, daily.

BELFAST

Belfast Zoo. *Fifty-acre mountain site.* Open all year, daily.

Botanic Gardens Park. *Extensive and impressive gardens with Victorian glass palm house and a tropical ravine.* Open all year, daily.

Ulster Museum, Botanic Gardens. *Important museum and art gallery with good collection of Irish art.* Open all year, daily.

BELLEEK

Belleek Pottery. *Famous for its Parian china. Small museum of showpieces, restaurant and shop. Craftsmen can be seen at work.* Open all year, daily; tours, Mon to Fri only.

BIRR

Birr Castle Demesne. *Splendid ornamental gardens; the castle is not open to the public.* Open all year, daily.

BUNRATTY

Bunratty Castle and Folk Park. *Classic medieval castle with a 25-acre museum of traditional rural life.* Open all year, daily.

BUSHMILLS

Old Bushmills Distillery. *Whiskey distillery with visitor centre.* Open all year, Mon to Fri (closed Friday afternoon).

CARRICKFERGUS

Carrickfergus Castle (AM), on shore of Belfast Lough. *Well-preserved Norman castle.* Open all year, daily.

CASHEL

Rock of Cashel. *Important historical location with impressive remains and an underground museum.* Open Jun to mid-Sep, daily.

CASTLETOWNROCHE

Anne's Grove Gardens. *Eighteenth-century botanical gardens by the River Awbeg.* Open Apr to Sep, daily.

CELBRIDGE

Castletown House. *Huge, splendid mansion with many treasures.* Open all year, daily.

CHURCHILL

Glenveagh Castle Gardens. *Important exotic gardens in Glenveagh National Park.* Open Etr to Oct, daily; closed Fri in Apr and Oct.

COOKSTOWN

Wellbrook Beetling Mill (NT). *Water-powered linen mill restored to working order.* Open Apr to Sep at varying times.

CORK

Blarney Castle. *The famous Blarney Stone is set into the battlements of this 15th-century castle.* Open all year, daily.

Blarney House and Gardens. *Scottish baronial mansion on the estate of Blarney Castle.* Open Jun to mid-Sep, Mon to Sat.

CRATLOE

Cratloe Woods. *Protected forest with an Irish longhouse. Magnificent views.* Open Jun to mid-Sep, Mon to Sat.

DONAGHADEE

Ballycopeland Windmill. *Complete working 18th-century windmill with wooden machinery. Visitor centre in Miller's House.* Open all year, daily.

DOWNPATRICK

Down County Museum, The Mall. *Museum in old county gaol.* Open all year; Jul to mid-Sep daily, rest of year Tue to Sat.

DUBLIN

Dublin Castle. *State Apartments, the Wedgwood Room, the Throne Room and others.* Open all year, daily.

National Botanic Gardens. *Lovely oasis with superb glasshouses.* Open all year, daily.

National Gallery of Ireland. *Huge collection of paintings and sculpture.* Open all year, daily.

National Library. *Collection of national importance.* Open all year, Mon to Sat.

National Museum of Ireland. *All aspects of Ireland's past and her treasures.* Open all year, Tue to Sun.

Chester Beatty Library, Ballsbridge. *Oriental and Middle Eastern art on display.* Open all year, Tue to Sat.

Dublin Castle's State Drawing Room ▼

DUNDRUM

Dundrum Castle. *Fine medieval castle with good views.* Open all year, daily.

DUN LAOGHAIRE

James Joyce Tower. *Defensive tower now housing a museum devoted to Joyce.* Open May to Sep, daily.

National Maritime Museum. *Nautical exhibits of all kinds.* Open May to Sep, Tue to Sun.

ENNISKERRY

Powerscourt. *One of Europe's great gardens which includes Ireland's highest waterfall.* Garden open Mar to Oct, daily; waterfall. Open all year, daily.

ENNISKILLEN

Castle Coole (NT). *Fine classical mansion filled with treasures.* Open Etr to Sep at varying times.

Enniskillen Castle. *Overlooking Lough Erne; houses two museums and a heritage centre.* Open all year, Mon to Fri and BH.

Marble Arch Caves. *Underground caverns, rivers and lakes.* Open Apr to Oct, daily.

Florence Court (NT). *Eighteenth-century mansion with forest park (not NT).* Open Etr to Sep at varying times (forest park open daily, all year).

FORE

Tullynally Castle. *Victorian castle in landscaped grounds with lake.* Castle open mid-Jul to mid-Aug; grounds open Jun to Sep, daily.

FOATY ISLAND

Fota Estate. *Arboretum on island in Cork Harbour with trees from every continent.* Open Apr to Sep, daily; Oct, Sat and Sun.

GIANT'S CAUSEWAY

Giant's Causeway Centre (NT). *Dramatic rock formation with a visitor centre.* Open all year, daily.

GREYABBEY

Grey Abbey. *Well preserved abbey ruins in parkland.* Open Apr to Sep, Tue to Sun; Oct and Mar, Sat only.

Mount Stewart House and Gardens (NT), on east shore of Strangford Lough. *Eighteenth-century house with fine contents, but most famous for lovely gardens.* Open Apr to Oct at varying times.

HOLYCROSS

Lough Gur Stone Age Centre. *Excavated tombs, stone circles and dwellings with visitor centre.* Open mid-May to Sep, daily.

HOLYWOOD

Ulster Folk and Transport Museum. *Impressive museum of reconstructed buildings plus the history of transport.* Open all year, daily.

HOWTH

Howth Castle Gardens. *Famous rhododendron gardens with fine views.* Open all year, daily.

Malahide Castle. *Turreted castle with period furnishings and portraits. There is a botanical garden in the grounds, plus a model railway centre.* Open all year, daily.

KENMARE

Derreen Gardens. *Luxuriant area of woodland with a subtropical garden containing many excellent shrubs.* Open Apr to Sep, daily.

KILDARE

The Japanese Gardens. *Gardens tracing human life, including stone ornamentation, bridges and a miniature village.* Open all year, daily.

The National Stud. *Guided tours enable visitors to see the stallions, the foaling unit and a museum depicting the evolution of the horse.* Open all year, daily.

KILKENNY

Rothe House. *Merchant's town house, now home to a museum.* Open Apr to Oct, daily; Nov to Mar, Sat and Sun.

KILLARNEY

Muckross House. *House now containing the Kerry Folklife Centre. Lovely grounds on edge of Muckross Lake.* Open all year, daily.

KINVARRA BAY

Dunguaire Castle. *Restored castle of ancient origin.* Open Apr to Sep, daily.

LISBURN

Lisburn Museum, Market Sq. *Museum of the linen industry and transport in the Lagan valley, plus works by local artists.* Open all year, Tue to Sat.

MITCHELSTOWN

Mitchelstown Caves. *Huge show caverns.* Open all year, daily.

MOHER CLIFFS

O'Brien's Tower and Cliffs of Moher. *Huge cliffs with 19th-century viewing tower and visitor centre.* Tower open May to Sep, daily.

NEW ROSS

John F Kennedy Arboretum. *Over 58 acres near the Kennedys' ancestral home.* Open all year, daily.

OMAGH

Ulster American Folk Park. *Outdoor museum tracing the history of Ulster's link with America.* Open Etr to early Sep, daily; Sep to Etr, Mon to Fri.

PORTAFERRY

Northern Ireland Aquarium, Castle St. *Interpretative centre for Strangford Lough, plus many marine animals and family facilities.* Open all year, daily.

PORTARLINGTON

Emo Court. *Neo-classical mansion with lovely formal gardens.* Gardens open all year, daily; house open Apr to Sep, Mon.

PORTRUSH

Dunluce Castle. *Spectacular castle ruins on cliff edge, visitor centre.* Open all year, daily.

QUIN

Craggaunowen Project. *Life in prehistoric Ireland reconstructed in lakes and hills.* Open all year, daily.

SAINTFIELD

Rowallane Gardens (NT). *Exotic 50-acre garden with plants from all over the world.* Open end Mar to Oct, daily; Nov to Mar, Mon to Fri.

SANDYFORD

Fernhill Gardens. *Includes rock, water, walled and woodland gardens.* Open Mar to Nov, Tue to Sun.

SKERRIES

Newbridge House. *Georgian mansion with dairy, forge, doll museum and aviary.* Open Apr to Oct, Tue to Sat; Nov to Mar, Sat, Sun and BH.

SKIBBEREEN

Creagh Gardens. *Informal woodland garden and a water garden.* Open Apr to Sep, daily.

STRANGFORD

Castle Ward (NT). *Interesting house on edge of Strangford Lough.*

House open Etr to Oct at varying times; grounds open all year, daily.

WEXFORD

The Irish National Heritage Park. *Replicas of monasteries, settlements and burial places overlooking the River Slaney.* Open Mar to Nov, daily.

Johnstown Castle Gardens. *Fifty-acre gardens, which include the Irish Agricultural Museum with horse-drawn vehicles and reconstructed workshops.* Open all year, daily.

SPORTS AND ACTIVITIES

This is just a taste of the many sporting activities that can be enjoyed in Ireland. Further information can be obtained from the contacts given or from the two tourist boards (see page 110).

ANGLING

Coarse fishing is possible all year in Ireland as there is no close season. In the Republic no licence is needed but permission from the owner is generally required. Bait can be obtained locally or from Irish Angling Services Ltd. In Northern Ireland a coarse rod licence must be obtained from the Fisheries Conservancy Board as well as a coarse fishing permit from the owner of the water.

In the Republic a state licence is required when game fishing for salmon and sea trout, but not for brown or rainbow trout. The seasons vary from county to county but the statutory dates are: salmon and sea trout 1 Jan to 30 Sep; brown and rainbow trout 15 Feb to 12 Oct (many trout fisheries close 30 Sep). Some salmon fishing is free, as are many brown trout waters, but almost all sea trout fisheries require a permit. Salmon are found in most rivers flowing north, west and east, but are most prolific in Galway; sea trout frequent the shorter coastal streams and their acidic lakes; hundreds of brown trout lakes are scattered throughout the country. Detailed information is available from the Central Fisheries Board.

To game fish in Northern Ireland you must obtain a rod licence from either the Fisheries Conservancy Board or the Foyle Fisheries Commission. In addition, you must obtain permission from the owner of the water. If the water is owned by the Department of Agriculture a permit or daily ticket must be obtained from an angling club.

▲ Roscommon holds four meetings annually, including races over hurdles

Licences and permits are available from the Northern Ireland Tourist Board and from local tackle shops. Further information is available from the Department of Agriculture.

A tremendous variety of sea fishing is available in Ireland, all of which is free and does not require a permit. On estuaries, however, a licence must be obtained to fish for sea trout. The various different types, which include shore, inshore and deep sea, depend upon the time of year.

Hundreds of angling galas and festivals take place throughout the year and most are open to all-comers. Details are available from the Irish Tourist Board and the Northern Ireland Tourist Board (see page 110).

The Central Fisheries Board, Balnagowan House, Mobhi Boreen, Glasnevin, Dublin 9 (01 379206).

Irish Angling Services Ltd, Ardlougher, Ballyconnell, Co Cavan (049 26258).

Department of Agriculture (Fisheries Division), Stormont, Belfast BT4 3PW (0232 763939).

Fisheries Conservancy Board for Northern Ireland, 1 Mahon Road, Portadown, Co Armagh BT62 3EE (0762 334666).

Foyle Fisheries Commission, 8 Victoria Road, Londonderry BT47 2AB (0504 42100).

CANOEING

This sport can be enjoyed all year round on Ireland's hundreds of navigable lakes and rivers. Slalom, down-river racing, white-water canoeing and surfing are available in winter, and sprint, long-distance, marathon and surfing in summer. Canoe touring is probably of most interest to visitors and details of tuition and holidays can be obtained from the Association of Adventure Sports and also from the Irish Canoe Union.

Association of Adventure Sports, Tiglin National Adventure Centre, Ashford, Co Wicklow (040 440169).

Irish Canoe Union, House of Sport, Longmile Road, Dublin 12 (01 501633/509838)

Canoe Association of Northern Ireland, House of Sport, Upper Malone Road, Belfast BT9 5LA (0232 381222).

CYCLING

Ireland's quiet roads and lanes are ideal for cycling, and bikes can be hired in most towns. Mountain bikes and children's bikes are often available as well. Raleigh operate a number of Rent-a-Bike offices in the Republic and Northern Ireland, and bicycles can be collected from one dealer and returned to another. Bicycles hired in the Republic cannot be taken into Northern Ireland, and vice versa. Several cycling holiday specialists operate in Ireland and lists of these are available from the Northern Ireland Tourist Board and from the Irish Tourist Board (see page 110).

GOLF

The island's 280-odd courses offer first-class golfing and most are open to non-members for modest green fees. Golfing holidays are widely available in Ireland, details of which can be obtained from the Irish Tourist Board and the Northern Ireland Tourist Board. Tourist offices can also provide information about local courses.

EQUESTRIAN PURSUITS

There are a number of residential and non-residential riding and trekking centres throughout Ireland offering a wide choice of facilities and tuition. The Association of Irish Riding Establishments (AIRE) inspects and registers riding centres, and a list of those which have been approved is available from both of the tourist boards.

One of the most popular kinds of riding holiday in Ireland is trail riding, which involves riding a different route each day, either from one base or spending each night at a different place. Horse-drawn caravan holidays are another favourite equestrian holiday.

Hunting is possible in Ireland as visitors are welcome at meets and horses can be hired for the day. Check, however, that you are adequately insured.

The Irish Tourist Board has information sheets on horse riding, trail riding, hunting, horse-drawn caravan holidays and a calendar of events which includes details of race meetings. Race details are also published in the Irish Racing Calendar, available from the tourist boards and from the Racing Promotions Group (see below).

Racing Promotions Group, Racing Board Headquarters, Leopardstown Racecourse, Dublin 18 (01 2897277).

The Show Jumping Association of Ireland, Anglesea Lodge, Anglesea Road, Ballsbridge, Dublin 4 (01 601700).

The Irish Horse Trials and Dressage Society, Anglesea Lodge, Anglesea Road, Ballsbridge, Dublin 4 (01 601417).

The All-Ireland Polo Club, Phoenix Park, Dublin 8 (01 776248).

Association of Irish Riding Establishments, 11 Moore Park, Newbridge, Co Kildare (045 31584).

INLAND CRUISING

The extensive, uncommercialised and unpolluted waterways of Ireland make cruising particularly pleasurable. The chief cruising areas are the River Shannon, the Grand Canal, the River Erne and the River Barrow, and Lower and Upper Lough Erne. Several companies provide self-drive, luxury cruisers for hire, but only members of the Irish Boat Rental Association (IBRA) are approved by the Irish Tourist Board, which can supply full details. Optional extras such as bicycles, fishing tackle and sailing dinghies are available. No licence or previous boat handling experience is required as basic tuition is given when you take charge of the boat. The Erne Charter Boat Association represents most cruise operators on the Erne system and can be reached at Erne Marine.

Erne Marine, Bellanaleck, Co Fermanagh (0365 82267).

SAILING

This is a popular pastime in Ireland and the many lakes – as well as the long coastline – mean that there are lots of opportunities to enjoy it. The Irish Yachting Association governs the sport in the Republic and can supply information to visiting yachtsmen. The Royal Yachting Association, Sports Council of Northern Ireland (see this page), governs sailing in Northern Ireland.

The Irish Association for Sail Training is the national organisation in the Republic which represents professional sailing schools, and details of reputable centres around the country which are affiliated to it can be obtained from Confederation House.

The Irish Yachting Association, 3 Park Road, Dun Laoghaire, Co Dublin (01 2800239).

Confederation House, Kildare Street, Dublin 2 (01 779801).

WALKING

This is becoming increasingly popular as a recreational activity in Ireland and since 1978, when the Long Distance Walking Routes Committee of Cospóir was founded to establish a network of trails around the Republic 13 routes have been completed. These total some 1,000 miles and another 12 routes are planned. All completed routes are clearly waymarked and a leaflet about each is available from the Irish Tourist Board. In the north, keen walkers can embark on the 491-mile Ulster Way. For more details, contact the Sports Council for Northern Ireland (see this page).

There are also 12 forest parks in the Republic, each featuring walks and nature trails, which are open to the public all year round. Booklets on each can be obtained from Coillte Teo (Irish Forestry Board). Northern Ireland also has forest and country parks (see below); the former are administered by the Department of Agriculture (NI), the latter by the Department of the Environment (NI). All are open all year (booklets available). Ireland's three National Parks also provide extensive opportunities for walking. For further information on these contact the Office of Public Works.

Coillte Teo (Irish Forestry Board). Leeson Lane, Dublin 2 (01 615666).

Office of Public Works, 51 St Stephen's Green, Dublin 2 (01 613111).

WATERSPORTS

Conditions around the coast of Ireland are ideal for diving and every aspect of the sport can be enjoyed here. Information about courses and clubs is available from the Irish Underwater Council or the Sports Council for Northern Ireland (see below).

The west coast provides top class surfing conditions, but although boards may be hired at some resorts they are not widely available. More information from the Irish Surfing Association or the Sports Council for Northern Ireland (see below).

Irish Underwater Council, Haigh Terrace, Dun Laoghaire, Co Dublin (01 2844601).

Irish Surfing Association, Tigh-na-Mara, Rossnowlagh, Co Donegal (072 51261).

USEFUL INFORMATION

Telephone numbers are given in brackets.
The Automobile Association

ADDRESSES

Breakdown numbers: Northern Ireland – Belfast (0800 887766); Republic – Dublin (01 779481).

The National Trust (NT)
Rowallane House, Saintfield, Ballynahinch, Co Down BT24 7LH (0238 510721).

Youth Hostel Association of Northern Ireland
56 Bradbury Place, Belfast BT7 1RU (0232 324733).

An Oige (Irish Youth Hostel Association)
39 Mountjoy Square, Dublin 1 (01 363111/364749).

The Sports Council for Northern Ireland
House of Sport, Upper Malone Road, Belfast BT9 5LA (0232 381222).

TOURIST INFORMATION

Northern Ireland Tourist Board
St Anne's Court, 59 North Street, Belfast BT1 1NB (0232 246609).

16 Nassau Street, Dublin 2 (01 6791977, Freephone 1800 230230).

11 Berkeley Street, London W1X 5AD (071 493 0601, Freephone 0800 282662).

Bord Fáilte (Irish Tourist Board)
Baggot Street Bridge, Dublin 2 (01 765871).

General postal enquiries regarding travel to and in the Republic
PO Box 273, Dublin 8.

53 Castle Street, Belfast BT1 1GH (0232 327888).

150 New Bond Street, London W1Y 0AQ (071 493 9065).

British Travel Centre, All Ireland Desk, 12 Regent Street, London – callers welcome, Mon–Fri, 9am–6.30pm, Sat and Sun, 10am–4pm.

Local Tourist Information Centres
The following centres are open all year; there are many others which are only open during the summer months.

Antrim, Council Offices, Steeple (084 94 63113).

Armagh, Bank Building, 40 English St (0861 527808).

Ballycastle, Sheskburn House, 7 Mary St (026 57 62024).

Ballymoney, Council Offices, 14 Charles St (026 56 62280).

Banbridge, Leisure Centre, Downshire Rd (082 06 62799).

Bangor, Tower House, 34 Quay St (0247 270069).

Belfast, 59 North St (0232 246609).

Belfast International Airport (084 94 22888 ext 3009).

Belfast City Airport (0232 457745).

Carnlough, Post Office, 38 Harbour Rd (0574 885210).

Carrickfergus, 19 North St (096 03 66455).

Cavan, Farnham St (049 31942).

Coleraine, Railway Rd (0265 44723).

Cookstown, Council Offices, 12 Burn Rd (064 87 62205).

Cork, Tourist House, Grand Parade (021 273251).

Cushendall, Car Park, 24b Mill St (026 67 71180).

Downpatrick, Down Leisure Centre, Market St (0396 613426).

Dublin City, 14 Upper O'Connell St (01 747733).

Dublin International Airport (01 376387/375533).

Dundalk, Market Sq (042 35484).

Dungannon, Council Offices, Circular Rd (086 87 25311).

Dun Laoghaire, St Michael's Wharf (01 2806984/5/6).

Ennis, Clare Rd (065 28366).

Enniskillen, Lakeland Visitor Centre, Shore Rd (0365 323110/325050).

Fivemiletown, Library, Main St (036 55 21409).

Galway City, Aras Fáilte, Victoria Place, Eyre Sq (091 63081).

Giant's Causeway, 44 Causeway Rd (0265 731855).

Hillsborough, Council Offices, The Square (0846 682477).

Kilkeel, Mourne Esplanade (069 37 64666).

Kilkenny, Shee Alms House, Rose Inn St (056 21755).

Killarney, Town Hall (064 3633).

Knock Airport (094 67247).

Larne, Narrow Gauge Rd (0574 260088).

Larne Harbour (0574 70517).

Letterkenny, Derry Rd (074 21160).

Limavady, Council Offices, 7 Connell St (050 47 22226).

Limerick City, Arthur's Quay (061 317522).

Londonderry, 8 Bishop St (0504 267284).

Lurgan, Town Hall, 6 Union St (0762 323757).

Magherafelt, Council Offices, 43 Queen's Ave (0648 32151).

Monaghan, Market House (047 81122).

Mullingar, Dublin Rd (044 48650).

Newcastle, Newcastle Centre, Central Promenade (039 67 22222).

Newry, Arts Centre, Bank Parade (0693 66232).

Newtownards, Council Offices, 2 Church St (0247 812215).

Omagh, 1 Market St (0662 247831/2).

Portadown, Town Hall (0762 353260).

Rosslare Ferry Terminal (053 33622).

Shannon Airport (061 61664/ 61565/61604).

Skibbereen, Town Hall (028 21766).

Sligo, Aras Reddan, Temple St (071 61201).

Tralee, Ashe Memorial Hall, Denny St (066 21288).

Waterford, 41 The Quay (051 75788).

Westport, The Mall (098 25711).

Wexford, Crescent Quay (053 23111).

Wicklow, Fitzwilliam St (0404 69117).

▲ The very Irish sport of hurling

CUSTOMS AND EVENTS

This is just a selection of the hundreds of customs, festivals and sporting events which take place in Ireland. Dates (and occasionally venues) may vary from year to year. It is always best to check with local tourist information centres (see pages 110–11) for further details.

FEBRUARY

Ulster Motor Show
King's Hall, Belfast (2nd week).

Ulster Harp National
Downpatrick Racecourse (3rd week). *Celebrated steeplechase.*

Dublin Film Festival
Dublin Cinemas (Feb/Mar). *The best in Irish and world cinema.*

MARCH

Belfast Musical Festival
Balmoral, Belfast (1st two weeks). *Youth speech, drama and music competitions.*

St Patrick's Day
Celebrations all over the country (17 March) *involving floats, bands, music and processions.*

Horse Ploughing Match and Heavy Horse Show
Fair Head, Ballycastle (mid-Mar).

EASTER

Circuit of Ireland Car Rally
(Good Friday–Easter Monday)

Irish Grand National
Fairyhouse (Easter Monday).

APRIL

Feis Ceoil
Dublin (end Mar/Apr). *Competitive music festival.*

European Championship Motorcycle Races
Kirkistown, Ards Peninsula (2nd week).

World Irish Dancing Championships
Jetland Festival Centre, Limerick (2nd week).

Pan Celtic Festival
Various venues in Galway city (3rd week).

MAY

Cork International Choral Festival
Cork (end Apr/May). *International competitions for choirs.*

Spring Show and Garden Festival
RDS Showgrounds, Ballsbridge, Dublin (1st week).

Belfast Civic Festival and Lord Mayor's Show
Belfast (2nd/3rd week). *Concerts, competitions, parades and similar events.*

North West 200
Portstewart (mid-May). *Fastest motorcycle road race in the British Isles.*

Listowel Writers' Week
Listowel (end May).

Dundalk Maytime Festival
Dundalk (end May). *Daily events, street entertainment and sports.*

FACT FILE

JUNE

Guinness Canal Festival
Newry (2nd week). *Floats and bathtub race on Newry Canal followed by civic celebrations.*

Music in Great Irish Houses Festival
Castletown House, Celbridge (2nd week).

An Tostal Druimseanbhoth
Drumshanbo (3rd week). *Traditional music and dance festival.*

Galway Hookers' Regatta
Strangford Lough (end Jun). *Traditional Irish vessels race on the lough.*

JULY

Northern Ireland Game and Country Fair
Shane's Castle, Antrim (1st week). *Field sports event covering all aspects of country life and sport.*

Castlebar International Four Day Walk
Castlebar (1st week).

North of Ireland Open Amateur Golf Championship
Royal Portrush, Causeway Coast (2nd week).

International Folk Dance Festival
Cobh (2nd/3rd week). *Street entertainment and folk dancers from all over the world.*

One of Ireland's many yachting centres; near Ardmillan on Strangford Lough in Co Down ▼

Sham Fight
Scarva (mid-Jul). *Traditional 200-year-old pageant.*

Galway Horse Racing Festival
Galway (end Jul/early Aug)

Mary from Dungloe International Festival
Dungloe (end Jul/Aug). *Festival of music and entertainment; Mary from Dungloe is selected.*

AUGUST

All Ireland Senior Road Bowls Final
Armagh and Cork (1st week). *Ancient game; metal bowls have replaced cannonballs.*

Kerrygold Dublin Horse Show
Ballsbridge, Dublin (1st or 2nd week). *Huge programme of horse-jumping events.*

Puck Fair
Killorglin (2nd week). *Horse and cattle fair, plus stalls and a fun fair.*

Kilkenny Arts Week
Kilkenny (3rd week). *All areas of the arts celebrated.*

Rose of Tralee International Festival (Festival of Kerry)
Tralee (4th week). *A beauty queen is picked from girls of Irish descent.*

Fleadh Cheoil na hÉireann
Venue changes (weekend before last Monday in August). *Notable cultural event with competitors from all over the world.*

Connemara Pony Show
Clifden (4th week).

SEPTEMBER

All Ireland Hurling Final
Croke Park, Dublin (1st week).

Clarenbridge Oyster Festival
Clarenbridge (2nd week). *Oyster tasting, music, song and dance.*

Waterford International Festival of Light Opera
Theatre Royal, Waterford (3rd week Sep to 1st week Oct).

All Ireland Football Final
Croke Park, Dublin (4th week).

Galway Oyster International Festival
Galway (4th week). *Festival of oyster tasting, music and dance.*

Listowel Racing Festival
Listowel (4th week).

OCTOBER

Dublin Theatre Festival
Various theatres in Dublin (2nd/3rd week).

Cork Jazz Festival
Cork (4th week). *Features many famous musicians.*

Wexford Opera Festival
Wexford (last week Oct to 1st week Nov). *Internationally acclaimed festival.*

NOVEMBER

Belfast Festival
Queen's University, Belfast (2nd to 4th week). *Major arts festival.*

Atlas

▲ On Lough Conn, Co Mayo

The following pages contain a legend, an atlas of Ireland, ten circular motor tours and fifteen planned walks throughout the length and breadth of the island.

MAP SYMBOLS

THE GRID SYSTEM

The map references used in this book are based on the Irish National Grid. They comprise of one letter and two figures.

Thus the reference for Cork appears W 67.

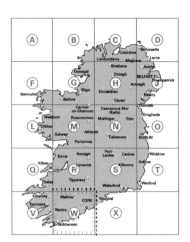

Each 100 kilometre square is identified by a letter eg W. These squares are then subdivided into 10 kilometre squares. The first figure shows which number along the bottom to locate, and the second figure which number up the side. These indicate the square in which the place name is found.

These 10 kilometre squares can be further divided into tenths to give a four figure grid reference. These are used for the walks to allow a more precise reference to locations on larger scale maps.

1 🚗	Start point of tour		Featured tour
➡	Direction of tour	②	Point of interest
▸▶	Alternative tour		

TOURS 1:350,000 - 1" to 5.25 miles

The above scale of mapping does not allow the inclusion of some minor roads.

Roads in the Republic of Ireland

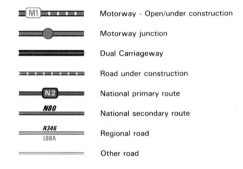

M1	Motorway - Open/under construction
●	Motorway junction
	Dual Carriageway
	Road under construction
N2	National primary route
N80	National secondary route
R346 / L98A	Regional road
	Other road

Regional roads: these road numbers are currently replacing the Link and Trunk road numbers. During the changeover, either the old or the new numbers may be seen on the signposts on the roads. On the tour maps, the previous Link and Trunk numbers are shown in red type. Distances on National Primary signposting are now in kilometres.

Roads in Northern Ireland

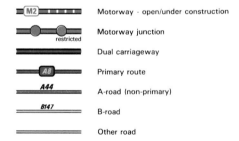

M2	Motorway - open/under construction
● ● restricted	Motorway junction
	Dual carriageway
A8	Primary route
A44	A-road (non-primary)
B147	B-road
	Other road

ATLAS 1:1,000,000-1" to 15.87 MILES

Roads in the Republic of Ireland

M1	Motorway
N17	National Primary Route
N54	National Secondary Route
R182	Regional Road

Roads in Northern Ireland

A4	Primary Route
A21	A Road
B75	B Road
	Road under construction
5	Distance in miles between symbols
▪ ▬ ▬ ▪	International Boundary
◆ Ⓟ	Frontier Post

GENERAL FEATURES

┼	Road toll
◄ 6 ►	Distance in miles between symbols
⌐	Frontier post
⌐	Border crossing - prohibited
---Ⓥ---	Vehicle ferry
⊕	Airport
	Railway line
─○─	Railway station
AA	AA shops (Northern Ireland)
AA	Outlets (Rep of Ireland)
☎	AA telephone

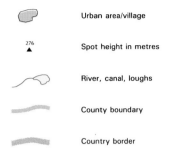 Urban area/village

276 ▲ Spot height in metres

River, canal, loughs

County boundary

Country border

WALKS

On each map there is an indication of the scale used

Start of walk

Line of walk

➡ Direction of walk

▻▻ Alternative route

① Point of interest

TOURIST INFORMATION

🄸	Tourist Information Centre	🐗	Wildlife collection-mammals
🄸	Tourist Information Centre (seasonal)	🐦	Wildlife collection-birds
🄰	Abbey, cathedral or priory	🐟	Aquarium
🄰	Ruined abbey, cathedral or priory	☀	Viewpoint
♜	Castle	⛩	Picnic site
🏛	Historic house		Hill fort
🄼	Museum or art gallery		Prehistoric monument
	Industrial interest		Steam centre (railway)
❋	Garden	◠	Cave
♣	Arboretum	★	Other places of interest
🤸	Country park	☐	Boxed symbols indicate attractions in urban areas
🐘	Zoo		National park
			Forest park

ROADS, RAILWAYS AND PATHS

═════	Main road
════	Minor road
=======	Track
-------	Path
+–+–•+–+	Railway line/station
+ + + + + +	Disused railway line

GENERAL FEATURES

⚑	Campsite	○	Cashel
🚐	Caravan site	○	Sink hole
🅿	Parking		Tumulus
⚑	Golf course	◉	Rath
⚡	Radio mast	—	Footbridge
🎇	Lighthouse	- - -	Stepping stones
✝	Church	—	Waterfall
✝	Monastic site	❯	Lock
✝	Stone cross		Rocks
			Cliffs

RELIEF

Metres	Feet	
900	2953	
750	2460	
600	1968	
450	1476	To convert metres to feet divide by 0.3048
300	984	
150	492	
75	246	
0	0	

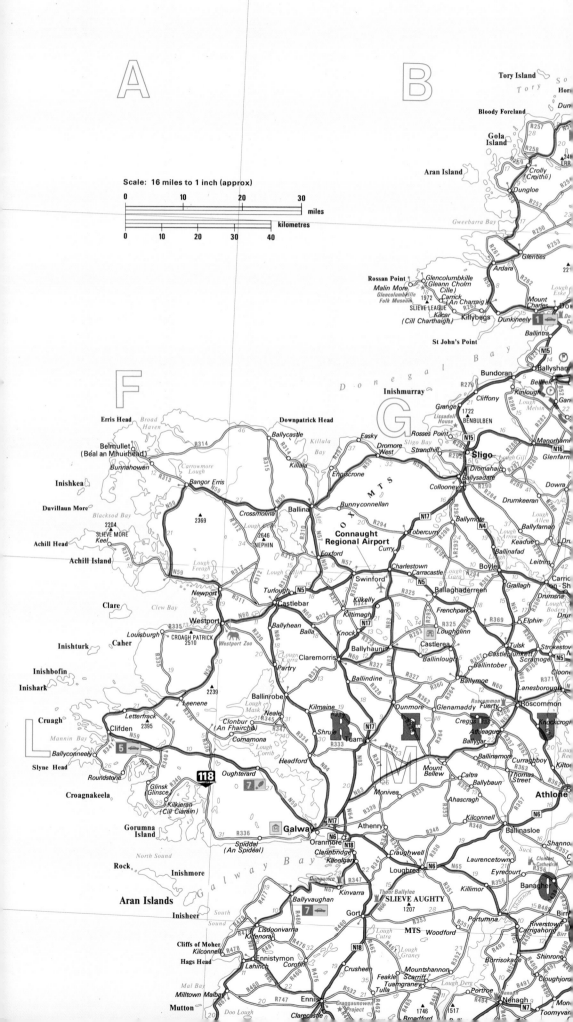

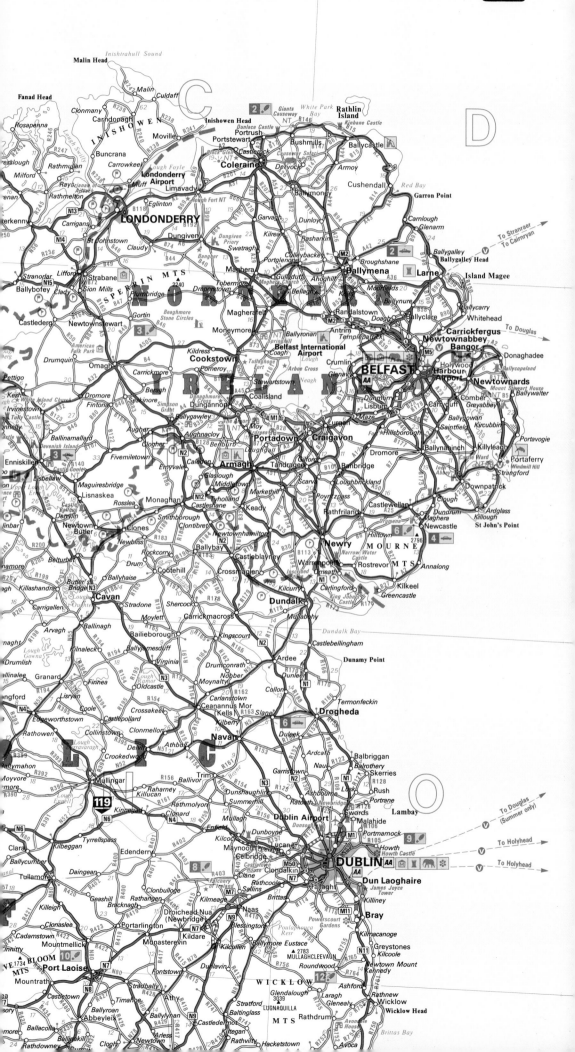

Achill Island

Lough Feeagh

Clare

Inishturk

Caher

Louisburgh

Clew Bay

Newport

Turlough

N5

Castlebar

Swinford

Charlestown

Carracastle

N57

N59

R311

R312

R320

Kilkelly

R325

Westport

N60

Ballyhean

N84

Balla

Kiltimagh

N17

R293

Castler

Croagh Patrick
2510

Westport Zoo

Ballyheart

Knock

13

Ballinl

Inishbofin

Inishbofin

Inishark

Partry

Claremorris

R327

Ballyhaunis

N60

Ballindine

R328

R366

Ballinrobe

Neale

Kilmaine

19

Dunmore

Gle

Cruagh

Leenene

Lough
Mask

Clonbur
(An Fhairche)

R333

Tuam

Mount
Bellew

Letterfrack

2239

R345

Shrule

N17

Clifden

2395

R344

Cornamona

Lough
Corrib

N83

Mannin Bay

R340

Headford

N84

Monivea

Ballyconneely

5

N59

10

Oughterard

7

116

N63

R339

Slyne Head

Roundstone

N63

Athenry

R348

Glinsk
(Glinsce)

Kilkieran
(Cill Ciaráin)

Galway

Oranmore

N6

Craughwell

N6

Croagnakeela

Gorumna
Island

R336

Spiddal
(An Spidéal)

Clarinbridge

Kilcolgan

Loughrea

R350

North Sound

Galway Bay

Kinvarra

Thoor Ballylee

SLIEVE AUGHTY

Wood

Rock

Inishmore

Ballyvaughan

Gort

1207

MTS

28

Aran Islands

Inisheer

South
Sound

7

R477

Lough
Cutra

Lough
Graney

R480

Lisdoonvarna

N18

Kilfenora

R476

Crusheen

Mountshanne

Scariff

Cliffs of Moher

Kilconnell

R471

Ennistymon

Corofin

Feakle

Tuamgraney

Kilconnell

Hags Head

Lahinch

R460

Tulla

Mal Bay

Milltown Malbay

R747

Ennis

Craggaunowen
Project

1746

Broadford

Mutton

Doo Lough

Clarecastle

Knappogue

Killaloe

Doonbeg

Newmarket-on-Fergus

Donegal Point

Kilkee

Cooraclare

Shannon Airport

N18

Sixmilebridge

Cloon

River Shannon

N19

LIMERICK

N7

Loop Head

Kilrush

N67

Killadysert

34

Mouth of the
Shannon

R487

R488

Tarbert

Foynes

Askeaton

N20

Patrickswell

R512

Ballybunion

Ballylongford

Glin

Shanagolden

Adare

N21

Croagh

Croom

Pallas

Kerry Head

Ballyduff

Listowel

Athea

Newcastle
West

Rathkeale

R520

Ballingarry

Bruff

Hospital

Causeway

R523

Bruree

Ballyheige

Abbeyfeale

Kilmeedy

R515

Kilmallock

Rough
Point

Artfert

Abbeydorney

N21

Kilkinlea

Broadford

Rath Luirc
(Charleville)

Kilfinnane

1696

11

Brandon
Bay

1170

Duagh

Dromcollliher

1341

Freemount

N20

BRANDON MTN
3127

BEENOSKEE

2713

2796

Tralee

Castleisland

Newmarket

Buttevant

Mitche

Sybil Point

Camp

2539

R559

N21

Scartaglen

Ballydesmond

Kanturk

Donerail

Dingle
(An Daingean)

Anascaul

BAURTREGAUM

Castlemaine

N22

Farranfore

Boherbue

Castletownroche

Slea Head

R561

Milltown

N23

Kerry County
Airport

Cloonbannin

Banteer

Mallow

14

Killorglin

R562

Killarney

Rathmore

Nad

Mourne
Abbey

1406

Rathco

Glenbeigh

Beaufort

Millstreet

BOGGERAGH
MTS

CARRANTUOHILL
3414

Muckross

2118

Glenville

Doulus Head

MULLAGHANATTIN

Killarney
National Park

Mangerton Mtn
2756

Carriganimmy

N20

Valentia

Cahirciveen

Molls Gap

Cloonkeen

Ballymakeery

Blarney

AA

Waterville

Sneem

N70

Kilgarvan

Macroom

N22

Dripsey

CORK

The Skelligs

Bolus Head

Kenmare

Ballingeary
(Béal Átha an
Ghaorthaidh)

Inchigeelagh

Kilmichael

Ovens

Crookstown

Cork Airport

Douglas

Castle Cove

Parknasilla

Tahilla

KNOCKBOY
2321

Lee

Ballinhassig

Scariff

Caherdaniel

Derrynane
House

Lauragh

Glengarriff

R585

Bandon

Inishannon

Cod's
Head

Ardgroom

2251

Adrigole

Dunmanway

Ballineen

Enniskean

Dunderrow

Belgooly

Dursey

Allihies

Castletownbere

Bantry

Durrus

Drimoleague

Timoleague

Kilbrittain

Ballinspittle

Bear

Sheep's
Head

Ballydehob

Leap

Ross Carbery

Courtmacsherry

Toormore

Schull

Skibbereen

Glandore

Clonakilty Bay

Old Head
of Kinsale

Goleen

Crookhaven

Castletownshend

Galley Head

Mizen Head

Roaringwater
Bay

Baltimore

Toe Head

Clear

TOUR 1

TO THE BLUE STACK MOUNTAINS

Straddling southern Co Donegal, the glorious Blue Stack Mountains, their tops often shrouded in mist, are easily explored on this tour which starts in the town of Donegal.

ROUTE DIRECTIONS

The drive starts at Donegal ①.

From the Diamond in Donegal follow SP 'Killybegs, Mount Charles' N56. Drive alongside Donegal Bay, passing Mount Charles after 3¾ miles, and ascend inland for several miles. Rejoin the coast at Inver Bay. After 7 miles (from Mount Charles) pass through Dunkineely, which lies at the base of a narrow peninsula separating Inver and McSwyne's bays. (This peninsula can be explored by an unclassified road.) In 1½ miles pass through Bruckless, and in 2 miles continue on to the R263 before driving alongside Killybegs Harbour and entering the town ②. In ¼ mile bear right and ascend, then in 1¼ miles descend to the edge of sandy Fintragh Bay. After 2¾ miles bear right SP 'Kilcar', and climb a low pass between Croaghbeg (260m) and Crowarad Hill (491m). Descend along Glenaddragh Valley into Kilcar. Meet crossroads and keep forward SP 'Coast Road' on to an unclassified road. In ½ mile ascend steeply, with distant views of the Co Mayo mountains to the left. Summit views extend across Teelin Bay to the famous Slieve League (601m). Rejoin the R263 and in 1 mile reach Carrick, a village which provides access to Teelin and Slieve League. Pass through Carrick, following signs for Glencolumbkille (Gleann Cholm Cille), shortly enter the Owenwee Valley, then climb to 180m before descending sharply towards Glencolumbkille ③. At the edge of the village keep forward on an unclassified road SP 'Ard an Rátha' (Ardara). A left turn here allows a detour to the Folk Village. In ¼ mile bear left over a river. Meet a T-junction and turn right SP 'Ard an Rátha', then in 1 mile cross a river and bear right. Climb to a 210m pass between Croaghnaleaba (271m) and Croaghloughdivna (310m), then descend to the Glen River valley. Bear left SP 'Ard an Rátha' then drive straight on to cross the river and enter the Crove River valley.

Follow an easy ascent past Crove village, with mountains ahead and to the right, and climb 270m below Croaghavehy (371m) at the head of Glen Gesh. Descend, with maximum gradients of 1 in 4 and hairpin bends, meet a T-junction and turn left on to the N56 SP 'Ard an Rátha'. In 1¼ miles enter the town of Ard an Rátha (Ardara) ④ and bear left SP 'Glenties', then ascend and bear right. Continue for 6 miles to reach Glenties. Pass the school and church on the right, and immediately turn right on to the R253, keeping the town to the left. Follow the Owenea Valley, and after 3¼ miles cross a river bridge and keep right. In ¾ mile the road affords views of Aghla Mountain (598m) on the left, plus Carnaween (519m), Silver Hill (600m) and, after several more miles. Lough Ea, all to the right. In 2¼ miles (from the lough) reach a 241m summit, then make an easy descent into the Reelan Valley. Ahead is Gaugin Mountain (568m) and views to the right include the glorious Blue Stack Mountains. Continue for 4 miles and bear right across a river, then in 1 mile join the valley of the River Finn. Follow the river for 3¼ miles and drive forward on to the R252, proceeding to Ballybofey. Turn right here on to the N15 SP 'Donegal', and skirt Lough Mourne after 4 miles. The mountains beyond the lough include Croaghnageer (544m) on the right, and Croaghconnellagh (523m) and Barnesmore (451m) ahead of you. Drive between the latter two mountains via Barnesmore Gap. Once you are clear of the range, pass Lough Eske (right) and later re-enter Donegal.

Ard an Rátha (Ardara), Co Donegal ▼

POINTS OF INTEREST

① Donegal, whose 'Diamond' forms an impressive town centre, contains ruins of a Franciscan friary (founded in 1474, but largely destroyed by an accidental explosion of gunpowder) and the better preserved remains of an O'Donnell castle.
② Killybegs is a busy fishing port with a memorial to the clan chief Niall Mór MacSweeney in its Roman Catholic church. A narrow road leads three miles south to Drumanoo Head, popular for both its views and walks.
③ Named after St Columba (Colmcille), Glencolumbkille is a place of pilgrimage on the saint's feast day (9 June), when pilgrims walk barefoot 3miles around the holy sites of the village. The Folk Village shows what rural Irish life was like at three different points in history.
④ The area around Ard an Rátha (Ardara) is good for game fishing, and the town itself is a centre for tweed and other handicrafts.

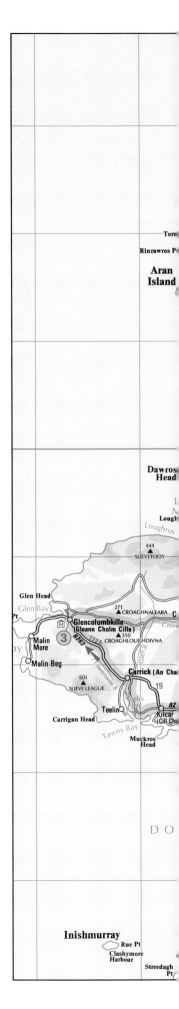

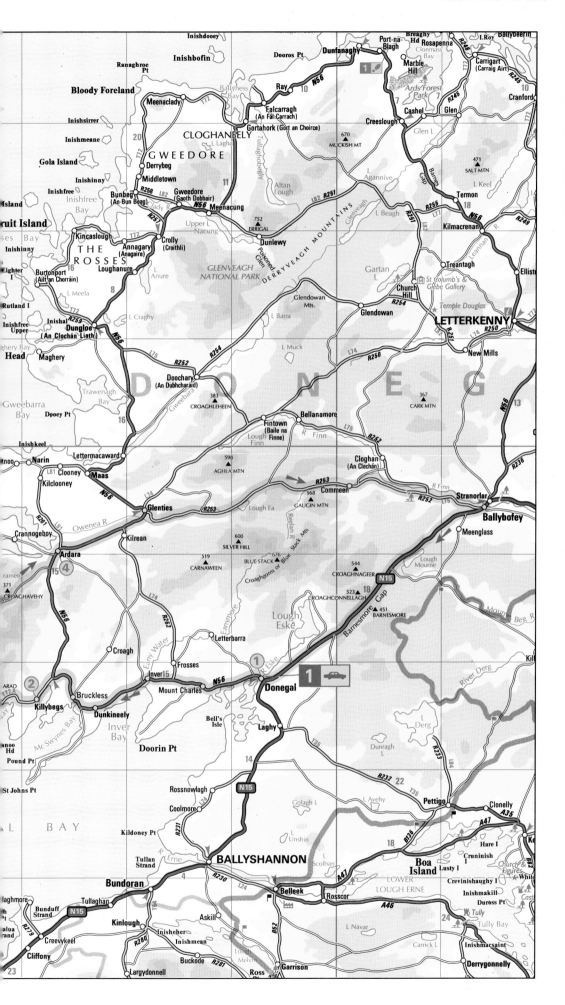

TOUR 2

A SPECTACULAR SEA DRIVE

This route follows part of the Antrim Coast Road – rightly considered to be one of the finest marine drives in the whole of Europe – through some of the spectacular scenery around the famous nine Glens of Antrim. Most of these glens are accessible from the road and comprise a series of deep, wooded rifts which cut across a range of coastal hills. The most distinctive is Glenariff, which extends 5 miles inland from Waterfoot and includes attractive waterfalls.

ROUTE DIRECTIONS

The drive starts at Larne ①.

From Larne follow SP 'Coastal Route, Glenarm' to leave by the A2 along the Antrim Coast Road ②. In 1¾ miles pass through Black Cave Tunnel to drive along Drains Bay and Carnfunnock Country Park, then round the 92m-high Ballygalley Head, in 2½ miles reaching Ballygalley ③. Continue along the coast for another 6 miles to enjoy lovely hill and sea views before reaching Glenarm ④, a village on the Glenarm River at the head of one of the nine Glens of Antrim ⑤. Leave the village by following SP 'Carnlough' and cross the Glenarm River, then continue along the coast to Carnlough ⑥. On leaving Carnlough pass beneath a stone arch, with the harbour to the right, following SP 'Cushendall, Waterfoot'. In 4 miles pass Garron Point Post Office, where Garron Point itself towers above the road and offers views which extend to the Scottish coast.

Veer west with the road to follow the shoreline of Red Bay. After 4½ miles reach Waterfoot. Drive to the end of the village, cross the Glenariff River, and at T-junction turn left on to the A43 SP 'Glenariff Forest Park, Cargan, Ballymena'. Begin the ascent to Glenariff ⑦. Keep the Glenariff River on the left and wind along the cultivated, tree-shrouded slopes of Lurigethan Mountain (349m) which rises to the right. This road afford fine views across the glen to the left, and to imposing cliffs with several waterfalls on the right. After 2 miles pass the entrance to Glenariff Forest Park on the left. Parkmore Forest is later seen to the right, and north of this is Trostan Mountain, at 554m the highest of the Antrim Hills. Proceed through rugged hill country with views of Cargan Water to the right, then descend to reach the village of Cargan. After 2½ miles of tree-lined road, drive through Martinstown, cross the Clogh River, and after another 2 miles (at crossroads) turn left B94 SP 'Broughshane'. Continue through undulating countryside for 4 miles, then enter Broughshane and cross the Braid River. In 1/4 mile turn left B94 'Ballyclare' and next turn right B94, again SP 'Ballyclare'.

Drive through pleasant, hilly country along a stretch of road which affords views of Slemish Mountain (438m) to the left, then after 6 miles at crossroads turn left A36 SP 'Larne'. Follow the valley of the Glenwhirry River and in 1¾ miles bear right. In ¾ mile cross the Glenwhirry River. Ascend through hilly countryside with fine views of the river, now on the left. In 1½ miles reach Ballyboley Forest. Beyond the forest climb for a short distance and attain the 309m Shane's Hill summit, then descend with bleak moorland on the left, the fertile 6-mile Water Valley lying to the right. Later pass the Kilwaughter House Hotel, and in 1 mile further turn left on to the A8 for the return to Larne.

POINTS OF INTEREST

① The Chaine Memorial Tower and the 13th-century Olderfleet Castle can be found in Larne, from which Scotland is visible on a clear day.
② The Antrim Coast Road runs from Larne to Cushendall. It was built in the 1830s and helped to ease suffering in the area from the potato famine.
③ The fine fortified manor house in Ballygalley village is now a hotel.
④ The chief attraction of Glenarm is the beautiful park and glen adjoining its imposing castle, built in 1636 but subsequently altered.
⑤ Some parts of the nine Glens of Antrim are still inaccessible to cars, and the hills contain nature reserves, indigenous forests and waterfalls.
⑥ Carnlough is beautifully situated at the foot of Glencloy – famous for its waterfalls – and features one of the mesolithic raised beaches for which this coast is famous.
⑦ Glenariff is often considered the most beautiful of the nine glens. A particularly attractive feature is the contrast between the green cultivated land and the black basalt cliffs.

Ballygalley Head, Co Antrim ▼

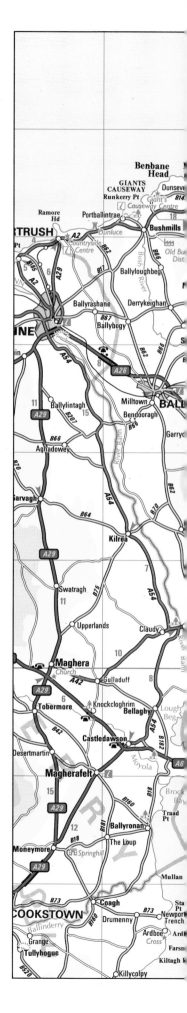

TOUR 3

THE LOWER ERNE SHORELINE

On its hilly island, Enniskillen, Fermanagh's county town, stands at the narrows where Erne's two loughs, the Upper and the Lower, meet. Head north and loop around one of Ireland's most beautiful lakes, its shores dotted with enigmatic heads of stone.

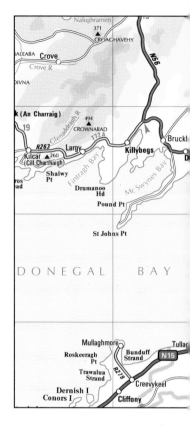

ROUTE DIRECTIONS

The drive starts at Enniskillen ①.

From Enniskillen follow SP 'Omagh' to leave the town on the A32. In 3¼ miles branch left on to the B82 SP 'Kesh' and pass the road to Devenish Island ②. After another 1½ miles pass Ballycassidy Post Office and cross the Ballymallard River via a hump-backed bridge. Beyond this the road offers a fine view over the island-studded waters of Lower Lough Erne. Continue through the small angling centre of Killadeas and follow the wooded shores of the attractive Rossclare Bay and the entrance to Castle Archdale Country Park ③. After a further 1 mile pass the road to Rossigh Bay Picnic Area on the left.

Continue through the village of Lisnarrick and in 1 mile turn left on to an unclassified road SP 'Kesh, Scenic Route', passing the entrance to Castle Archdale Forest Recreational Area, Loughshore Paths and Picnic Areas on the way. Ascend through part of Castle Archdale Forest and reach a stretch of road which offers further excellent views of Lough Erne. Drive through more open, undulating countryside, still with views of the lough. In 3½ miles at T-junction turn left SP 'Kesh' and proceed to the cruising and angling centre of Kesh village, then turn left on to the A35, cross the Kesh River and pass SP 'Muckross Quay Recreation Area'. In a further ¾ mile turn left A47 SP 'Boa Island, Belleek' to pass through pleasant scenery alongside the north shore of Lower Lough Erne. In 2¼ miles cross a bridge on to narrow Boa Island, the largest of many islands in the lough, in 2 miles pass the ferry point to Lusty Beg Island, and in another 2¾ miles cross over to the mainland.

In ½ mile bear left SP 'Belleek', and in 3¼ miles pass the entrance to Castle Caldwell Forest Recreation Area and Wildlife Park (left) ④. Continue to Belleek ⑤, then leave this small town on the A46 SP 'Enniskillen' to cross the River Erne. After ¼ mile follow SP 'Garrison, Forest Drive' on to the B52.

Ascend, and in 1¼ miles turn left on to an unclassified road SP 'Derrygonnelly, Forest Drive'. Continue through barren, hilly countryside with distant views of Lough Navar Forest and Corral Glen Forest ahead, plus Big Dog Forest to the right. After 5 miles join an occasionally tree-lined road, and in 3¼ miles pass the Lough Navar

Forestry Office and then (at 4 miles) the entrance to the circular Lough Navar Forest Drive. The latter offers an interesting diversion from the main drive and visits two viewpoints, the first at Aghameelan with Picnic Area and Walks, and the second at Magho Cliffs. The magnificent panorama includes Lough Erne, the distant Donegal Hills and far-off Donegal Bay on the west coast. The signposted return follows a descent past Lough Achork with picnic area and walks and rejoins the main road, where a left turn is made, SP 'Enniskillen', to complete the circuit, and once again pass the forestry office. A road opposite the entrance to the Forest Drive leads into wooded Glen Corral.

Continue along the unclassified road which forms part of the main route, and in ¾ mile pass picturesque little Carrick Lough. Follow SP 'Lough Erne', then in 4 miles meet a T-junction and turn right on to the A46 SP 'Enniskillen'. In 1 mile pass the road to Camagh Bay on the left, then after another 1½ miles pass the track to Carrickreagh Viewpoint on the right. Skirt the shore of Lower Lough Erne and pass the entrance to Ely Lodge Forest Loughshore Trail, car-park and picnic area on the left, then drive through part of the Ely Lodge Forest. Later, pass a road leading right to Monea Castle ruins ⑥, and continue along the A46 for the return to Enniskillen. Portora Royal School can be seen on the hill before the route enters the town.

POINTS OF INTEREST

① Enniskillen is an island town strategically sited in the River Erne between Upper and Lower Lough Erne. Its position has made it of great military importance for hundreds of years and as such it has been the centre of numerous battles and the site of several castles.
② Situated in beautiful Lough Erne, Devenish Island boasts one of the most complete monastic settlements in Ireland. St Molaise first founded a monastery here in the 6th century, and the small, rectangular oratory which carries his name is typical of many such structures built by the early-Irish church. Other interesting remains to be seen on the island (which can be reached by passenger ferry) include the Great Church and an 85ft round tower of 12th-century date.
③ Castle Archdale Country Park is a

popular spot for camping and caravanning, and is also a centre for boat hire.
④ Next to Castle Caldwell Recreation Area and Wildlife Park is the 18th-century Fiddle Stone, which carries a curious inscription. The castle which gives its name to the park was one of the numerous Plantation structures which dot the shores of Lough Erne.
⑤ Belleek is known throughout the world for its delicate pottery, particularly the basketwork designs which are woven from strands of china.
⑥ Monea Castle is a remarkable well-preserved 17th-century fortification set back from Lower Lough Erne.

OPTIONAL CROSS-BORDER DRIVE

Along the shores of Lough Melvin and Lower Lough Erne. 71 miles.
From Enniskillen follow signs Sligo A4. In 2¾ miles the A32 on the left leads to Florence Court (5 miles – see page 90) and Marble Arch Caves (9 miles – see also page 90). Continue with the A4 to Belcoo and then cross the border on the N16 to reach Glenfarne. Turn right on to the R281 and continue via Kiltyclogher to Rossinver. At crossroads turn right; then in ¾ mile turn left shortly, alongside Lough Melvin. In 6¼ miles branch right to reach Kinlough. Turn right on the R280 to Bundoran. Turn right again to reach Ballyshannon. On the nearside of the River Erne turn right on the R230 and later cross the border to the edge of Belleek. Keep forward on the A46 and later pass alongside the southern shore of Lower Lough Erne for the return to Enniskillen.

TOUR 4

THROUGH THE MOURNE MOUNTAINS

A dozen summits top the Mournes, nestling beside the sea in south-east Co Down. Ringed by scenic roads, just one route runs right through them past lakes, streams and dry-stone walls. Newcastle, where the mountains sweep down to the sea, is the start of the tour.

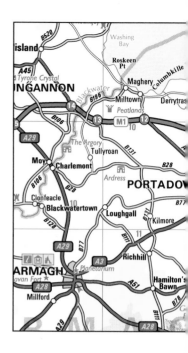

ROUTE DIRECTIONS

The drive starts at Newcastle ①.

Leave Newcastle with SP 'Bryansford'. After 1½ miles pass the Tollymore Forest Park entrance, then in ½ mile meet a T-junction and turn left. In a further ½ mile follow SP 'Hilltown' through Bryansford and pass Tollymore Forest Park below the Mourne Mountains ②. After ¾ mile pass Moneyscalp Road and in ½ mile pass the entrance to the Northern Ireland Mountain Centre (left), with Moneyscalp (246m) on the right. Gradually ascend with further summits on the left and views of Lough Island Reavy below Tullynasoo Mountain (279m) on the right. After several miles reach a 204m summit and descend along the Kinnahalla Valley, then after 1½ miles pass the road to Goward Dolmen (AM) on the right. Views to the left extend across the upper Bann Valley to Hen (360m) and Cock (505m). In ½ mile turn right on to the B27 SP 'Hilltown', and in 1 mile turn left on to the B8. Shortly, cross the River Bann to enter Hilltown, then continue on the B8 SP 'Newry'. After 1½ miles bear right and continue the ascent for ¾ mile, then descend into Mayobridge. At crossroads turn left on to the B7 SP 'Warrenpoint', then climb through hilly country beneath Craignamona (286m) and Slieveacarnane (295m). Descend and in 3½ miles pass through the unsignposted village of Burren. After another 1 mile, turn left at crossroads SP 'Warrenpoint'. After 1½ miles turn left A2 Warrenpoint. The Carlingford Mountains rise to over 460m on the south side of Carlingford Lough. Follow SP 'Kilkeel' through Warrenpoint. Proceed along the lough shores with mountain views to the right and Kilbroney Forest on the slopes of Slievemartin (487m) ahead. After 1 mile cross the Moygannon River, and in a further 1 mile cross the Ghann River into Rostrevor.

Here the main drive route keeps straight ahead with SP 'Hilltown B25', and in ½ mile branches right on to an unclassified road SP 'Spelga Dam' before crossing the Kilbroney River in ½ mile. Climb the Kilbroney Valley, with part of Kilbroney Forest ahead and to the right; Leckan More (351m) rises to the left. After 1¾ miles cross a bridge and enter the forest. In 1½ miles pass a picnic area on the right and reach a 205m summit.

Gradually descend along the valley of Shanky's River, with views of Rocky Mountain (402m) ahead, and after 1½ miles pass a picnic area to a fork and bear right SP 'Spelga Dam'. Pass Rocky Mountain on the right and in 1¼ miles cross the Rocky River to a further picnic site. In ¾ mile cross the River Bann, meet crossroads, and turn right on to the B27 SP 'Spelga Dam, Kilkeel'. Follow the River Bann past Hen Mountain and the wooded lower slopes of Kinnahalla, then ascend steeply (1 in 10) into barren country between Spelga (454m) and Cock Mountain. This section of the road is part of the Spelga Pass hillclimb route. Shortly, reach the edge of the Spelga Dam reservoir, with some of the higher points in the Mourne range ahead. In ¾ mile at a T-junction turn right, SP 'Kilkeel, Silent Valley' to continue at over 380m above sea level.

In ¾ mile cross the infant River Bann, then pass between Slieve Muck and Pigeon Rock Mountain (531m) towards 'Kilkeel'. After 1¾ miles skirt a small forest, with picnic area on the right, and in another 1½ miles branch right on to an unclassified road, SP 'Attical'. Descend through agricultural country, and in ¾ mile reach the small village of Attical. After another ½ mile cross the White Water River, with Finlieve (573m) ahead and the wooded slopes of Knockchree (306m) on the left. Follow the White Water past Knockchree and the woods of the Mourne Park Estate, then continue the descent with some views of Carlingford Lough to the right. At T-junction, turn right A2 SP 'Warrenpoint', and in 1½ miles turn sharp left on to the unclassified 'Cranfield' road. Skirt Mill Bay with views of the Carlingford Mountains, and the sturdy remains of Greencastle (right). In a further 2½ miles cross the White Water bridge, then at crossroads turn left SP 'Kilkeel'. In ¾ mile bear left then turn right. In ½ mile at a T-junction turn left to proceed to Kilkeel. Enter this town and follow SP 'Newcastle' to join the A2. The road to the right leads to Kilkeel Harbour. Reach the end of the town, cross the Kilkeel River, and in ¼ mile pass an unclassified road on the left leading to the Silent Valley reservoirs ③, situated deep in the Mourne range. The lower reservoir lies to the left of Slieve Binnian (743m).

In 1¾ miles pass through Ballymartin, descend almost to the shore, then after 2 miles (from Ballymartin) enter the straggling fishing village of Annalong ④. In 1 mile pass the harbour and a marina park (right). Cross the Annalong River and continue along the A2 with views of Slieve Binnian to the left and Chimney Rock Mountain (653m) ahead. Follow the coastline, with views across Dundrum Bay to St John's Point, and after 4 miles (from Annalong) cross Bloody Bridge ⑤. Slieve Donard, the highest of the Mourne Mountains, rises to 852m on the left. Rejoin the cliff edge, and in ¾ mile pass a ravine known as Maggie's Leap ⑥. Beyond this is the edge of extensive Donard Lodge Forest, and to the right are further views over Dundrum Bay. After 1 mile (from Maggie's Leap) pass Newcastle Harbour, and in ¾ mile re-enter the town.

POINTS OF INTEREST

① Newcastle is a pleasant seaside resort which also serves as a centre for hill-walkers visiting the Mournes. The area is surrounded by attractive forest parks which are popular picnic spots.
② The Mourne Mountains were made famous by Percy French's song, and are now extremely popular with walkers as they command excellent views over Co Down and the Republic.
③ The road to Silent Valley is the only one running into the centre of the Mournes. Here you will find parkland and picnic areas.
④ The picturesque fishing village of Annalong is also home to a working corn-mill.
⑤ A massacre took place at Bloody Bridge during the 1641 rebellion.
⑥ Maggie's Leap is a rift in the rocks which a local girl is said to have jumped while being chased by an unwanted admirer.

TOUR 5

INTO JOYCE'S COUNTRY

This is a tour of contrasts; high rocky peaks, low, rolling bogs, windswept Atlantic shores and sheltered seaweed-fringed bays.

ROUTE DIRECTIONS

The drive starts at Clifden ①.

Take the unclassified Sky Road to leave Clifden, and follow the coast of a peninsula which is bounded to the south by Clifden Bay. Climb above the bay to cliff tops, which afford superb island views and Atlantic seascapes. In 4 miles keep right in order to return along the north side of the peninsula, and later follow the shore of Streamstown Bay. This part of the drive gives distant views of the Twelve Pins, the highest of these mountains, Benbaun, rising to 730m. After 3¾ miles turn left on the N59 SP 'Westport' and continue through open moorland, extensively cut for turf. In 1¾ miles bear right to cross more blanket bog, with further views of the Twelve Pins to the right. After another 1¾ miles the views to the left take in Ballynakill Harbour, backed by Tully Mountain (357m). Continue and later drive alongside Barnaderg Bay to reach Letterfrack ②. Leave Letterfrack and continue, with Doughruagh (529m) ahead, before following the valley of the Dawros River and entering the Pass of Kylemore. The late 19th-century Kylemore Abbey ③ is later passed on the left.

Proceed to the attractive shoreline of Kylemore Lough. The stretch after the lough affords views of the Maumturk Mountains to the right. After 3 miles it is possible to catch a glimpse of Lough Fee to the left. Descend to the shores of picturesque Killary Harbour, from which views of the Mweelrea Mountains can be obtained. The rafts in the water are used for growing mussels. The 819m-high Mweelrea dominates the range to which it gives its name and is the highest peak in Connacht. Continue to Leenane ④, which is pleasantly situated near the head of Killary Harbour, and branch right on to the R336 SP 'Maam Cross, Galway'. Cross higher ground for a short distance then gradually descend through moorland scenery to enter the area known as Joyce's Country ⑤. Follow the valley of Joyce's River with the Maumturk Mountains prominent to the right. Continue on the R336 to Maam Bridge, then turn right on to the 'Maam Cross' road. Cross Joyce's River and continue over higher ground with Corcogemore (613m) to the right.

Proceed through open countryside to Maam Cross, and at crossroads go straight on SP 'Casla, Rosmuck, An Cheathrú Rua'. After 5½ miles turn right on to the R340, and continue through lake-studded and afforested moorland, skirting the numerous inlets of the Atlantic Ocean which form a main feature of the South Connemara coast. Partrick Pearse's cottage is on the left at Rosmuck. In 4¾ miles cross a river bridge, then keep left and later follow the west shores of Kilkieran Bay to reach the village of Kilkieran ⑥. Continue with R340 between small, stone-walled fields to the outskirts of Carna, meet a T-junction, and turn right SP 'Cloch na Ron, An Clochán, Glinsce' to turn inland. More views of the Twelve Pins are offered ahead. After 3½ miles rejoin the coast and skirt Bertraghboy Bay.

In a further 4 miles turn left on to the R342 SP 'Cashel, Roundstone', then after 1 mile pass Cashel Bay with its rich orange seaweed-covered boulders. In 4 miles turn left R341 SP 'Roundstone', crossing the Ballynahinch River, famous for its salmon and sea trout, then in 1 mile turn left again. The next section of the route offers extensive coastal views before taking the drive to the little fishing village of Roundstone ⑦. Continue along the Clifden road and skirt Gorteen Bay and Dog's Bay, with Errisbeg (310m) to the right, then Ballyconneely Bay to reach Ballyconneely.

Proceed northwards and shortly pass Mannin Bay with its 'coral' strands, with excellent views of the Twelve Pins ahead. In 3¼ miles pass a track to the right which leads to the spot where famous aviators Alcock and Brown landed after the first transatlantic flight in 1919. A memorial and viewpoint commemorating the event lie ½ mile to the left. In order to complete the drive, cross Ballinaboy Bridge and turn left, then later pass Salt Lake before returning to Clifden.

POINTS OF INTEREST

① Clifden is a picturesque town containing the 1815 Clifden Castle and is within easy reach of white sandy beaches.
② Under the shadow of Diamond Hill (445m), Letterfrack lies next to the Connemara National Park.
③ One of Ireland's last castle houses, Kylemore Abbey is a castellated granite structure. It was built in 1860 for a rich Liverpool merchant and is constructed from stone from Dalkey Quarry, Dublin.
④ Leenane is a lovely village, providing a centre for walkers and fishermen.
⑤ The unofficially named Joyce's Country derives its title from a Welsh family who moved there in the 13th century. Many of the local people count these early settlers as their ancestors.
⑥ A seaweed factory can be found beside the pier in the village of Kilkieran.
⑦ Roundstone is another attractive fishing village which stands on Bertraghboy Bay.

Inishbofin

Inishark

Slyne Head

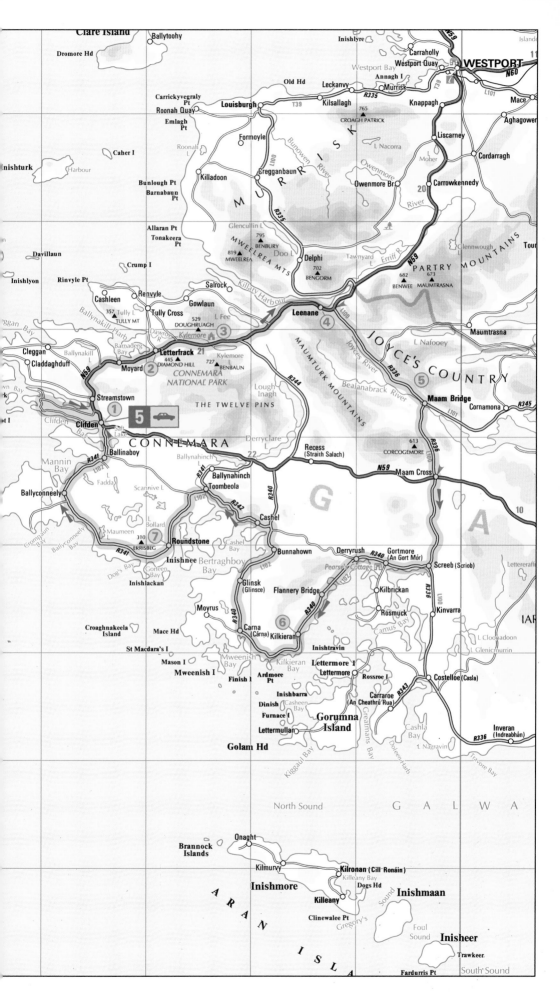

TOUR 6
THE HISTORIC BOYNE VALLEY

In the rich farmland of the Boyne Valley the earliest human settlements in Ireland can be found, along with medieval castles and religious sites.

ROUTE DIRECTIONS

The drive starts at Drogheda ① The scale of mapping used does not allow the inclusion of some minor roads.

Leave central Drogheda via West Street and turn right into George's Street N1 SP 'Dundalk, Belfast'. In 4½ miles turn left SPs 'Monasterboice Abbey, Round Tower' and 'Boyne Drive', and in ½ mile turn left again. In ½ mile pass ruined Monasterboice Abbey ② on the right. Continue with SP 'Mellifont Abbey' and in 1½ miles turn right SP 'Dublin, Drogheda'. In 1 mile turn right SP 'Mellifont Abbey', and in another 1 mile meet a crossroads. Go forward for ¼ mile to ruined Mellifont Abbey ③ beside the Mattock River. Return to the crossroads and turn right. In 1¾ miles at a T-junction turn right and shortly go straight on at a crossroads, SP 'Newgrange' into King William's Glen. In ¾ mile turn right N51 SP 'Slane', beside the River Boyne. In ¾ mile turn left SP 'Dowth', pass Dowth ④ on the left, and in 2½ miles turn left at T-junction SP 'Newgrange'. Pass Newgrange ④ on right and then follow narrow road passing Knowth ④ on left to rejoin N51 SP 'Slane' after 3 miles.

Pass the cottage of the poet Francis Ledwidge on the right, and then after 1¾ miles enter Slane and at a crossroads go straight on with the N51 SP 'Navan'. In 1 mile with the Slane Castle estate on the left, turn right R163 SP 'Kells L17'. In ½ mile turn left, and in 2½ miles meet a T-junction. Turn right SP 'Kells', then in ¼ mile turn left. In 1 mile bear left, and in a further 1 mile reach the village of Kilberry. At a staggered crossroads turn right then immediately left, and in 1 mile drive straight over a level crossing. In 2¼ miles at crossroads go straight on, then in 1½ miles bear right then left through Oristown. In a further 2½ miles cross the River Blackwater and in 1 mile bear right into Kells ⑤. Pass the Headfort Hotel, branch left, then turn right N52 SP 'Mullingar'. In ¼ mile branch left and in a further ¼ mile turn left R164 SP 'Athboy'. In 6½ miles turn right, N51; the left turn leads to Rathmore Church ⑥. In 1¼ miles, on entering Athboy, turn left R154 SP 'Trim' and follow the River Athboy. In 2½ miles bear right and continue to the town of Trim ⑦.

Continue forward, and on meeting a T-junction turn right into the High Street. Cross the River Boyne into the town square, and turn left R154 SP 'Dublin L3'. Pass castle ruins (left) and in ¼ mile bear left to follow the River Boyne. Shortly, turn left (ruined cathedral on the right), cross the Boyne, then turn right R161 SP 'Navan'. After 3 miles turn right SP 'Kilmessan'. Pass ruined Bective Abbey ⑧ on right, recross the Boyne and at crossroads keep forward SP 'Kilmessan'. In 2¼ miles reach the pleasant village of Kilmessan and turn left SP 'Tara, Navan' to cross a river bridge. Keep straight ahead, and in 1 mile turn right SP 'Tara'. Climb towards the ancient royal hill of Tara ⑨, then in ½ mile turn left (turn right for Tara), and in 1 mile cross the N3 SP 'Skreen Cross Church'. After 1½ miles pass Skreen Church and Cross ⑩ on the left, meet crossroads and go forward, then in ½ mile at next crossroads go forward again and later descend. After 2¼ miles reach Edoxtown crossroads and turn left SP 'Drogheda', then in ¾ mile meet more crossroads and drive forward. In ¼ mile bear left SP 'Duleek, Drogheda'.

In 1 mile at crossroads turn left N2 SP 'Slane'. Keep forward for 6¼ miles along the N2 to crossroads and turn right L21 SP 'Donore'. In 1¾ miles pass left turn SP 'Battle of the Boyne' ⑪ (the first of several such SPs). Shortly, bear left (more SPs 'Battle of the Boyne') to reach the Boyne, then in 3¾ miles enter Donore and turn left SP 'Drogheda'. After ¼ mile pass SP 'Battle of the Boyne', bear right and in 2¾ miles re-enter Drogheda.

POINTS OF INTEREST

① Drogheda is a historic town at the mouth of the Boyne, and is now becoming prosperous as a seaport and manufacturing centre.
② Monasterboice Abbey was a monastic site from the 8th century onwards. It is noted especially for its high crosses and the round tower (which may be ascended).
③ The first Cistercian abbey in Ireland, Mellifont Abbey's most striking ruin is the Romanesque lavabo.
④ Brugh na Bóinne, the prehistoric necropolis which includes the huge burial cairns of Dowth, Knowth and Newgrange, is one of the most important prehistoric sites in Europe, dating back some 4,000 or so years. Newgrange is open to the public, with guided tours on offer.
⑤ The quiet country town of Kells was founded in 1193. There is a fine high cross and round tower at nearby Kilree.
⑥ Rathmore Church is a curious 15th-century combination of church and castle, with some interesting tombs of the Plunkett family.
⑦ A principal stronghold of the English Pale in the Middle Ages, Trim is dominated by the huge castle of the de Lacy family. The town and castle were the scene of many battles.
⑧ Bective Abbey was the first daughter house of Mellifont. The ruins date from the 12th to 13th centuries.
⑨ Seat of the early High Kings of Ireland, the ruins of Tara today are extensive but unspectacular.
⑩ The ruined Skreen Church once housed the relics of St Columcille; there are also two fine crosses here.
⑪ The decisive Battle of the Boyne in 1690 confirmed William III's position on the English throne. The Jacobite army, drawn up around Donore, was beaten by the larger Williamite army, part of which crossed the Boyne further west and outflanked the Jacobites.

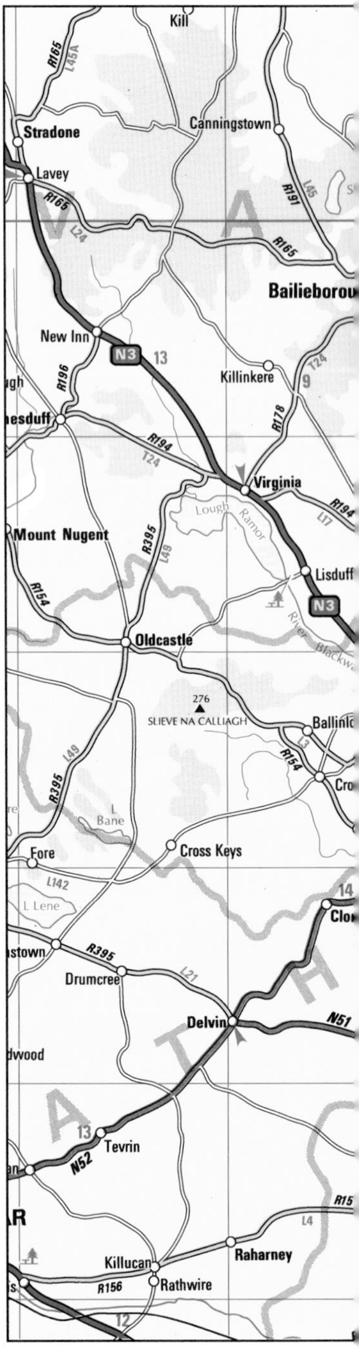

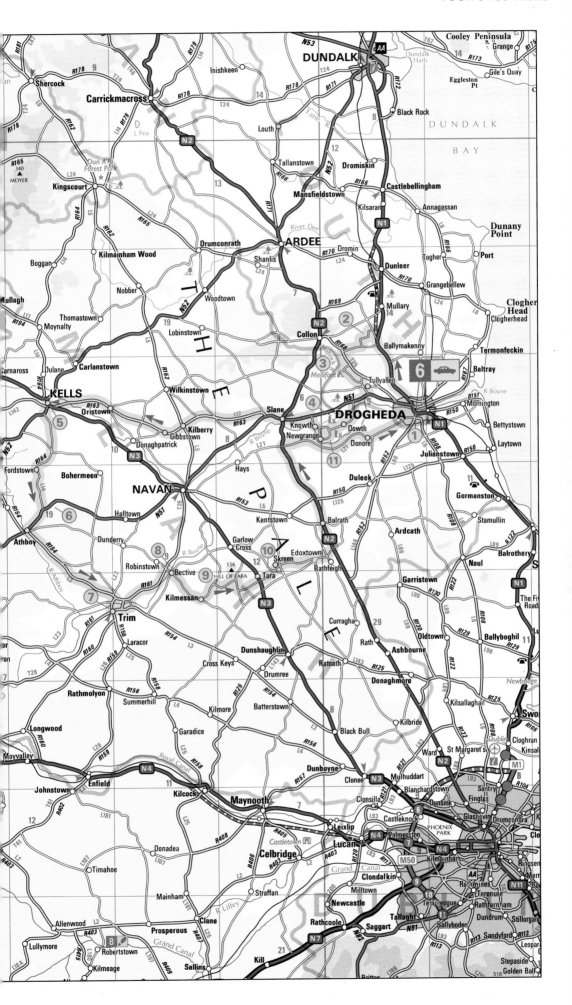

TOUR 7
BURREN LANDSCAPES

This tour explores one of Ireland's most remarkable landscapes, with seemingly bare limestone terraces being host to a unique flora as well as the highest vertical cliffs in Ireland.

ROUTE DIRECTIONS

The drive starts at Ballyvaughan.

Depart from the waterworks fountain in Ballyvaughan with SP 'Lisdoonvarna via coast road' on the R477 and drive along the shores of Ballyvaughan Bay. Pass beneath Cappanawalla (312m) and Gleninagh Mountain (319m), and pass Pinnacle Well on left and Gleninagh Castle on right. After 6 miles round Black Head for views of the Aran Islands. In 1½ miles pass through the tiny village of Fanore, and in a further 2 miles pass Creagach Post Office, right, with Slieve Elva (346m) to the left.

Continue, passing Knockauns (298m) on the left, then after 4 miles (from Creagach) turn inland and ascend with the 15th-century Ballynalackan Castle visible ahead. Galway Bay and the Aran Islands can be seen behind during the climb. After 1¾ miles reach the castle gates and turn right on to the R479 SP 'Doolin'. Pass through farmland with distant forward views of the famous 180m high Cliffs of Moher ①. Descend to Doolin, cross the River Aille, and in ¼ mile turn left SP 'Harbour View B&B'. The road leads to Doolin Strand (1 mile). In 1¼ miles turn right at crossroads on to the R478 SP 'Lahinch'. Ascend with fine views to the right and Knocknalarabana (207m) on the left. After 4½ miles pass a right turn leading to the Cliffs of Moher car-park. Steps from here lead up to the cliff-top O'Brien's Tower ②. After another 1¼ miles along the R478 pass St Bridget's Well and a monument to Cornelius O'Brien on the right. In ¾ mile meet a T-junction and turn left SPs 'Lahinch' then 'Liscannor', then in 1½ miles enter Liscannor on the shores of Liscannor Bay. Continue with the R478 along the shore and in 1 mile pass a fine (but dangerous) beach. Follow SP 'Lahinch', cross the Inagh River by O'Brien's Bridge ③, then skirt Lahinch Championship Golf Course among the sand dunes on the right. At a T-junction, turn right on to the N67 then immediately left into the main street of Lahinch ④. Drive to the church, then turn right, then immediately left SP 'Milltown Malbay'. Ascend and in 1 mile turn right SP 'Milltown Malbay' to continue along the coast road. Proceed through farmland with hilly country to the left and, after 4 miles, views ahead of Mutton Island. After a further 2½ miles turn right into Milltown Malbay, continue to the end of the town, and turn left on to the R474 SP

'Ennis, Inagh'. In 1½ miles turn left at crossroads on to the R460 SP 'Ennis' and follow a winding road. After another 4 miles pass between several loughs as the drive approaches Inagh. Enter the village and turn left on to the N85 SP 'Ennistymon' to follow the valley of the Cullenagh (or Inagh) River. Reach Ennistymon ⑤, proceed through the town and climb on the N67 SP 'Lisdoonvarna', and in 1 mile branch right on to the R481 SP 'Kilfenora' to enter low, hilly country. In 4½ miles enter Kilfenora with the Burren Centre, drive to the end of the village and turn left on to the R476 SP 'Lisdoonvarna'. Climb steadily with views ahead and right of the Burren ⑥ and after about 2 miles pass through bogland. Continue, and in another 1 mile turn right on to the N67 across the Aille River at the spa. Enter the town of Lisdoonvarna ⑦, follow SP 'Galway, Ballyvaughan', and in ¼ mile bear left. In another ½ mile meet a T-junction and turn right SP 'Galway' to follow a narrow road between some walls with rocky fields on both sides. Slieve Elva – the highest point in this area – rises to the left as the route climbs steadily into the heart of the Burren. After 6 miles (from Lisdoonvarna) reach Corkscrew Hill ⑧, descend steeply through hairpin bends, and in 3½ miles re-enter Ballyvaughan.

POINTS OF INTEREST

① The Cliffs of Moher are one of the most outstanding of such features in the British Isles. Composed of dark sandstone, they contain many rare fossil remains.
② O'Brien's Tower was constructed in 1835 to provide a look-out. Magnificent views of the cliff range are afforded from here.
③ The ruins of Kilmacreehy Church and Dough Castle can be found beside O'Brien's Bridge.
④ Lahinch lies on Liscannor Bay and is a popular seaside resort. It was also home to the reputed inventor of the submarine, John Holland.
⑤ The fishing town of Ennistymon was home of the well-known Gaelic poet, Brian Merryman.
⑥ The Burren is a vast, bare karst landscape which is of particular interest to geologists and those seeking out its rare flora.
⑦ Lisdoonvarna is Ireland's main spa resort where the waters are recommended for their health-giving properties.
⑧ Corkscrew Hill offers magnificent views over the Burren and is close to several sites of historic interest.

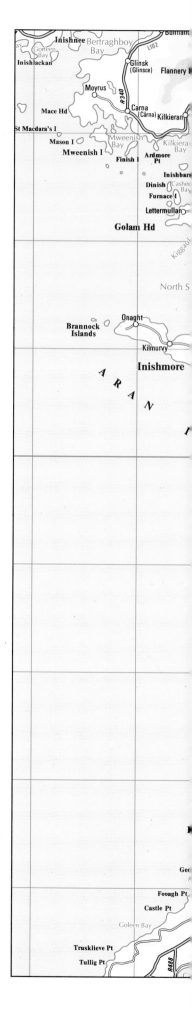

TOUR 8

SEA VIEWS AND THE WICKLOWS

A wide variety of landscape – from attractive shores north of Arklow to wooded valleys and the raw beauty of the Wicklow Mountains – make this a particularly rewarding tour.

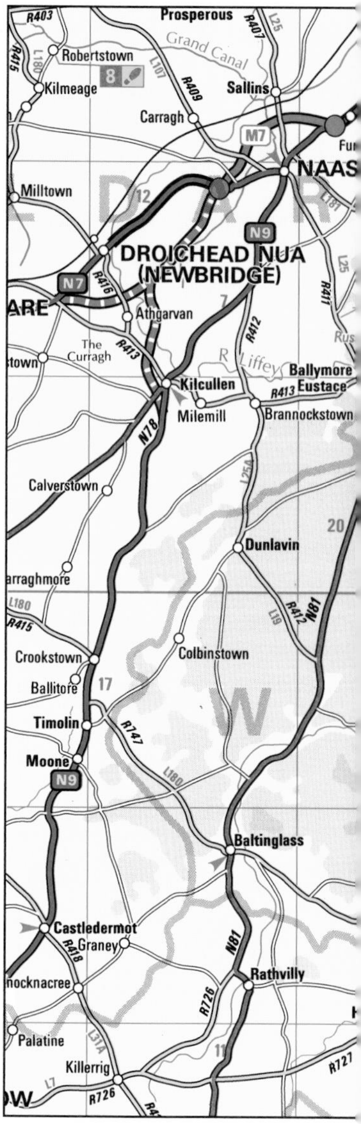

ROUTE DIRECTIONS

The drive starts at Arklow ①.

Leave Arklow's main street to go northward on the N11 SP 'Dublin'. Cross the Avoca River and in ½ mile where the main road swings left, branch right on to the R750 SP 'Brittas Bay'. After 6 miles reach the shores of Brittas Bay ②, and 5 miles further turn right SP 'Coast Road, Silver Strand'. The road follows the coast, then descends into Wicklow town ③. Continue straight ahead through the town. In 2 miles enter Rathnew and bear right on to the N11 SP 'Dublin'. After another 2 miles cross the Vartry River in Ashford ④ and turn left on to the R763 to follow the Vartry Valley. In ¼ mile keep left SP 'Glendalough, Annamoe'. In ½ mile bear left and descend to recross the Vartry River, and 1 mile further bear right SP 'Annamoe, Glendalough' up a steep ascent. In 5 miles descend and turn left on to the R755 to cross the Avonmore River into Annamoe.

Follow a broad main road, with tree-framed views of the Wicklow Mountains, to Laragh ⑤. Bear left across the Glenmacnass River SP 'Laragh, Glendalough'. Turn left with the R755 SP 'Rathdrum' (straight on at this junction leads to Glendalough, see page 74). Bear right SP 'Glenmalure, Rathdrum' and cross a river bridge, then in ½ mile branch right uphill on to an unclassified road SP 'Glenmalure'. Climb to a 377m summit with Kirikee (472m) on the left and Cullentragh (466m) to the right, then descend towards Glenmalure ⑥ with views directly ahead of Lugnaquilla (926m).

Reach the valley bottom, and at the crossroads go forward SP 'Rathdangan, Aghavannagh'. Cross Drumgoff Bridge over the Avonbeg River. Climb through forestry to a 448m summit, with Croaghanmoira (662m) on the left. In 5 miles descend to Aghavannagh and turn left SP 'Aughrim'. In ½ mile bear left uphill. To the left is Croaghanmoira. Ascend a rough narrow road to a 366m summit. In 2 miles descend and meet a crossroads. Go forward SP 'Ballinaclash' and continue the descent into the Avonbeg Valley. After 3 miles, on the outskirts of Ballinaclash, bear right on to a main road. In ¼ mile, in Ballinaclash, turn left on to the R753 SP 'Rathdrum' and cross the Avonbeg River, then turn left again SP 'Rathdrum'. In 1 mile turn right on to an unclassified road, and in ¼ mile go straight across a main road SP 'Avondale House'. After a further ¼ mile bear right; the road

on the left leads to Avondale House ⑦. Follow a ridge between the Avonmore and Avonbeg rivers, then make a steep descent through woodland. Meet a main road at a T-junction, turn left on to the R752 and shortly cross the Avonbeg River where it joins the Avonmore at the Meeting of the Waters.

Enter the Vale of Avoca ⑧. In 2¼ miles reach the edge of Avoca village and turn right SP 'Woodenbridge'. In 2 miles reach Woodenbridge ⑨. At the hotel turn right on to the R747 SP 'Aughrim' and follow the Aughrim River. In 2¼ miles bear left, and after another 1 mile turn left, then right to cross the Aughrim River. In ¼ mile bear right again and in 1¼ miles pass the edge of Aughrim town, SP 'Tinahely, Carnew'. Continue forward with the R747 to follow the Derry Water, in 6½ miles (from Aughrim) meet crossroads and turn left on to an unclassified road SP 'Gorey'. In 3½ miles keep straight on SP 'Gorey'.

Pass through the low Wicklow Gap ⑩ between Croghan Mountain and Annagh Hill (454m), and soon come to crossroads. Turn left SP 'Coolgreany'. The road climbs up and down skirting the southern slopes of Crogham Mountain. At Ballyfad Post Office and church turn left SP 'Coolgreany'. Descend into Coolgreany and turn left SP 'Arklow'. In 1 mile turn right and in another ¼ mile bear left. After 3¼ miles meet a roundabout and bear left to re-enter Arklow.

POINTS OF INTEREST

① Arklow is a seaside resort and fishing port, with a well-known pottery.
② Follow the coast past the low Mizen Head and the long sandy beaches of Brittas Bay, a favourite summer resort for Dubliners and others.
③ The road passes the lighthouse on Wicklow Head before descending into Wicklow town, where the Vartry River enters the sea.
④ Mount Usher Gardens are situated just outside Ashford on the Wicklow road. To the west of Ashford up the Vartry Valley are the woods, gorge and waterfall of the Devil's Glen, and Tiglin Adventure Centre.
⑤ At Laragh the Glenmacnass River flows into the Avonmore. The beautiful valley of Glendalough with its many monastic remains lies 1 mile west.
⑥ The route from Laragh to Aghavannagh follows an old military road which originates in Rathfarnham in Dublin. Through Glenmalure flows

the Avonbeg River which rises on the slopes of Lugnaquilla (923m), Wicklow's highest mountain.
⑦ Avondale House was the home of Charles Stewart Parnell, and is now a State Forest Park.
⑧ The Avonbeg River joins the Avonmore at the Meeting of the Waters, made famous in song by Tom Moore. The united rivers take the name of Avoca to flow through the Vale of Avoca to Arklow. On the eastern slopes of the Vale is the mansion of Castle Howard. The remains of a formerly extensive copper, lead and zinc mine can also be seen.
⑨ At Woodenbridge the Aughrim River, which rises below Lugnaquilla as the Ow and flows through Aghavannagh and Aughrim, meets the Avoca, and is joined by the Goldmines River.
⑩ From Woodenbridge to Arklow the route describes a partial circuit of Croghan Mountain (604m), a southern outlier of the Wicklow Mountains. The descent toward Arklow gives fine views of the coast and neighbouring low hills.

TOUR 9

THE DINGLE PENINSULA

The Dingle Peninsula is rich in sites of archaeological interest. It is also a Gaeltacht (Gaelic-speaking area) hence most of the road signs west of Dingle town are in Gaelic. (Many villages have no name signs on entering.) Some claim the Dingle peninsula to be the most beautiful part of Ireland.

ROUTE DIRECTIONS

The drive starts at Tralee ①.

Leave the Mall by turning left into Bridge Street. Follow SP 'Dingle (N86)' along Prince's Quay and turn right to drive between the ship canal (right) and the River Lee and narrow gauge railway (left), turning left over the river into Blennerville with its restored windmill which is in working order.

Follow the R559 (T86), with the Slieve Mish Mountains on the left, then, after a considerable distance, pass through Stradbally village. Bear left 2 miles beyond for the Connor Pass and Dingle, first crossing the end of the deep Glennahoo Valley, then climbing steeply from the Owenmore River valley to the upper slopes of Slievanea (617m). As the road climbs, many small loughs come into view in the valley below with Brandon Mountain and its paternoster lakes further north. On a sharp bend a small waterfall provides a high outlet for tiny Lough Doon.

After reaching the dramatic summit of the 454m Connor Pass, a long descent gives panoramic views across Dingle Bay to the Iveragh peninsula. On entering Dingle, turn left, then immediately right, and proceed to the roundabout, taking the second exit to go round by the harbour with its marina. After ¾ mile turn left across the Milltown River. The route now follows the brown 'Slea Head Drive' or 'Ceann Sléibhe' signs. Dingle Harbour is visible on the left.

As the road swings north-west towards Ventry, Mount Eagle (514m) rises beyond Ventry Harbour and its beach. Go through Ventry and rejoin the coast after 3¼ miles. Dunbeg Promontory Fort is on a small headland on the left; about 1 mile beyond, on a sharp bend, Glenfahan Stream runs over the road on cobblestones. Continue above the sea through Fahan ②, then drive around Slea Head, high above the shore and below Mount Eagle with the Blasket Islands coming into view.

In another mile pass above Coumeenoole Strand and behind Dunmore Head before returning to the coast. Continue through Dún Chaoin (Dunquin) ③ and pass Clogher Head on the left 1½ miles on, with views ahead across a small bay to Sybil Point and the pointed bumps of The Three Sisters. After 2½ miles drive through Baile an Fheirtéaraigh (Ballyferriter) and 3 miles beyond,

where the main road turns left, the road to the right leads to the Gallarus Oratory ④. A further mile on enter An Mhuiríoch (Murreagh), turn right and continue for 2¾ miles, passing the Raidio na Gaeltachta transmitter and then views of Dooneen Cliffs (both on the left) to An Fheothanach (Feohanagh). In Feohanagh turn sharply left SP 'Brandon Creek, Cuais'. With Ballydavid Head on the left continue to a crossroads. The road to the left leads to Brandon Creek ⑤. Turn right and with the Brandon Mountains on the left continue straight on to drive along the Milltown River valley towards Dingle Harbour. In 4 miles (having completed the Slea Head Drive) turn left at Milltown into Dingle ⑥ by the main street. Follow the one-way system, turning right, then left and bearing right to the roundabout.

Take the Tralee exit at the roundabout (R559). Ascend gradually for several miles, then descend to cross a wide valley surrounding a coastal inlet. About 5½ miles from Tralee drive through Lispole and follow a long winding stretch of road to the edge of Anascaul. Before entering the village turn right on to R561 for Inch Strand, following the Owenascaul River between high hills. Meet the coast and drive along the Red Cliffs with views of Dingle Bay and the mountains on the Iveragh peninsula to the right. The Inch peninsula, with its fine sandy beach extending 3 miles into the estuary, lies ahead.

Pass through the village of Inch at the base of the peninsula, then bear right for Castlemaine. Shortly, drive close to the shores of Castlemaine Harbour, with the Slieve Mish Mountains on the left. Continue to Castlemaine and turn left on to the N70 for Tralee.

In 1 mile turn left on to an unclassified road SP 'Viewing Point'. Drive up this narrow mountain road for 2½ miles to reach a car-park and a 302m viewpoint. The Maine Valley, Castlemaine Harbour, and the Laune Valley as far as Killarney and the Macgillicuddy's Reeks can be identified. From a second car-park a short distance on, the views north include Tralee Bay, Tralee town and the Stack's Mountains. Descend to a crossroads and keep straight on. In 4 miles at a T-junction turn left on to the N70 for Tralee. After ¾ mile turn left into Castle Street and drive into the town centre.

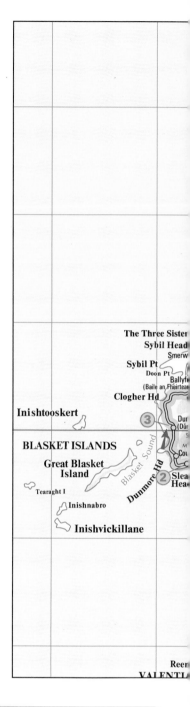

POINTS OF INTEREST

① The elegant and historic town of Tralee serves as a base for walkers travelling in the Dingle Peninsula.
② At Fahan you will find the sites of about 400 stone beehive huts, known as clocháns, some of which are indicated and can be visited.
③ Dún Chaoin (Dunquin) is claimed to be Europe's most westerly place of habitation.
④ The ancient Gallarus Oratory (see page 71) is the only perfect example of its kind in Ireland.
⑤ Brandon Creek is the point from where St Brendan the Navigator is reputed to have set sail for America long before Christopher Columbus.
⑥ The small town of Dingle lies in a breath-taking landscape and is a centre for Gaelic students who come to visit the Gaeltacht.

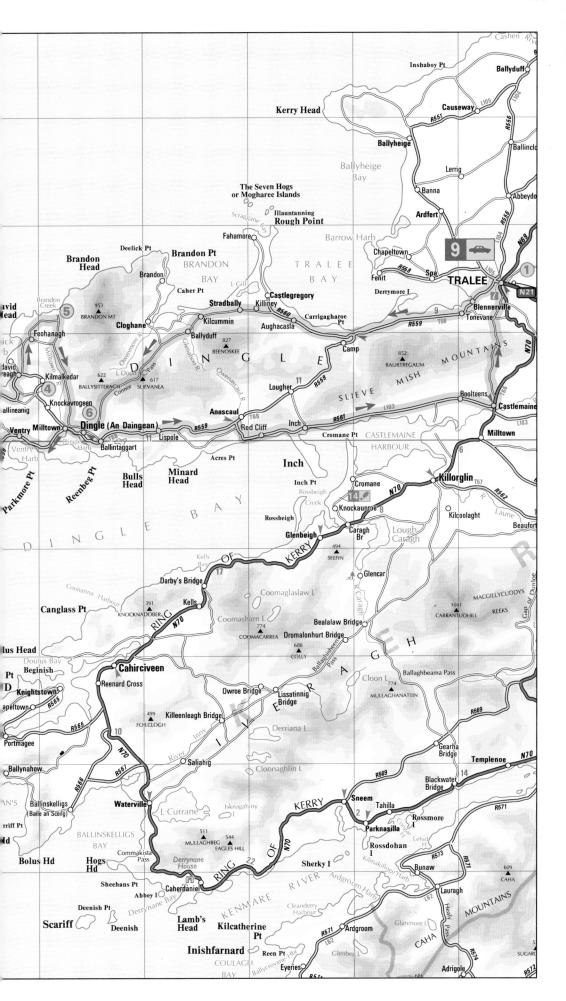

TOUR 10

RIVERS AND VALLEYS, MOUNTAINS AND THE SEA

Beginning and ending in the thriving market town of Dungarvan, this tour takes you through spectacular scenery and past historic towns along the coast, along river valleys, and through two mountain ranges.

ROUTE DIRECTIONS

The drive starts from the square in Dungarvan ①.

From the square follow signs to Cork to join N25, the main Waterford–Cork route. The N25 climbs to heights overlooking panoramic views of the harbour, then dips through a gap in the Drum Hills. (After 9 miles consider an interesting 6 mile side trip, turning left on to the R673, SP 'Ardmore' ②.) Continue on N25 another 7½ miles, with good views of Youghal Bay, cross the River Blackwater to an unclassified road turning right SPs 'Cappoquin', 'Lismore' and 'Blackwater Valley Scenic Route', 2 miles outside the historic fishing town of Youghal ③.

Follow the Blackwater, and after 1½ miles pass Templemichael Burial Ground and ruined castle (unmarked) on right. In another ½ mile, pass gates to ruined Molana Abbey on right. In about 1 mile bear right to follow SP 'Scenic Route', through a small valley, climb past Carnglass Wood (right), then Strancally Wood ④ on the left to a T-junction and turn right SP 'Cappoquin', 'Lismore'. Cross the River Bride, and continue above the Blackwater, where Killahaly Wood (left) faces Dromana Forest across the river. Follow SP 'Scenic Drive', with good views of Knockmealdown Mountains, to junction at Killahaly Wood entrance on left. Continue straight for 4 miles to historic Lismore ⑤.

At monument in town centre, turn right SP 'Clogheen', 'The Vee' and cross the Blackwater. Take second left turn on to R668 SP 'Clogheen', 'Cahir', 'The Vee' and continue for 9½ miles through the Owennashad Valley, turning left at T-junction SP 'The Vee' and climbing steadily to The Gap pass ⑥ at a 337m summit of the Knockmealdown Mountains. After a hairpin turn, descend through Bohernagore Wood and a series of sharp bends to the outskirts of Clogheen. Turn sharp right on to unclassified road SP 'Newcastle', and continue for 5¼ miles along the Tar Valley through Goats Bridge to crossroads and follow the River Tar on your left. Continue for 2 miles to T-junction and turn right for 7 miles into Newcastle, set on the southerly bend of the River Suir. Bear right, SP 'Clonmel' and follow signs for 9 miles to outskirts of Clonmel ⑦.

At first roundabout, continue straight, and at second roundabout turn right on to unclassified road SP 'Golf Club', climbing along Comeragh Mountain foothills. After 3¼ miles pass Lyreancarca Wood (right), and in another ¾ mile, turn right SP 'Nier Church' and climb 330m to a layby with good views of the Suir Valley and Comeragh Mountains. Descend towards the Nier Valley to a T-junction, turn right and follow SP 'Comeragh Drive' ⑧, past Nier Wood and crossing the River Nier. Shortly, turn right at junction SP 'Ballymacarbry' and continue for 3 miles to edge of Ballymacarbry ⑨. At crossroads, turn sharp left and climb to 240m. After 5¾ miles, turn left and follow 'Comeragh Drive' signs to SP 'Kilbrien Church' and continue (leaving Comeragh Drive), following SP 'Dungarvan '. Cross the Colligan River and turn left, still SP 'Dungarvan'. In ¾ mile pass through Colligan Wood (park and picnic grounds) and in ½ mile turn left on to R672. In 1 mile turn left on to the N72 and branch right to rejoin R672 for the return to Dungarvan.

POINTS OF INTEREST

① Once an important port and military centre, Dungarvan has an excellent small museum in the 1691 Town Hall, as well as remains of the 1185 castle built by King John.
② Ardmore is noted for its fine 10th- to 14th-century ecclesiastical remains, its perfectly preserved, 97ft round tower, and its long sandy beach.
③ Sir Walter Raleigh first introduced both the potato and tobacco to Ireland in the picturesque fishing harbour and seaside resort of Youghal. Its 1777 clock gate and many of the original city walls are well preserved.
④ Just past Strancally Wood on your right are fine panoramic views of the valley where the tidal rivers Bride and Blackwater meet.
⑤ Lismore was an important monastic settlement from the 7th to 12th centuries. Its majestic castle, built by King John in 1185 on the monastery site and once owned by Sir Walter Raleigh, is still occupied and is floodlit on summer nights. The Cathedral of St Carthach has grave slabs from the 9th and 11th centuries, and the Heritage Centre in the Old Courthouse features an excellent audio-visual town history.
⑥ The Gap, a V-shaped pass through the Knockmealdown Mountains, opens up breath-taking panoramic views of Co Tipperary's Golden Vale and heather-covered mountainsides.
⑦ In 1815, Charles Bianconi began Ireland's first coaching service in Clonmel, once an important garrison town. Its impressive West Gate is a survivor of the original town walls, and its streets are lined with fine traditional shop-fronts.
⑧ The Comeragh Drive climbs and dips, twists and turns through remote wooded mountainsides, mountain pastures dotted with sheep and cattle, and valleys sprinkled with small, traditional farmhouses.
⑨ The little village of Ballymacarbry sits on the slopes of the Comeragh Mountains, where a rough, unclassified road SP 'Knockanaffrin Republican Cottage' leads to the remote mountain cottage where Irish leaders once met to discuss an end to Ireland's bloody Civil War.

▲ Views such as this – looking towards Great Blasket Island from Clogher Strand on the Dingle peninsula – await keen walkers

Walking in Ireland

Ireland possesses some of the finest scenery in Europe, but it is not always easy – or particularly safe – to appreciate it on foot. The following pages contain 15 walks, fairly evenly spread throughout the island, which provide a variety of types of terrain and places of interest. They are of differing levels of difficulty and so will *not* be suitable for all walkers. Please read the following section before embarking on any walk, either in the Republic or in Northern Ireland. If you are at all unsure as to whether you should start a walk, perhaps because you do not have the correct clothing or because you may not have enough time, you are strongly advised not to begin the walk. Do not be beguiled by the majesty of the landscape; mountains can be as dangerous as they are beautiful. It may only take a short walk from the road to escape the hordes, but if anything goes wrong you are equally remote from help. In many parts of Ireland, you are walking in true wilderness country; the island's comparatively small population is reflected in the few people that you will meet, wherever you are.

Walking and the law
That you will not meet many fellow walkers is especially true in the Republic of Ireland. Here, current legislation can mean that if an accident happens on private land, and if negligence is proven, it is the responsibility of the landowner, even if he or she is wholly unaware of anyone walking on his or her

property. This has understandably caused some landowners to discourage the use of their land for recreational purposes which, in turn, has meant that footpaths tend to be few and far between. (Walking for purely recreational purposes is therefore not as widespread as in Great Britain, for example.) There are moves afoot for this law to be repealed, but at the time of publication it still stands and looks set to be in force for some while. In Northern Ireland, however, you will find more footpaths, perhaps better defined, since there is no comparable law to that in operation in the Republic.

Grading the walks
The 15 walks which follow are divided into three distinct categories: easy, moderate and difficult. These categories are determined by assessing a number of factors; ease of navigation, the distance of the walk, the terrain covered and the amount of climbing involved. Because a walk is classified as easy, it does not mean that is necessarily short. Similarly, a difficult walk is not necessarily long. Walk 15 (Dunboy Castle and Woods) is at present classed as difficult, but improvements are, at the time of publication, being carried out which should ultimately give rise to an 'easy' walk. As a very general rule, it is not recommended that children under 14 years of age tackle any of the difficult walks, nor should children under 8 be taken on the moderate routes.

Precautions
In Ireland, with its maritime – and so fairly mild – climate, the weather can change almost instantaneously as the next weather system, bringing sun or rain, sweeps in from the Atlantic. Accordingly, you should set out on even the easiest of walks equipped for every eventuality. Waterproof (not simply showerproof) clothing and stout shoes (preferably boots) are essentials wherever you are walking. On higher or boggier ground – and Ireland has more than its fair share of both – proper waxed walking boots and a small supply of provisions are also imperative. For all walks you should tell somebody of the route you intend to follow and the time you intend to finish. If you do not appear at the prearranged time, the alarm can then be raised. For similar reasons, walking on your own is not advised. Be aware of what time darkness falls and only set out if you are sure you can easily complete the walk before nightfall. If the walk includes a stretch on the shore, make certain that there is no possibility of being cut off by the incoming tide. Do not stray from the path; it is probable that you will be trespassing.

Further information
For further information on walking in Ireland, refer to the walking section of the Fact File, on page 110, or contact the Northern Ireland Tourist Board or Bord Fáilte (Irish Tourist Board).

WALK 1

STRANDS AND DONKEYS IN DONEGAL

A walk which meanders along a twisty little lane, used more by cattle than cars, running between old stone walls. For much of its length, the walk follows a strand of clean golden sand washed by Atlantic breakers. The sea views are particularly fine on a clear day.

ROUTE DIRECTIONS

5 miles. Allow 2 hours.
Start at the lay-by at Edward Mullen's shop opposite the Cove Restaurant, 1½ miles east of Dunfanaghy (in north Co Donegal) and 18 miles north-west of Letterkenny (grid ref: C004307). Easy.

From the lay-by take the road (N56) uphill for a few hundred yards ①, then turn left at SP 'Scenic Route' ②. This quiet road through typical Donegal coastal scenery forms the majority of this simple walk; follow the road as it goes down to the shore, skirts the cove ③ and then eventually rejoins the N56 road. Here, turn right and follow the main road back to your car, and the start of the route.

POINTS OF INTEREST

① Co Donegal in general, and the area of this walk in particular, is a beautiful land of mountains, lakes and sea loughs, although the traditional picture of thatched cottages with stacks of turf propping up the gables is largely a thing of the past. Nevertheless, it still possesses a unique atmosphere where people have time to stop and talk to walkers, or simply pass the time of day. Like the 'leafy lanes of County Down', the little roads of Co Donegal 'go winding here and there, and none can tell you where they go and no one seems to care'. It is inevitable, however, that some of those roads have been widened and straightened, and that the houses now have electricity.
② The road to Marble Hill is small and narrow, with twists and turns giving different views every minute. It rises and dips with small farmsteads here and there. In front are lovely views of Sheep Haven, one of Donegal's most attractive sea loughs. Beyond lies the peninsula of Rossguill and to the left is the massive Horn Head. As you meander along the lane the chances are that you will see a donkey or two poking its head over the bars of a gate.
③ The road meets the sea at Marble Hill Beach, a beautiful stretch of sand that is aptly named. A map of the area is mounted on a board. There is also a notice which refers to the regular analysis of water quality, although this hardly seems necessary.

▲ The scenery on this walk is typical of the remote beauty of Co Donegal

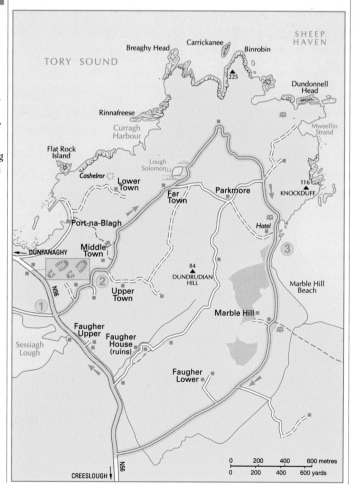

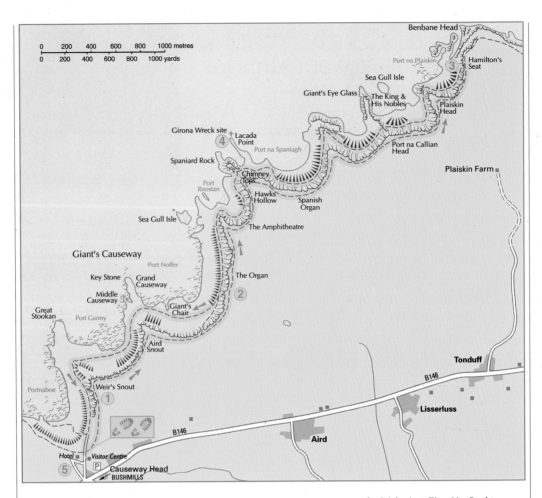

WALK 2

GIANT'S CAUSEWAY
AND CLIFF PATH

A walk which includes both the spectacular Giant's Causeway, one of Europe's finest geological sites, and the magnificent cliffs of the Antrim coast. The area has been designated a World Heritage Site.

ROUTE DIRECTIONS

5 miles. Allow 3½ hours.
Start at the Causeway car-park
7 miles east of Portrush (grid ref: C945439). Moderate.

Enter the visitors' centre and pass through to the open ground overlooking the sea. Take the cliff path on the right (signposted). In wet weather this path may be muddy so strong shoes are recommended, and when strong winds are blowing special care is necessary in places. At Weir's Snout and Aird's Snout, a little further along, excellent views are provided of the cliffs and the causeway below ①. A ¼ mile further on, a path (the Shepherd's Path) leads off to the left and descends to the shore by a series of steps. Do not take this, but instead continue on along the cliff path ② for about another 2 miles as far as Hamilton's Seat (signposted) ③. Here, take the path on the left which descends to the shore. Follow this path to the Grand Causeway and then take the wide, clear path leading back to the visitors' centre.

POINTS OF INTEREST

① To most people it is the extraordinary rock formations of the Giant's Causeway which are the chief attraction, but the whole area is rich in history and legend, being of interest to botanists, ornithologists and wildlife lovers in general. Geologists explain that the causeway is the result of volcanic action; the area was covered by a sheet of lava which, as it cooled, formed the curious basalt columns, numbering in all over 37,000. There were in fact several outflows of lava, separated by a period in which there was an almost Mediterranean climate. The different flows can be seen as dark red bands in the cliffs. Local people of course know better, and will tell you that the Causeway was built by the Irish giant Finn MacCool to enable him to get at a Scottish giant on the (now uninhabited) island of Staffa in the Hebrides, where there is a smaller version of the causeway.
② From the cliff path numbers of fulmar petrels may be seen gliding around on the rising air currents. Rock doves are common and occasionally gannets may be seen diving spectacularly into the sea for fish. Plants such as sea spleenwort, red broomrape and frog orchids can also be found.
③ Coming along the path from Hamilton's Seat, sections of the rock formations have been given individual names, including: the king and his nobles; Lord Antrim's parlour; the Spanish organ; and the chimney tops.
④ At Port na Spaniagh, the *Girona*, the largest ship of the Spanish Armada, was wrecked on 26 October 1588 with the loss of as many as 1,300 lives. The ship contained not only its own treasures but those of two other ships wrecked on the west coast of Ireland. About 10,000 objects were recovered in 1967 and 1968, and these are now on display in the Ulster Museum in Belfast.
⑤ In the visitors' centre, the National Trust has a café and shop. Video shows are screened in the theatre to describe the scenery, and to explain the causeway and its formation. There are also many models, maps and diagrams of the surrounding area.

WALK 3

GORTIN GLEN FOREST AND THE ULSTER HISTORY PARK

An enjoyable walk along paths through a conifer forest and beside a mountain stream, with a visit to the remarkable history park.

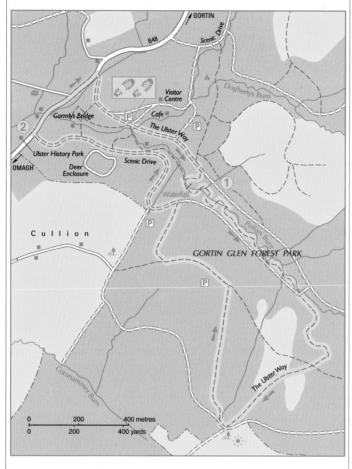

▲ ...at The Ulster History Park

times by rustic bridges. Continue to follow the Ulster Way signs until the tarmacadamed Scenic Drive is reached. Turn left, following the blue arrow and Ulster Way up through the forest. On reaching the forest drive, turn right, then soon left up through the forest to the Ladies' Viewpoint, with a wide panorama over the forest and hills beyond, including the hills named Mary Gray and Bessie Bell, hence the name of the viewpoint.

At this viewpoint take the path SP 'Ladies View Trail', which runs down through the trees to a forest road. Turn left at the road and follow it down to join the Scenic Drive once more. Turn right and keep to this road to join the B48 main road. The deer enclosure is passed on the way. To visit the Ulster History Park ② which is almost opposite, turn left – the entrance to the park is then on the right. Return to the Gortin Forest car-park by the B48 and the history park entrance.

POINTS OF INTEREST

① The total area of Gortin Glen Forest is some 3,500 acres, of which roughly half has been planted. The Pollan Burn running through the forest is a most attractive stream. The mammal life of the forest includes hedgehogs, red squirrels, badgers, stoats and sika deer. Birds include redwings, pheasants, treecreepers, goldfinches, kestrels, and long-eared and barn owls.

② The Ulster History Park is of very great interest, both to archaeologists and to the general public. It contains full-size replicas of an ancient Irish round tower (circa AD 900); a crannog (an ancient artificial island built in a lake for protection, with thatched huts lying within a wooden palisade); a Norman motte and bailey castle; a neolithic house; a dolmen; an (original) ogham stone, with its curious writing, found in the area; and many other interesting features. The park is open all year.

ROUTE DIRECTIONS

4½ miles. Allow 2 hours, plus time to explore the history park.
Start from Gortin Glen Forest car-park, 300yd in from the entrance to the park on the Omagh–Gortin road (B48), 6 miles from Omagh (grid ref: H485821). Moderate.

From the car-park, turn down over the small bridge and follow the Ladies View Trail and Pollan Trail. The path runs through Gortin Glen Forest ① along the Pollan Burn. At the waterfall turn off to the right, following the Ulster Way sign, and go down the steps to the bridge. Cross the bridge and continue on up the next set of steps, crossing and recrossing the Pollan Burn several

Traditional Irish buildings on display... ▼

WALK 4

A LOUGHSIDE COASTAL PATH AND GLEN

A walk along the North Down Coastal Path and through a steep-sided glen. The route passes through some glorious countryside rich in wildlife, and a variety of birds and mammals may be seen from the path.

ROUTE DIRECTIONS

4½ miles. Allow 2½ hours (including visits to Crawfordsburn village and the countryside centre).
Start from the car-park (free) near the shore at Helen's Bay, 9 miles north-east of Belfast, (grid ref: J458828). Moderate.

On leaving the car-park, turn right and take the path on the left down to the beach. Follow this path around the bay to the wooded headland at Quarry Point. Continue along the strand at Crawfordsburn Bay. On reaching the stream (Crawford's Burn ①), do not cross the footbridge but take the path to the right. Follow the path along the stream to the car-park and two wooden bridges. Do not cross either of these, but take the small path from the end of the next (stone) bridge. It follows close to the burn to reach a wooden footbridge ②. Cross this and then turn right. Continue along this path until near the railway viaduct, then turn down a path on the right ③. Pass under the viaduct and along the burn until a path comes down sharply on the left. Take this path; after about 350yd another path is met. Turn right, following SP 'Ulster Way', where a narrow zigzag path goes down to the right. Follow this as indicated by an 'Ulster Way' sign. On reaching the path by the burn, turn left and follow this to a wooden footbridge. Cross the bridge and go up the steps to the waterfall ④.
Return back up the zigzag path. Turn left back to SP 'Ulster Way' and left again down to the burn. Cross the footbridge and walk uphill. Turn left at a T-junction and a short distance later take a turning on the right up to the footpath adjacent to a field. Turn left and follow the path to reach Crawfordsburn village. After exploring this attractive village, retrace your steps to the T-junction, then continue straight along the path past a farm. On joining the main drive, turn right down to the car-parks and countryside centre ⑤. Return to your car along the coastal path ⑥.

POINTS OF INTEREST

① Crawfordsburn Glen and the land around it has a fascinating history. The first recorded owners were the monks of the great monastery of Bangor, Co Down, founded by St Comgall in AD 588. The glen and adjoining coastal path are now owned by the Department of the Environment for Northern Ireland.
② Many of the trees here are of interest. Along the path between the stone bridge and the wooden footbridge you can see huge giant western red cedar and Monterey cypress trees. Further on, some of the beech were planted early in the 19th century.
③ Just before passing under the viaduct there is an old salmon pool, originally built as a private fishing pool. Along the stream you may catch sight of a dipper, a dumpy, dark brown bird with a white bib. It walks along the bed of the stream under water in search of food. Foxes, stoats and badgers, and many other birds may be seen. Seals, too, can often be spotted offshore. The 80ft-high viaduct was built in 1865 to extend the railway, which until then had run from Belfast to Holywood, as far as Bangor. This event even caused the railway to change its name from the Belfast and Holywood Railway to the Belfast and Co Down Railway.
④ The stream at the waterfall was used at various times to power a corn-mill, a flax-mill and a saw-mill. Later, it generated electricity to light the house and the waterfall.
⑤ The well-equipped countryside centre houses an exhibition hall, an information counter and the welcome sight of a café.
⑥ On Grey Point, close to the Helen's Bay car-park, is the relic of an old fort used for the defence of Belfast Lough during the two world wars. It has a sister fort on the other side of the lough at Kilroot, and has been partially restored. Containing two huge 6-inch guns and a number of other relics, Grey Point Fort is open to the public from Easter until October.

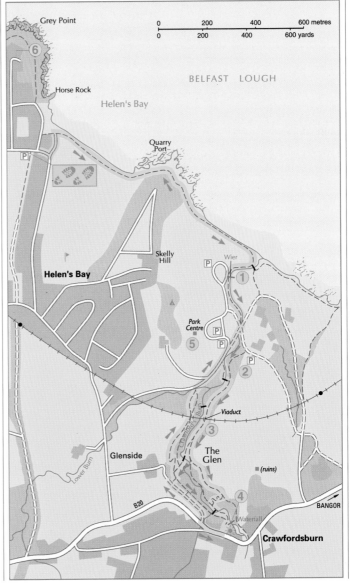

WALK 5

CLADAGH GORGE AND MARBLE ARCH CAVES

A walk up the Cladagh Gorge to the stunning Marble Arch Caves, with their remarkable stalagmites, stalactites and underground lakes below the Cuilcagh Mountains. From the Marble Arch Centre, a quiet, scenic road is taken with wide views over the moors and the lakes.

ROUTE DIRECTIONS

6 miles. Allow 2½ hours plus an additional 1½ hours if the caves are visited.
Start at the parking area (free) at Cladagh Bridge, 3 miles west of Florence Court and 9 miles (as the crow flies) south-west of Enniskillen (grid ref: H128357). A recommended alternative in high season is to start at the caves and book your tour before you begin the walk. Moderate.

From the parking area take the track with the white gates. It follows the Cladagh River into the glen and gorge. Some way up, enter the Marble Arch National Nature Reserve ①. Continue on up the road to the Marble Arch, a natural limestone arch over the river. Go up the series of steps to the visitors' centre ②. Having explored the caves, take the wide road leading up to the Marlbank Scenic Road. Turn right here and follow the road for about 2½ miles to a farm lane on the right, 100yd past a white bungalow on the left. There is a cattle grid at the entrance to the lane. Sections of the lane have been concreted, but in other places a green grassy strip runs down the centre of it ③. At a crossroads the concreted road turns off to the left. Ignore this and carry straight on down a grassy, winding lane. After ¾ mile (from the start of the lane) a group of large, curious boulders on the left marks the remains of an ancient chambered grave.
On reaching the main road, turn right for a few hundred yards back to the car. Make sure that you close all gates behind you.

POINTS OF INTEREST

① The Marble Arch National Nature Reserve has something to interest everyone. As well as containing good examples of ash, there are rowan, birch and hazel trees growing on the limestone. The bird life of the reserve is important and includes, amongst many other species, goldcrests, treecreepers and wagtails. Dippers may also be seen along the river. Both red and grey squirrels, as well as feral goats, may be glimpsed during the walk. A spectacular sight, especially so after a period of heavy rain, is the emergence of a sizeable stream gushing out from the limestone rock.
② These caves were discovered in 1895 by Edouard Martel, a French geologist. The complex of wide underground tunnels and lofty caverns with their masses of stalagmites and stalactites – one is known as the Porridge Pot – in Marble Arch Caves is claimed to be one of the finest in Europe. They are skilfully lit by concealed lights and at one point an underground lake is crossed by boat. Visitors must be escorted by a guide. The caves are open every day from April to September, but occasionally a spell of particularly wet weather means that they must be closed. Tours are booked in advance at busy times. There is an admission charge.
③ This lane is of great interest, spring probably being the best time to appreciate it. You will pass banks of whin (gorse), with a delightful aroma of almonds discernible on warm afternoons. A line of fine old beech trees stands on the right of the lane at one point. For most of the way the lane runs through rolling moors containing rushes – proof, if needed, that it can be damp. On cresting a hill about a mile along, there is a magnificent panorama, with Lough Macnean in the distance. The lane then descends steeply between moss-covered banks thick with primroses in spring, as well as a sprinkling of bluebells and violets. On the opposite bank are patches of stitchwort with lesser celandine growing in the shade; such sights are now uncommon. Far across the moor the mountains are a deep purple.

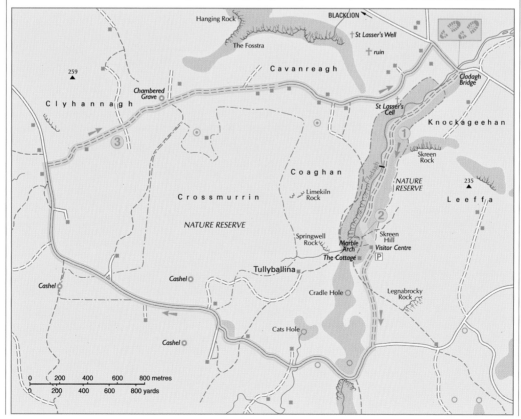

WALK 6

MOURNE MOUNTAINS AND TOLLYMORE FOREST PARK

A most attractive walk through the Forest Park on the slopes of the Mourne Mountains, including a section up the Spinkwee Gorge.

◀ The magnificent Mourne Mountains can only be properly explored on foot

river and the mountains rise to almost 1,000m.

② The Hermitage is a peculiar folly, consisting of a mass of stones built to form a chamber 12ft long, and commanding a fine view of the river far below. It was built by the second Earl of Clanbrassil as a memorial to his friend, the Marquis of Monthermer, who died in 1770.

③ On the way up to the Spinkwee Gorge, a large boulder at the side of the road invites you to 'Rest Awhile. To Nassans Bridge 1865.' The name Spinkwee is Gaelic for 'the yellow cliff'; other Gaelic place-names on this walk are Tollymore (meaning 'big hill'), Altavaddy (meaning 'the height of the dog') and Shimna (meaning 'reeds' or 'rushes').

④ As many as 18 species of mammals have been seen in Tollymore Forest. Foxes, badgers and red squirrels are relatively common, although there is no evidence of the grey squirrel. Rarest of all is the pine marten, which has only been seen on a few occasions over the years. Otters are not so rare, however, and fallow deer may also be seen. The birdlife includes jays, bullfinches, dippers and kingfishers.

⑤ Old Bridge, the oldest of many bridges over the Shimna, is dated 1726. On the parapet opposite is the inscription 'Repaird 1822' (note the spelling).

ROUTE DIRECTIONS

3 miles. Allow 2 hours.
Start at the south car-park (small fee) of Tollymore Forest Park (grid ref: J344326). The entrance to the forest park is on the Bryansford Road (B150) 2 miles north-west of Newcastle, Co Down. Moderate.

From the mounted map of the park, follow the orange arrow down the Azalea Walk ① and pass under the curious stone bridge. Take the path on the right and continue down to a path which crosses at right angles. Cross over this path and go down some steps to the T-junction and the Shimna River. Turn right and keep to this path along the river. Go up the steps into the Hermitage ② and out at the other end. Continue to follow the path along the river as far as the Rustic Bridge, passing two sets of stepping-stones and a simple footbridge on the way. Cross the Rustic Bridge and turn left.
In ¼ mile you will reach Altavaddy Bridge. Do not cross it but take the path to the right, SP 'Cascade' – this takes you up the Spinkwee Gorge ③. A shelter with a seat is at hand and viewpoints have been provided so that you can see the waterfalls which give the river its alternative name of Cascade River. Just beyond is the Spinkwee Bridge. Do not cross the bridge but continue along the path to a T-junction. Turn left, SP 'Drinns, Old Bridge'. Pass over Hore's Bridge

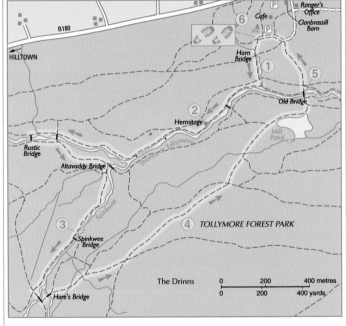

and continue straight on down to the lake ④. Walk along the path by the lake and then turn down to the left to Old Bridge ⑤. Cross this and follow SP 'Car-Park' to the end of the walk ⑥.

POINTS OF INTEREST

① As its name suggests, the Azalea Walk is a blaze of colour in spring and early summer. Before you, the

⑥ The Arboretum beside the car-park contains a valuable collection of trees of many species, all labelled for easy identification. Adjoining the upper car-park is the interesting Clanbrassil Barn which was erected in about 1757. It houses a small lecture theatre and an interpretive centre. A café lies close to the south car-park and an attractive caravan park is open to the public.

WALK 7

OUGHTERARD

Along quiet lanes, paths and river banks, the walk circles the pretty village of Oughterard, gateway to Connemara.

ROUTE DIRECTIONS

6¼ miles. Allow 3 hours.
8 miles if including Old Bog Road and visit to pier. Allow 4 hours.
Start from the public car-park beside the health clinic at the east end of the village (grid ref: M113243). Easy.

With care, cross the N59 to the petrol station and Welby's Garage, beside which is Porter Lane ①. Enter and continue almost to the end of the lane. Just before the private gateway, look for the low stone stile on the left, giving access to a narrow belt of woodland. The short path, slippery if wet, leads to a second stone stile on to Cregg Road, a quiet laneway. Pass the two lions guarding the entrance to Cregg House and continue to follow the lane ② as far as the crossroads; here carry straight on. Continue on the narrow surfaced lane, under the small bridge of the old railway line to Canrawer, and at a T-junction go left for 100yd. Immediately after the house on the right (Derrybrien), watch for stone pillars with a green gate (also on the right). Take a narrow path which leads between stone walls (left) and trees (right), down steps, to the watch-tower, viewing point and footbridge over the Owenriff River ③. Cross the footbridge and go up the steps and along the path to emerge at a red gate on the N59 (Oughterard–Clifden road). Go right on the footpath past the Sweeney's Oughterard House Hotel. Half a mile on is the bridge leading into the village. Unless you wish to see the two village churches, remain on this side of the river to take the by-road straight on. Almost immediately, directly in front of you is a stile beside a gateway, SP 'Owenriff Way'. Continue along this mile-long walk on the river banks with footbridges provided where necessary. A metal bridge at Fough East (Camp Street) takes you across the river. Go left and immediately right, following fingerposts to the boat moorings ④. The riverside walk, now on the southern bank, reaches the road leading from the village to the pier. Either turn right and reach your car in ¼ mile or, to extend the walk, turn left. This gives two options: a walk to the pier at Lough Corrib ⑤ with (or without) a detour to the right along a track SP 'The Old Bog Road' ⑥.

POINTS OF INTEREST

① Porter Lane is so named as it was used for the delivery of ale to the rear of the premises backing off it.
② Just by the crossroads is the old railway station, now a factory for V'soske–Joyce carpets. Behind is the site of the Union Workhouse, which offered some relief to the hungry in the potato famines of the 1840s.
③ The round tower overlooking the tumbling waters was a watch-tower for the former Waterfall Lodge, built possibly to deter poachers from fishing the well-stocked river.
④ At the end of Camp Street, on the land enclosed by the bend in the river, was the site of a British ordnance barracks, used when the 'natives were restless'. Oughterard also claims to have Ireland's oldest angling club.
⑤ Lough Corrib, one of Ireland's largest lakes at 7 miles wide, is said to have 365 islands. One, Inchagoill, has a ruined 5th-century church. A cruise (three trips daily in season) is available. Across the lake are the mountains of Mayo with the grounds of Ashford Castle in the foreground.
⑥ From the peaceful Old Bog Road you may see turf-cutting, harvested by hand for domestic fires.

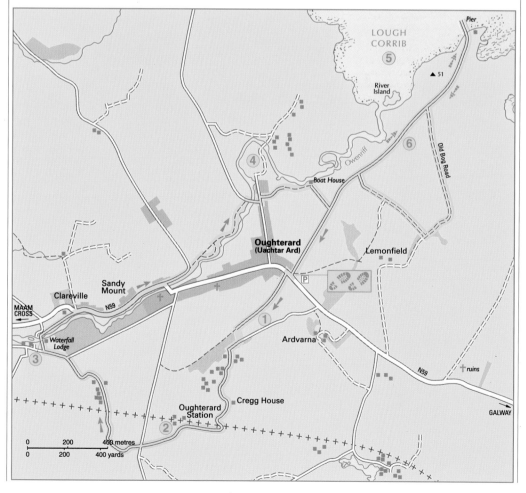

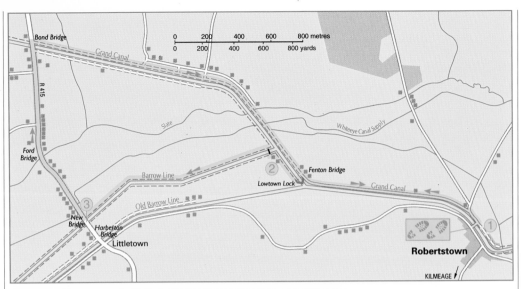

WALK 8

THE CANALS OF KILDARE

An undemanding walk along the extensive canal system of the flat, but by no means uninteresting, agricultural lands of Co Kildare, crossing or passing on the way several old hump-backed bridges and other evidence of more than 200 years of canal transport. This walk is suitable for families, but a narrow footbridge may prove awkward for pushchairs.

ROUTE DIRECTIONS

4 miles. Allow about 1½ hours. Start at Robertstown (grid ref: N790249). Easy.

From Robertstown ①, cross to the northern side of the Grand Canal and follow the road for a short distance. Where the road swings right, continue along the canal bank to reach Lowtown, about ½ mile away. Cross left over Fenton Bridge here, turn right and walk along the quays past the canal buildings ②. Beyond these, cross a high footbridge over the Barrow Canal. Turn left and follow the canal bank as far as the first bridge ③. Turn right here on to tarmac, cross a bridge over a river and turn right directly beyond the next bridge, Bond Bridge. Walk the towpath here back to Lowtown, and keep to the same bank to reach the bridge at Robertstown.

POINTS OF INTEREST

① Robertstown was founded when the canals were a main means of transport for passengers as well as goods. The large building on the south bank just to the east of the bridge was once a hotel, catering primarily for travellers on the canal. ② Lowtown was once the nerve-centre for the control of the Grand and Barrow Canal systems, regulating water-levels as well as traffic. The main building, which once housed the horses that pulled the barges, is now in use as a boat repair depot. From this junction canals radiate to Dublin, the Shannon and the Barrow, the last of these with two branches which join a short distance away. As you cross the footbridge, note the far-off destinations on the signpost, culminating in St Mullins, all of 70 miles away.
③ From this bridge both the tower-crowned Hill of Allen, famed in Irish history and mythology, and the cooling tower of the power station at Allenwood, which uses fuel from the boglands in the vicinity, are visible in opposite directions.

WALK 9

HOWTH

The attractive fishing village of Howth lies only 9 miles from the centre of Dublin, but the sea cliffs and rocky hillsides traversed on this walk could be a thousand miles away. Far from remote, this area none the less retains much of its atmosphere as a peninsular community quite distinct from the nearby city.

ROUTE DIRECTIONS

5½ miles. Allow 3 hours. Start near the east (far) pier of the harbour in Howth (grid ref: O288392). Moderate.

Walk east up Balscadden Road ①② and at the end of the road take the cliff path ③ which forms its continuation. Within sight of the Baily Lighthouse (it is on a nose of land reaching out into Dublin Bay) the cliff path joins a track. Continue straight ahead, cutting across the headland.
Cross the tarmac road, and on the far side follow the path just to the left of the house 'Gale Point', turning right, still on a path, a few yards further on. Turn left at the T-junction where a plaque at ground level indicates a right of way.
Take the right path at the first fork to stay above the cliffs. There is another fork further on at the edge of a garden, to the left of which is a continuation of the coastal path, but ignore this and turn right on to tarmac at Ceanchor Road (the bollards marking the end of the road will be just about visible from the path). At the end of Ceanchor Road turn left on to Thormanby Road, and a few yards beyond the last house on the right, turn right uphill at a path to face a summit of Howth Head. Do not take the main path which heads resolutely uphill. Instead, take the minor left turn and walk up through gorse bushes and ferns, (which grow tall in the summer) to round the hill ④. At a ruined house at the edge of the golf course, follow the line of white stones across the course and so enter a narrow valley beyond, a rocky spur of Howth Head on the right and a small wood on the left.
The path tends to disperse into a maze of sub-paths towards the end of the wood, so perhaps the simplest guide is to keep, on lower ground, to the right of the golf course (not the same course that was crossed

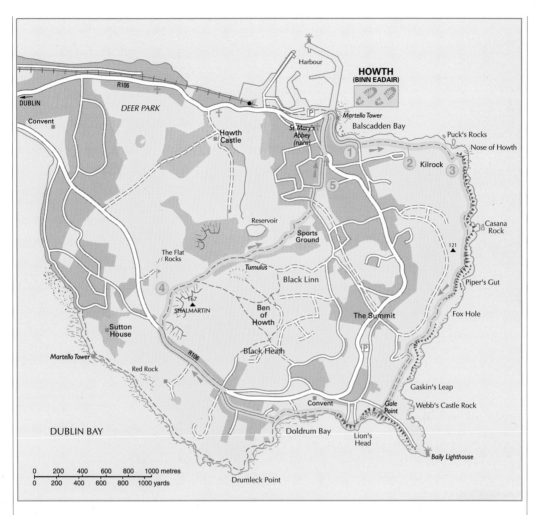

previously) and to watch out for goal posts just beyond it. Keep the playing field close on the right to descend on a short, narrow path to Balkill Road. Turn left here and walk downhill through Howth to return to the start ⑤.

POINTS OF INTEREST

① As you ascend Balscadden Road, the views of Ireland's Eye (near) and Lambay Island (further off) open out. Lambay is a bird sanctuary and was the first landing place (late in the 8th century) of the Norse invaders of Ireland. The name Lambay is of Norse origin, 'ey' meaning 'island'.
② The plaque on a house on the left states that the poet W B Yeats lived here in the years 1880–3, when he was a teenager. There seems to be some doubt about this because a recent biography states that the family were lent the house for only six months, after which they moved to a house nearer the harbour.
③ The cliffs here are a favourite haunt and nesting place for many varieties of sea-bird, including herring gulls, black-backed gulls, kittiwakes and cormorants.
④ Visible from this is the long sandy island to the left of the neck of the peninsula. This is Bull Island. It developed after the Bull Wall at its far end was constructed about 150

years ago. The salt marsh to the right of the island is of international importance for brent geese. It is believed to have the highest density of waders of any Irish wetland.
⑤ The village of Howth has retained its distinct individuality in spite of

the city's proximity. It was probably founded by the Norse invaders (indeed the name is of Norse origin). Many of the older houses and cottages to be seen on the descent, although simple, are architecturally very pleasing.

A wonderful prospect; the view of Ireland's Eye and Howth Castle on a fine day ▼

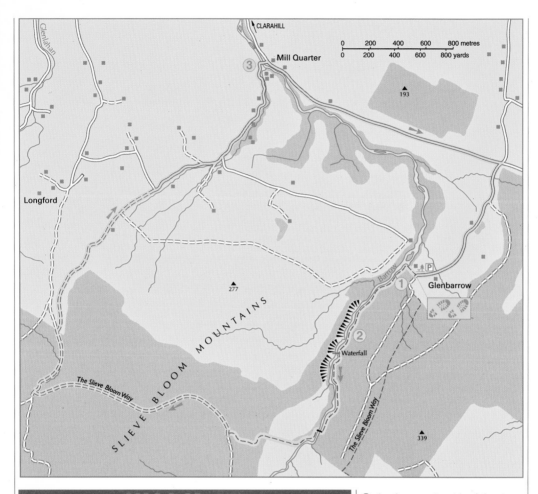

WALK 10

THE SLIEVE BLOOMS

An upland walk by the turbulent River Barrow, through a forest and on narrow hill roads with fine panoramas.

ROUTE DIRECTIONS

6½ miles. Allow 3½ hours.
Start at the car-park at Glenbarrow, which is well signposted from the R422 (grid ref: N367079). Difficult.

From the car-park, take the Slieve Bloom Way ① on the path SP 'Tinnahinch', descend to the river bank and continue upstream along the edge of a wood ②. Pass a waterfall and beyond it cross the river on a wooden footbridge. (Since the next stretch can be extremely wet and boggy – waterproof footwear essential – this is a good point to turn back if you do not intend to do the whole walk.) Continue along the path on the opposite bank and then ascend steeply, bearing left at an indistinct T-junction to reach a forest track. Turn right here and continue along the track for about 1 mile. Turn right downhill at the first crossroads, thereby leaving the Slieve Bloom Way. After negotiating a gate, fork right to keep on the main track and, ignoring a right turn, continue down to a major track at a bend. Continue straight ahead here, passing the first of three small bridges. Once you have

reached the minor road after the last bridge ③, turn right on to it and then take the first right turn after about 1 mile. Walk uphill for about ½ mile to the start point of the route.

POINTS OF INTEREST

① The Slieve Bloom Way is about 30 miles long and is in the form of a loop, threading through the valleys surrounding the gently sloping Slieve Bloom Mountains. Glenbarrow is the recommended starting point.

② On the opposite side of the river is a steep bank of unconsolidated material, about 100ft high. This is glacial drift and is composed partly of rocks and other debris, much of it of limestone origin, carried here during an ice age. This limestone explains the presence of lime-loving plants such as blue fleabane and carline thistle, both of which grow happily in sandstone country near the drifts.

③ The farm buildings here, just before the bridge, are worth a second glance. Some of them are beautifully built of local sandstone, and one of them has slightly bulging walls. The smaller features such as the gates are also nicely designed. Even the modern buildings fit in quite well. This area is called Mill Quarter, 'quarter' being an ancient Gaelic land measure.

WALK 11

GREEN WOOD AND BALLYHOURA MOUNTAIN PARK

The woods and moorland near Kilfinnane provide energetic walking with plenty of interest, contrast and good views.

ROUTE DIRECTIONS

6 ½ miles. Allow 4 hours plus extra time if you decide to detour to Glenosheen village, to the birdwatching point or on the

nature trail.
Start at the Green Wood car-park (grid ref: R658183). Stout and waterproof footwear is particularly recommended for this walk. Difficult.

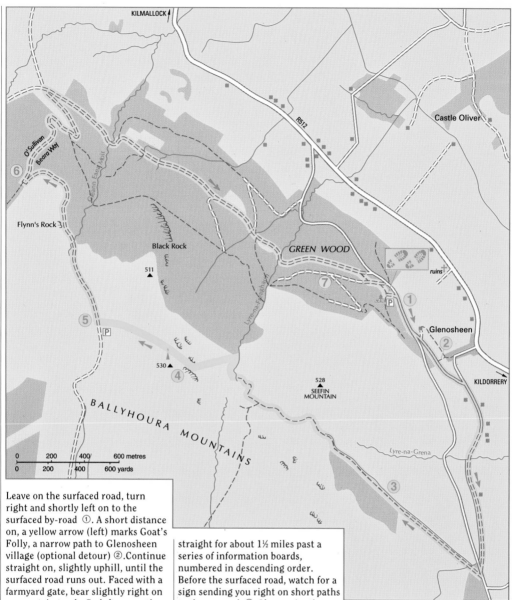

Leave on the surfaced road, turn right and shortly left on to the surfaced by-road ①. A short distance on, a yellow arrow (left) marks Goat's Folly, a narrow path to Glenosheen village (optional detour) ②. Continue straight on, slightly uphill, until the surfaced road runs out. Faced with a farmyard gate, bear slightly right on a mountain track. Go left across the surfaced road and then right through the gate to the forestry track, which can be a torrent after rain. This leads north-west to the saddle between Seefin Mountain and Black Rock ③. Over the saddle, and now on open moorland, keep right at the fork in the track, and at its end continue straight for 100yd as markers lead to a low earth bank. Go left on to the top of the bank to the prominent rocks on the hilltop ④. (Alternatively, cross the open moorland aiming straight for the radio mast between the prominent rocks on the hilltop.) Back on the earth bank, go downhill below the trigonometric point and radio mast, through the portals formed by rocks to the car-park, and right on to the forest track. Detour on the path, left, to the birdwatching point ⑤. At the first of a series of loops, just before re-entering Green Wood, a yellow arrow on a post shows that you have joined the O'Sullivan Beara Way ⑥.
Following the zigzags downhill, disregard a track right uphill. Where four tracks meet, go right and then

straight for about 1½ miles past a series of information boards, numbered in descending order. Before the surfaced road, watch for a sign sending you right on short paths to the car-park ⑦. If you miss the paths, at the end of the track simply go right on the road for 150yd.

POINTS OF INTEREST

① Directly east is Castle Oliver, a Gothic mansion. Robert Oliver, a Cromwellian captain, was granted the estate in 1666. The present building, dating from 1847, has a window for every day of the year. On the hill above is Oliver's Folly, known locally as 'The H'.
② In former years, a herd of 30 or so goats was called by their owner, Ellie Walsh, down Goat's Folly at milking time. Glenosheen (Gleann Óisín) is a Palatine village, built for descendants of 18th-century German refugees.
③ A border of conifers on the green road gives way to whin, heather and whortleberry. Patience and silence on the forestry track should reward you with sightings of wildlife.
④ The Ballyhoura Mountains are composed of old red sandstone with Silurian rocks exposed along the crest. The large boulders are said to be limestone erratics deposited during an ice age. The concrete pillar

is a trigonometric point, a base for instruments used by the Irish Ordnance Survey. The impressive panorama from here is: south, the town of Fermoy and the Nagle Mountains; west, the mountains of Kerry; north, the fertile Golden Vale, Limerick port and the hills of Clare; east, the Galtee and Comeragh Mountains.
⑤ Among the birds to be seen here are ravens, skylarks, merlins, hen harriers, red grouse, curlews and meadow pipits.
⑥ The Way follows the route of a certain O'Sullivan Beara who, on 31 December 1602, after the fall of Dunboy Castle (see Walk 15), led his followers north on a mid-winter 300-mile march. Only 35 of the 1,000 marchers reached Leitrim 15 days later.
⑦ The original oak forest of Green Wood was once part of the Oliver estate. The wood as it exists today consists largely of commercial trees, although there are still a few native deciduous trees as well as a rich understorey.

WALK 12

ABOVE GLENDALOUGH

This walk, which is almost all on forest tracks, reveals the magnificent beauty of Glendalough – its two lakes, its cascading waterfalls and its secret tributary valleys – as well as the monastic settlements which have made this once remote valley a famous centre of medieval Ireland.

ROUTE DIRECTIONS

4¾ miles. Allow 3 hours.
Start from the upper car-park, Glendalough (grid ref: O112964), about ¾ mile west of Glendalough's round tower. Moderate.

From the car-park, take the path skirting the park to the nearby Upper Lake ① and follow it, with the lake on the right, passing a footbridge before reaching two bridges which span the turbulent stream that enters the lake. Take the right-hand bridge – it is the footbridge – and follow the path beyond to Reefert Church ②.
From the church take the path onward, signed Poulanass Waterfall, to a forest track and turn right on to it. Follow it into the narrow valley through which the Poulanass Waterfall tumbles as a series of spectacular cascades in a deeply cut bed ③.
Ignoring the path back to the car-park, take the first turn left, thereby crossing two bridges. Between the bridges there is a pillar on the right which displays samples of local rock. Take the right fork immediately after the second bridge. Go straight ahead past a track which comes in from the right and continue ahead to stay on the main track. Further along, take the left track which leads to the valley floor.
Turn left here on to a path ④ and right at the second bridge which leads directly to the monastic settlement ⑤. Return to the path and continue along it past the Lower Lake to a sign pointing right to the car-park a short distance away.

POINTS OF INTEREST

① The waterfall at the far end of the Upper Lake, and clearly visible from the lakeshore, marks the boundary between the highly resistant metamorphic rocks to the west and the softer rocks nearer here. The latter were cut down by glacial action during an ice age.
② Reefert Church dates from the 11th century. The site here is reputed to be the burial ground of local chieftains. In the surrounding cemetery are some early Christian gravestones and a cross with interlacing decoration.
③ Silt carried by the Poulanass Waterfall has formed a delta in the main Glendalough Valley. At one time there was only one lake in this valley, but the accumulating silt split the lake so that there are now two – Upper Lake and Lower Lake.
④ The old mixed wood here, partly oak but also with beech and holly, may be one of the very few remnants of the ancient forests which once clothed most of Ireland. This wood is now a conservation area.
⑤ The main concentration of the medieval monastic ruins lies in this area. Each ruin is fully described at its site and there is a visitors' centre near by. There are several churches, a gateway and an impressive round tower which is about 100ft high.

St Kevin's Kitchen, so-called because of the squat chimney, at Glendalough ▼

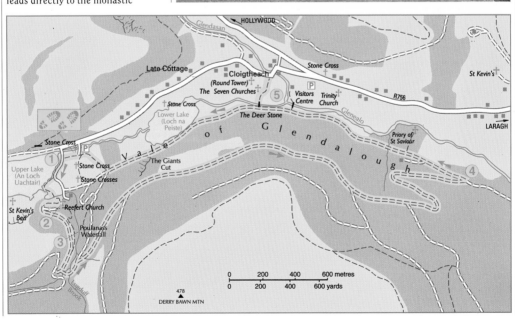

WALK 13

WATERFORD HARBOUR

Mostly on tracks and country roads between the attractive villages of Passage East and Cheekpoint, this walk takes you along high ground above the estuary which was formed by the meeting of three of Ireland's great rivers. The return is through a wood and pleasant agricultural upland.

ROUTE DIRECTIONS

8 miles. Allow 4 hours.
Start from the village of Passage East at the end of the R683. Park in the square close to the ferry crossing (grid ref: S703103). Moderate.

Walk along the main road (the R683) from Passage East ①, taking the first track right after 1 mile. Follow this track through a mixed wood to the crest of a hill, descend beyond it into a small valley and continue upwards on the same track to a T-junction close to a school. Turn right here and walk towards Cheekpoint, turning left (rather than taking the cul-de-sac straight ahead) near the village ② to gain the estuary bank.

Walk through the village with the estuary on the right, and at its end follow the road uphill. Take the first turn right, a narrow turning after a 90-degree bend to the left. At the first fork, either go right and take the path which forms its continuation through a field and into a wood, or (as is quite possible in late spring or summer) if thick vegetation has made this field impassable, take the left fork on a track leading to a T-junction. Turn right, then left, to rejoin the main road close to the village of Faithlegg (a detour down the first right turn for 100yd takes you to a fine viewpoint). If you decide to risk the field, ignore the fork left just inside the wood and continue along the main path high above the River Suir ③.

Still on this path, cross through a gap in a stone wall and 100yd beyond it turn left to go steeply uphill on a forest path. At its end, on tarmac, turn right to reach a viewing point. Take the track running left which starts just below the front of the viewing point. It ends on tarmac; turn right here to reach the main road close to the village of Faithlegg. Pass the church on the left ④ and beyond it turn left towards Passage East. Walk along this road for 1¼ miles and turn left at the T-junction. Walk for ½ mile and take the first track on the right. Ignoring the right turn, continue to a T-junction, turn left here and take the steps steeply downhill into Passage East.

POINTS OF INTEREST

① Passage East is neatly tucked in below cliffs that harbour a herd of easily encountered feral goats. The village has had a chequered history with both Strongbow and Henry II landing here shortly after the Norman invasion of Ireland in 1169. A car ferry links Passage East with Ballyhack across the estuary. The crossing takes five minutes or less, but can save a trip of 50 miles or so. The ferry runs all year, every day.
② Cheekpoint lies near the junction of three rivers: the Suir, the Barrow and the Nore. At one time in the 18th century it was the mail packet station for Ireland. Have a look at the battered old milestone as you enter the village.
③ There is an excellent viewing point here overlooking the marshland and water channels bordering the River Suir. The hills in the distance are the Blackstairs.
④ Beside the 19th-century church at Faithlegg are the ruins of its 13th-century predecessor which has a chancel arch and doorway in carved red sandstone. The tombstones in the churchyard are interesting; one is in memory of a sailor who sailed around the world with Captain Cook.

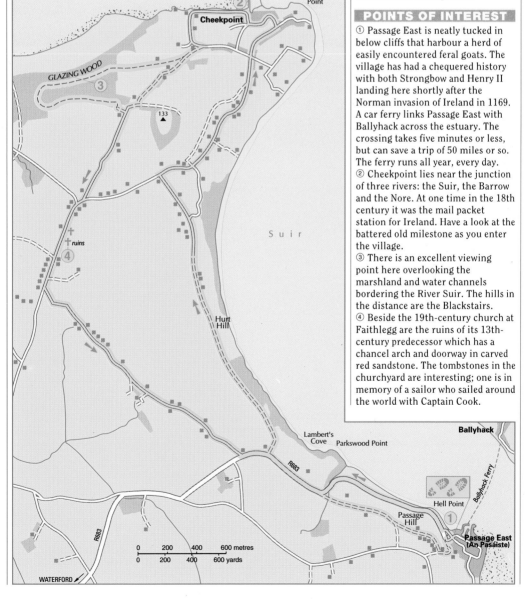

153

WALK 14

DOOKS (DOOAGHS) MOUNTAIN AND BEACH

This gentle walk, all under the 30m (100ft) contour, around the townland of Dooks introduces you to a variety of habitats (moor and bogland, sand dune and seashore) with an opportunity for swimming or golf.

ROUTE DIRECTIONS

4½ miles. Allow 2 hours.
Start at Dooks Slip (grid ref: V685956).
Park near the slipway. Easy.

Having checked the state of the tide for the later leg along the beach, return south along the Burkett's Road which gave access to the slipway ①. After approximately ¾ mile, turn right at the crossroads and 300yd later watch for the narrow entrance on the left to a grassy road, bordered mainly with whin (gorse). Follow it, swinging slightly left at the entrance to bogland ②. Approaching the 'mountain', circle right with the green road, with fine views to the north and west ③. As the green road meets a semi-surfaced laneway, a copse of trees gives temporary shelter on a hot day. Continue to the T-junction. Turn right and after approximately ½ mile turn left beside a pillar with a postbox. Pass Buncar House, on your left, and go right and then left to the mouth of the Caragh River and the beach ④. Go right along the beach and around Black Point, skirting Dooks Golf Club ⑤. Continue on the beach. Depending upon the state of the tide, it may be necessary to leave the sand and go along the boulder and pebble beach for short stretches, or to walk along the edge of the sand dunes. At the Slip, you will find your car ⑥.

POINTS OF INTEREST

① Dooks Slip is the mooring point for the small open boats used for generations by fishermen on the Caragh River. While salmon and trout are netted, the principal harvest of the area has been mussels from the natural beds of Castlemaine Harbour.
② Intensive turf-cutting can be seen to the right and left of the green road. This area enjoys a subtropical climate, thanks to the Gulf Stream. This explains the lush growth, including rich fuchsia and whitethorn hedges, seen earlier and again later. The bogland, seemingly bleak, is also rich in flora and teems with wildlife. The small concrete bridge crosses the stream running from Lough Yganavan (Loch Gainimh Bháin, or 'white sand lake', in Irish) to the sea. This may be the origin of the local place-name Clashdyne (Clais Doimhin or 'deep stream').
③ From the green road, the view

south-east is of the hills surrounding Lough Caragh and, behind them, MacGillycuddy's Reeks, Ireland's highest mountain range.
④ Dooks Beach is popular for family swimming and windsurfing. The views west are of the coombs of Coomasaharn and Drung Hill, site of the legendary Kingdom of Drung.
⑤ Dooks Golf Club claims to be the oldest in Ireland, the course having been developed in the 1880s as a golf links for use by the British Army. Aside from good golf, the links' present-day importance is as a habitat of the rare natterjack toad. The Club has adopted the natterjack for its crest and has adapted the course to ensure the toad's survival.
⑥ From the beach, the view is of long fingers of sand projecting into Dingle Bay – west is Rossbeigh Spit and north is Inch Spit. North of Dooks Slip, closer to the northern shore of Dingle Bay, is the site of the sinking in 1902 of the *Manchester Merchant*. The ship was on its maiden voyage from São Paulo in Brazil to Liverpool when its cargo of cotton

▲ Despite staying at a low level, the walk at Dooks Slip gives many wide vistas

spontaneously ignited, and the captain decided to run her into the bay and scuttle her as near to shore as possible.

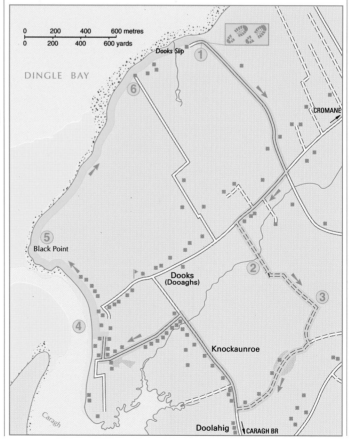

WALK 15

DUNBOY CASTLE AND WOODS

A gentle walk through the woods near Dunboy Castle becomes a journey through history, enhanced by spectacular scenery. There is also the possibility of doing part of the journey on horseback.

ROUTE DIRECTIONS

3½ miles. Allow 2 hours.
Start at entrance to Dunboy Castle (grid ref: V657443). Park outside the gateway or drive as far as Puxley's Mansion. Either way, there is a small entrance fee. After rain, footwear suitable for muddy paths should be worn. Difficult, but after current improvements, easy (see page 140).

Walk through the castellated gateway with two ruined gate lodges, through the tubular steel gate and straight on beside the water. The riding stables are to your right ①. Leaving Puxley's Mansion on your right, continue straight on the track. Before the forest gate, on the promontory (left) stand the ruins of Dunboy Castle ②. Return to the track and go left over the stile beside the forest gate (if renovation work here is not complete, negotiate collapsed fence), to follow a forest path which circles by the shoreline. At the fork, keep left, leaving the car-park and picnic tables on your right ③. The path meets a forest track. Go left here past a small beach and continue uphill on the path to the forest gate. Unless recent signposts allow, do not go beyond the gate ④.
Return on the path, join the forest track and go straight ahead. At the T-junction, go left (not straight on to the car-park) to meet the remains of the farm buildings for Puxley's Mansion. Go right between the ruins to follow a track and over a stile at the forest gate ⑤. Shortly after the stile, stakes with arrows lead right and left on a path (again, if renovation work is incomplete, negotiate wire fence rather than forest gate and then follow indistinct path) to take you back to Puxley's Mansion – to be admired from the outside only since the ruinous building is by now far from safe ⑥. Follow the road back to return to the entrance gateway.

POINTS OF INTEREST

① To your left is The Creek, an inlet of Bear Haven. Locals claim the harbour to be the second safest in the world, surpassed only by Sydney Harbour.
② The 15th-century O'Sullivan Beara castle was destroyed in June 1602 when besieged by English forces. After the fall of Dunboy, the clan chief led his followers on a 300-mile mid-winter march north (see Walk 11). Across the water on Bear Island can be seen the tunnel-like openings of the British gun batteries of a more recent era.
③ From the path, the view north-east up the harbour is of the might of Hungry Hill, the name of the Daphne du Maurier novel based on the Puxley family.
④ There is now a fuller view of the harbour mouth, Bear Island and lighthouse. The name comes from a Spanish Princess, Beara, who landed near here on her journey to marry a Munster king. On a high point of the island are the remains of a signal tower, shattered by lightning some years ago.
⑤ There are plans to restore the farm buildings which were placed sufficiently far away from the mansion so as not to offend sensitive noses and eyes. The large walled enclosures, left, now paddocks for the riding stables, were the orchards – there are a few remaining apple trees.
⑥ The Puxleys replaced the O'Sullivans as landowners, the latter family deriving their fortune from the Allihies copper mines further along the Beara peninsula. The mansion was built in three stages but was never completed. When Mrs Puxley died in 1872, her husband went to England, never to return. Locals say that materials remained in packing cases until the 1920s, when the mansion was burned down by the IRA for strategic purposes. The tall monkey puzzle trees across the water are evidence of the former gardens, once magnificent.

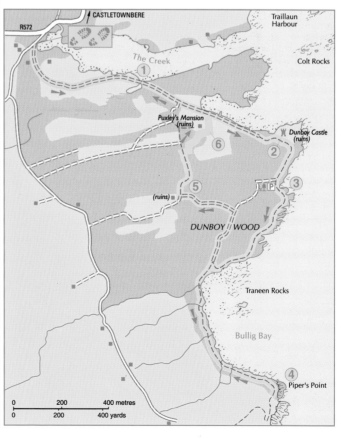

▲ Glenarm, on the Antrim coast. The popular belief is that it means the glen of the army

Page numbers in bold type indicate gazetteer entries.

▲ Garnish Point, at the extreme end of the Beara peninsula, typifies the beauty of the far south-west

ACKNOWLEDGEMENTS

The Automobile Association would like to thank the following photographers, libraries and associations for their assistance in the preparation of this book.

BORD FÁILTE 16 Benbulben, 17 Leenane area, 20 Aran Islands, 20/1 Staigue Fort, 22 & 23 Irish food, 26 Royal Dublin Horse Show, 34 Ardmore, Ardee, Aran Islands, 35 Aran sweater, knitting, 38 Ballina, 39 Bandon, 58 Croagh Patrick, 61 Drogheda, 68 Ennis, 70 Fermoy, 74/5 Glenmalure, 75 Gort, 82 Knappogue Castle, 91 Monasterboice, 95 Parknasilla, 109 Horse racing, 111 Hunting
H CHEVALLIER 16 Above Kylemore Abbey/Maumturk Mountains
Z GOODWIN 154 &155 Dooks Slip
C HARLEY 141 Donegal scenery
MARY EVANS PICTURE LIBRARY 25 Childhood of Fionn MacCumhail, 28/9 *Gulliver's Travels*
NATURE PHOTOGRAPHERS LTD 10 Large marsh grasshopper, 11 Great crested grebe (P R Sterry), 12 Dense flowered orchid (R B Burbidge), 13 Bewick's swan (C B Knights)
NORTHERN IRELAND TOURIST BOARD 18 Rowallane Gardens, 27 Show-jumping, 38/9 Ballintoy harbour, 45 The Minnionburn, 60 Donaghadee harbour, 69 Enniskillen, 70 Grey Mans Path, 77 Hillsborough, 94/5 Omagh
THE MANSELL COLLECTION 8 Easter Rising, D O'Connell, 28 G B Shaw, 29 W B Yeats, 30 Swift
All remaining pictures are held in the Association's own library (AA PHOTO LIBRARY) with contributions from:
L BLAKE, J BLANDFORD, D FORSS, T KING, G MUNDAY, THE SLIDE FILE, W VOYSEY & P ZOELLER